SUNSETS OVER
CHARLESTON

Acknowledgements

I t seems that we cannot be islands unto ourselves. The interaction we enjoy teaches and inspires us. In the performance of a task that is as daunting as interviewing three dozen or more people of the loftiest imaginable profiles, there had to be as much luck as there was toil. The luck prevailed. And there were unforeseen connections.

Established writers are exciting subjects for interviews. I started with Ken Burger, an author of greater significance than we will appreciate in our generation. Burger loves to write and has penned books of great entertainment beyond his newspaper career. I sheepishly asked him if he would consider writing my foreword. Who better? Getting to interview Burger was like getting on a train ride through the Alps. Every emergence and turn brought out something else to admire or gain insight. The writers always get my attention. Pat Conroy agreed to the interview early, but his schedule made me really appreciate any small piece of his time. His classical eloquence graces the typeset herein.

The intertwining of iconic personalities made this process both exciting and worthwhile. I had a lunch interview with former South Carolina governor Mark Sanford. I asked my six questions. I then put my pen away. We talked for two and a half hours more. Bobby Clair, the project manager for our bridge, deserves a whole book. So does Admiral Bill Schachte. Well, actually, there could be a book done about each of these characters. That idea may be too late for some. Those books were already written. You could fill a bookshelf with Ralph Friedgen, Martha Rivers Ingram, Angie LeClercq,

Pat Caddell, John McKissick, Nancy Mace and others. So to get a chance to sit and chat with any of them would be a memorable achievement—and I am giddy with memorable interviews. I can tell my recently born twin grandchildren that I had an extraordinary time speaking with the former executive director of the United States Olympic Committee. If that doesn't pique their interest, I would add two three-star generals who may have changed our world, a bishop, a mother superior, an actor-comedian, a well-known national attorney, a country music artist, the "winningest football coach ever," the mayor of our largest metropolitan-area city, an admiral, a Presbyterian minister, a college president, a jazz musician turned politician, a public utility CEO, a major-league catcher, the aforementioned two writers, the lady who will put wind turbines off our coast, the guy who foresaw the Charleston real estate market, the former president of the PGA, the lady who runs tourism in Charleston, two entrepreneurial builders, the first female graduate of The Citadel, a local television personality, an internationally acclaimed garden expert, a former governor, a BCS football coach, a court judge and a syndicated political guru. There are even more, but my mind is out of breath.

There were some coincidental connections I wanted to cover here, not in the essays. This was not part of a plan. In separate chapters, Pat Conroy contrasts the careers of two Pentagon generals from that fine Citadel class of 1967, John Sams and Mike Steele. Yet another classmate, Tommy Ford, was part of the interview on golf in Charleston and assisted me with his fabulous photography. Somberly, I am reminded that Tommy Ford's brother, Frank Ford Jr., perished in the same crash of Eastern Airlines flight 212 on September 11, 1974, as Elizabeth Colbert-Busch's father and two brothers. There were seventy-two casualties in all. One of my father's best friends, Chuck McDonald, died in that same crash. He was at my wedding the previous Saturday. Tragedy reaches into families beyond the dwindling decades.

When stellar baseball player Richard Wieters, Matt Wieters's father, came to The Citadel in 1973, I was the corps squad commander (head of the athletic cadre) who taught him to march. He played baseball better than he marched. Ralph and Gloria Friedgen attend my parish church, where eighty-nine-year-old Reverend Bishop David Thompson still celebrates the early Sunday Mass. Warren Peper played basketball against me in high school. We became friends through recreational basketball leagues over the next thirty years. He retired from playing when he was fifty. I retired from the leagues at forty-nine. The only injury he mentioned in those thirty years was because of me. He landed on my ankle. I sent him an ACE bandage so he could do the sports report on Channel 5. The Rivers family owned WCSC-TV Channel 5 until 1987. Martha Rivers Ingram once worked for her father at Channel 5 after returning from Vassar College. Mark Sanford and Pat Caddell are both "on call" as contributors to FOX News in New York. They are often from diametrically different viewpoints but are quite respectful of each other.

Somebody had to reel me in. I left it up to my first publisher, The History Press. They made a few exceptions to accommodate me, and I am most appreciative. Adam Ferrell has done this with great personal care. He had to be very patient. The History Press's work in getting me published for a second time has made several of my college English professors lose sizable bets. I am elevated by the editing, photo and formatting work extended, especially the expertise of Julie Foster and Annie Martz. Marketing publicist Katie Parry is also back to assist me in "getting the word out."

I should also thank my friend Fred Whittle, a Yank-turned-*pluffmudder*. A retired U.S. Marine Corps lieutenant colonel and Citadel regimental commander from the class of 1980, Fred is well read and reads well. He noticed that I turned the Marquis de Lafayette, a general, into an admiral in my first book. He has been there for more than my confusion of military insignias. I had casually passed the rough manuscript to Fred out of my profound confidence in his wide historical knowledge and acute literary abilities. He took it upon himself to respond and read the entire manuscript with the insights of a classically trained PhD. He gets the facts right while enhancing the style. In so many cases, you are reading the benefit of Fred Whittle's amazing grasp of the art of language. Thanks, Fred.

There are others who edified me, including family. Thanks to my children, Billy, Joey, Katie and Thomas. They made me do my sixth-grade homework over and over again. Thanks to Mandy, my wife, who cries when I've tried to make her laugh and laughs when I've tried to be serious. I think I've confused her for a lifetime.

Having eight brothers and sisters, twenty-seven nieces and nephews and eleven great-nieces and great-nephews in addition to my twin grandchildren, Cullen and Will (born during this process), makes me realize that belonging is a subscript to living. I love them all.

There was a somber side to this process.

Nearing the end of the project, my mother, Charlotte Simmons McQueeney, passed away after a seven-year battle with cancer. She inspired me in ways that I made sure she knew. I was with her over the last eighteen months almost daily. Four days before she died, she pulled me to her and said the simple words, "I love you." They were the last words she ever said to me. Just writing that made me tear up all over again. She slipped away into a wake-less drift with all of the transitional anointments like morphine, Ativan and the constancy of her nine children. She was an artist. That word expands for her beyond the product of her talent and well into the mindset of her life. She could do anything. She did everything. Her inspiration will remain with me in time indeterminate. She is my final-chapter profile as a loving commemoration of what she accomplished that is yet unmeasured. She left lessons of kindness.

The first book, *The Rise of Charleston*, found me in an inspirational mindset to channel whatever funds the enterprise would bestow back into something worthwhile. I selected Our Lady of Mercy Community Outreach on John's Island. Its mission is explored within these pages through the leadership of Sister Mary Joseph Ritter (Chapter 10). They have something special there, and when you consider their impact on those who transition from poverty into productive lives, they provide an exemplary service beyond the material world. They breed hope.

Encouraged, I have selected another charity for the proceeds of this effort. My first cousin Winn Tutterow—and his lovely wife, Mary Bissell Tutterow—were blessed with the birth of a special needs child on March 11, 1992. Mary Addison Tutterow is vivacious and outgoing. She has the daily struggle of developmental disabilities. She has shouldered a lifetime of difficult seizures. Yet, she is loved and appreciated by all. Her mother, Mary, is a brilliant University of Georgia graduate who had the predisposition to think well beyond self. She became a prime mover in the 1998 founding of Healing Farm Ministries (chartered in 1999). That conceptual plan is now a reality. She has helped to institute a "roadmap" and programs beyond the sphere of the caregiver's lifetime. Her simple question that could not be readily resolved then was: "Who takes care of these special people when their parents and caregivers age or die?" Healing Farm Ministries builds an infrastructure in an actual farming environment to foster real world skill sets for these special children. Healing Farm Ministries has effectively altered the way society views people with disabilities right here in our midst. The entire Charleston community is further edified by its passion and resolve. People of care and caring people have combined to underscore that we are all people of value. *Sunsets over Charleston*, no matter how scant the sales might be, will help someone in need. It is my wish that someone who knows this challenge personally will see you reading the book and thank you. Mary Addison Tutterow thanks you. Humbly, I thank you.

So, give this book as a gift to someone you care about and benefit someone else in the process. I hope I have the opportunity to personally thank you.

Assuming we remain above ground after the Mayans scared us enough to study the alignment of the heavenly bodies anew, do not give this hardbound book away. Apologies are hereby made to those who downloaded this chunk of verbiage on Nooks and iBooks. The hardbound copy has a greater projection of value. Let me explain.

If things go as I suspect, in a millennium or so, someone might find this book in a garage sale for only $200,000. So I acknowledge those listed above who unwittingly helped to make some unsuspecting someone in the future rich, if only in today's dollars. After you've read this book, place it in a Glad bag, seal it while letting all of the air out and then bury it—or place it in a cave near the Dead Sea. There's got to be some future in real weighty and textured books.

Introduction as Indoctrination

This book is dedicated to those of you who contemplated the safety of underground bunkers with plans to return in December 2017 to celebrate the fifth anniversary of the world's end. My Mayan calendar keeps me above ground because I cannot decipher the symbols. I wrote this companion volume to *The Rise of Charleston: Conversations with Visionaries, Luminaries and Emissaries of the Holy City* with the idea that it would be published by the fall of 2012, in plenty of time for disaster planning. *Sunsets over Charleston* is an attempt to sew the people back into the fabric of the Holy City after a definitive expansion of the weave. The two books should realign our identity from what we once were to what we are now. Together, more than seventy of our mainstream characters are examined and tagged like the Department of Natural Resources might suggest, before they are let back into the wild. So the two-volume set will allow sporadic reading about the people of an era. Perhaps they will be read about underground! I envisioned there would be nothing as comforting in a bunker as a good book—assuming this effort reaches beyond mediocre. My reasoning is sound. A hardbound copy can be read, discussed as a means of bleary-eyed cave therapy, criticized for its inherent personal commentary—and then, in observance of a proctored green energy plan, used as kindling. I hope the effort stretches to five years before the nuclear winter sets in.

Being cynical of cynics, leery of the lyrical and accepting that the poetic and prosaic are on Prozac, I decided to thrust my banality on the unsuspecting as one who is immersed within the state of aloofness. Being considered "aloof" is better than being considered a fool. Aloof is me.

This book is based on the same format as the first. It made the "Pest Seller" List. Yes, I pestered everyone to buy it, with proceeds going to a great charity, Our Lady of Mercy (OLM) Community Outreach on John's Island, South Carolina. You can read more about the OLM Outreach in the chapter on Sister Mary Joseph Ritter. The format of interviewing some of the Charleston area's more distinguished, high-profile and otherwise intriguing personalities and relating these interviews to the reader in essay form was continued in the second book of the series. There are no plans for a third book in this genre. No trilogy, just a soliloquy here. So you are holding the end piece to the effort. I hope that I have captured, for posterity if not for other edification, the essence of the people who have both changed Charleston and furthered the Holy City's world status. The essays are meant for you to "meet" those in the metropolitan Charleston area whom you might already know but not know their sentiments, especially as they relate to our fair city. They might give you some insight as to Charleston's meteoric elevation over the last half century. Citing *Conde Nast Traveler*'s Readers' Choice Awards of October 2012, this Geechie-Gullah enclave is designated as the number one travel destination in the world! The colossal leap of stature, for someone having grown up in the bygone era, is exhilarating. We placed ahead of Paris and London, Rio and Rome. Amazing! As a *benya*, I had no idea what was in store for the simple and austere city of my birth.

Those celebrities herein might relate a story or two about their childhoods, their adulthoods, what their life's work has been or the joy of some uniquely Charleston-styled event. The main character has jumped from the pages of the first book to the second. It is our dear city. Like all protagonists, there are quaint quirks and quintessential qualities.

The interim times have changed for me. Actual academics have asked questions of me as though I had graduated to a sleeve-patched tweed blazer and a swooping unlit pipe. Cagey as I pretend to be, my reluctance to speak out on any subject of great study camouflaged me as possibly being one of them, at least for a time. You know that I am most certainly not! They are mostly PhDs and fellows of some distant and honored fellowship. I am what I always was: a child of the pluff mud. Listening to their factually ascertained postulations made me realize the wide range of scholarship that should be associated with my favorite subject outside of baseball: Charleston present and past. If it is research that compels a labor like this, then there is tedium. So, I decided not to pursue the data as much as I pursued the upper strata. I went to the people to hear their stories. I am but the scribe, like Ezra, Geoffrey Chaucer or Pliny the Younger. But my Israel, my Canterbury and my Pompeii detail your Charleston. The coming generations may come to know us.

The Charleston that had been cocooned for a century in placid ambivalence has awakened. We're now the brightest kid in the class. There are others who look to us to ask how we did it. The answer is not that simple. I've penned two books interviewing people of profound importance to this community to see what it was, how it is and that which subtly resonates within each of them as the why for.

My six decades above the caverns have been quite an experience. My childhood among a downtown Charleston family with eight siblings and two loving parents gave me a sound basis and harmonious perspective. It grew within a neighborhood and a close-quartered peninsular city. That two-mile by mile-and-a-half elbow of land separating two minor southern rivers surely emulates Eden. Those rivers embrace a civility that overcame the twin torments of semi-constant wars and natural disasters. It is that now-famous civility that was the continuum, the lifeblood and the substance of our Charleston. It is variously called friendliness, good manners and hospitality. I suppose it touches all of those. To be sure, civility reigned here even during the pirate raids of the early 1700s, the American Revolution, the War Between the States, the Great Fire of 1861, the earthquake of 1886, the Great Hurricane of 1912 and Hurricane Hugo (1989). There were other troubles sewn in between, such as malaria, smallpox, two secessions, the Denmark Vesey uprising and the harsh closing of the Charleston Naval Shipyard (1996). Neighbors always depended on neighbors to become friends. Some intermarried and gave us the pretend names of an aristocracy. With the inflective Charleston brogue, all names roll from the tongue as likely country club presidents or debutantes. Their relative importance is no less.

Make no mistake, despite myriad challenges—or in observance of them— there remain centuries of innate pride. The historic surnames morphed into place names and reverted back again to become the first names of the children and grandchildren. The monikers Tradd, Calhoun, Rutledge, Legare (la GREE) and Huger (U-GEE) designate Charleston personalities as well as streets. The names Cooper and Ashley are exceedingly popular. They are also our two converging rivers easily mistaken for the biblical Tigris and Euphrates. The barrier islands are represented in children's names as well: Seabrook, Capers and Sullivan ("Sully"). I have not as yet heard the potential first-name placements like Folly (Beach) or Goose (Creek), though one of my best friends named his dog Edisto (Beach).

The eponymous names arose as restaurants, law firms, insurance agencies and auto dealerships. They have become the brand as well as the person. Charleston is resplendent in the recognition of the old families of the Holy City. Yet they are now much the minority. Nearly 80 percent of the citizens of Charleston are not born-and-bred Charlestonians. That fact is of prodigious consequence. We needed them as part of us. Better said, they have enhanced us in ways inestimable.

Yet the value of one's welcomed acceptance seems to expand to necessitate belonging to part of Charleston. Particularly, Charleston societies define the expansive curricula vitae of our populace. One could be placed on a long waiting list to become a member of the St. Cecelia's Society. The propriety of Charleston's best and longest-running ball hangs in the balance. A proper pedigree well researched could enable a lucky young man or lady to be invited to join the French Huguenot Society. The Hibernian Society of Irish revelers entitles use of the city's finest Greek Revival edifice. Wedding weekends are planned years in advance—sometimes before the engagement rings are presented. The German Friendly Society, the St. Andrews Society, the Arian Society, the Washington Light Infantry and others are sewn into the fabric of Charleston life. These vaunted associations are unique to Charleston, found no place else.

The cultural and religious mix is compelling. They all were assuaged by John Locke's *Fundamental Constitutions of Carolina*, a presage to the U.S. Constitution. The Holy City was built on religious freedom—and commerce. Those who came include the foundation Episcopalians and Anglicans, the second-largest Jewish settlement in colonial America, the Presbyterians, John Wesley's early Methodists, the German Lutherans, the aforementioned Huguenots and the Catholics of both French and Irish extraction. There also remains a vibrant Greek community, several African church affiliations and even a larger than might be expected Lebanese culture. The Quakers famously came and left. The Baptists came from Maine, restocked the bookshelves and developed the strong Southern Baptist faith principally out of Charleston. Oddly missing were those European cultures that settled north and south of Charleston: the Dutch, the Scandinavians, the Italians, the Spanish and the Portuguese. In time, they found us, too!

The planting of rice, cotton, tobacco, indigo and plentiful vegetables commercially supported the settlement. The dark days of the detestable practice of slavery brought the business of human trade through Charleston in numbers greater than any other North American port. Their ironically propitious legacy has adorned the entire community in sculpture, brickwork, architecture, cuisine, furnishings and the two-thousand-year-old art of sweetgrass baskets.

Charleston did not develop as much as it emerged. The birth was from sacrifice, strife and a lot of praying. It is, irrefutably, this generation of Charlestonians that has cracked the egg open from the inside. The world sees us as we have never been seen before—in admiration.

I love Charleston—the broken slate of the sidewalks and the clip-clop of the carriage tours. I love the salt air, the leftover milling stones and the shadowy saunter through the oaks at White Point Garden. I might volunteer information to lost tourists, even if they don't ask. I might pull my car over to show a guest a building that I know has an engaging story to recall. I proudly call it home when I am nowhere near it and especially when I am standing amidst its splendor.

There was an amazing artist from Charleston, Elizabeth O'Neill Verner, who gave lessons to my mother. "Miss Beth" wrote a book in 1941, titled *Mellowed by Time*, when Charleston was not on anybody's serious travel list. In it, she expresses a sentiment that one could never attempt to improve:

> *I feel it when I glide in through the narrow channel at the jetties and see across the harbor the sky-line of the city with the gleam of St. Philip's cross, St. Michael's white spire, the copper domes of the old Scotch Church and far uptown the slender steeple of St. Matthew's, still our skyscrapers. What a world of heroism that narrow channel has witnessed, so close Ft. Moultrie on one side and Fort Sumter on the other, and yet between these two a gap was once so wide that it split a nation. Such a very small city it is, compared to most cities, so confined by its rivers and harbor that it has been compressed and become an essence of itself.*
>
> *It is impossible for me to enter Charleston from any side, whether by land or sea, and not feel that here the land is precious; here is a place worth keeping; this, of all the world, is home.*

The eloquent outlook she espoused is as true today as when she wrote it. Those churches are still our skyscrapers. "Miss Beth" passed away in 1979, more known for her artwork. But she was a fine writer as well.

In the vista vision of grandeur, you would surely find this deep and wide harbor and its golden salt marshes, nourished by the warmth of soothing sunlight. You would certainly find the delicate sustenance of rain and the pulsed breezes of a caring God. You would find the joy of children at play and the quaint memories of healthful happiness among people of constancy and endearment. Our native accents welcomed people from afar. They can feel at home here. After all, it is now *your* Charleston as well as mine.

So, the story is really "us." It was in our depths that we found our heights. It was the common people among us who performed in uncommon ways. There existed a multigenerational dormancy of cultural and geographic pride, now awakened and alert to the possibilities of tomorrow. Our fate had always been before us, forged in the toil of our past. Indeed, the concoction of greatness has many parts, none more important than the people. They arose together. With them were patience, tolerance, creativity and a refined sense of hospitality. Add in the grandiose idea that Charleston could be the last temporal stage before Eden. People changed us and, in doing so, enhanced a stunning tapestry. It is a fine weave of personalities.

There are sunsets. They represent the consummation of a good day spent in the Holy City. Those wondrous views happen elsewhere, I'm told, but not in the same deepened hues with the famously low profile of a high fantasy beneath them. That recurring sunset is our Charleston, and it lights up all of America.

A Tour with Charleston Tour Guides

Jane Thornhill, Rhetta Mendelsohn, David Compton and Fran Bennett

W hy are all of the flags flying in the same direction?" "Is it true that the mosquitoes don't bite on the second-floor porches?" "What kind of money do you use here?"

These are samples of the daily questions that Charleston tour guides answer. They range from the hilarious to the absurd. But God love 'em, the comments come from our best advertising network: the Charleston tourist.

Some of these comical questions are heard from the friendly horse-drawn carriage drivers of Old South Carriage Tours, owned and operated by David Compton. They get even better.

"Oh, we hear everything you can imagine on our carriages. We once had someone ask if our horses were real because they were not moving," Compton offered. "Some others?"

"Do the horses like their jobs? Does Charleston close on Sundays? Is it just windy here or will it be windy on the tour, too? Do people live in those houses? How many dead people are in that cemetery? Do you have to feed your horses? How long will a horse stand in the rain? Does this carriage tour go to Fort Sumter?"

Compton noted that he seems to get another great question every day. In a way, the tourists entertain the drivers.

"How much does it cost to see the harbor? When do they celebrate Christmas here? What time do the noon bells ring at St. Michael's? Which beach is closest to the ocean?"

David Compton gives a view of Charleston from its primary early transportation, the horse and carriage. *Courtesy of David Compton.*

"There is just no telling what humor you'll hear on a tour," Compton indicated. "I'll have a few more good ones next week!"

His thirty years in the business have given him a broad view of how Charleston and tourism have changed: "There are more tourists now. And it seems they're more educated. Some know much about Charleston history. And the city has certainly changed, too. I personally think that that hurricane, Hugo, in 1989, changed us for the better. Everybody was restoring everything at the same time. There was a great surge of community pride. In the next season tourists came to see the damage, a great deal of restoration had already taken place. The market was upgraded. While I miss the lower rents and the relaxed regulations, I'm glad to still be in business doing what I enjoy. Under Mayor Riley's leadership, the city's transformation from the early '80s to what we have today has been extraordinary."

The tour business in Charleston was not always so vibrant. Jane Thornhill knows this better than anyone. She's proudly eighty-seven and still working.

"The best of all was Liz Young. She knew everything there was to know about Charleston. She died recently at age ninety-two. She was both my mentor and my friend," Thornhill acknowledged.

"My husband, Van Noy, and I used to be gazelles. He's eighty-nine now. Now we're more like caterpillars to be stepped on. But I keep moving. I love to take people around. They are just amazed at Charleston. After all, I call it 'America's greatest living museum.' People here are so very friendly. I have some places where Charlestonians invite me and my tourist guests into their backyards. You wouldn't find that kind of friendliness anywhere else on a constant basis than in Charleston," Thornhill asserted.

"Some things that the tourists find interesting are that we didn't put windows on the north side of our houses out of respect for our neighbors' privacy. They just cannot believe the beauty of the private gardens here, and they are simply astonished to meet our citizens on the street who nod or say hello. That little bit of manners goes a long way," Thornhill intoned.

A person who has seen the growth and significance of Charleston tourism, Grand Dame Jane Thornhill. *Courtesy of Jane Thornhill Schachte.*

Thornhill has been taking tourists around since 1954. She has a classical Charleston inflection in her description of places. They're grand! Her downtown home exudes the pace of times past. There are exquisite family pieces and an atmosphere of prideful heritage. She is authentic Charleston.

"I remember much from my family. I heard my grandmother talk about the earthquake of 1886. It gives me a perspective of a major event to personally relate to my tourist guests," Thornhill said, smiling. "Since I give more private tours and some by automobile,

I have had a variety of unique requests. One I remember was taking two couples on tour. When I picked them up, they wanted to go to a bar first. So I took them to one back near Calhoun and King Streets at Burns Lane. They went in while I waited. They stayed in the bar for maybe two hours and then went on the tour. I guess they thought I worked as a taxi, too."

Rhetta Mendelsohn gives group, bus and private tours. She's seen a few fun times while touring: "Somebody asked me, 'If I give you a dollar, what kind of change would you give back?' I wasn't sure that the man was serious, at first. But he was. I told him that Charleston is a special place, but it's still in America. I'd give back four quarters.

A most knowledgeable tour guide, Rhetta Mendelsohn knows Charleston and the difficult times of the past. *Courtesy of Tommy McQueeney.*

"Mike Duffy, a federal judge, hosted an event for judges here and had asked me to give the attending judges a walking tour. It was high humidity and the temperature was in the mid-nineties. They all showed up as judges would. [Her husband, Joe Mendelsohn, is also a judge.] They all had coats and ties. After the first block there was no judge with a coat still on. By the second block, the ties were gone, too! We went for two and a half hours, as prearranged. They were all dripping with sweat. I asked if they wanted to stop on several occasions, but they all wanted to go on. They had never been here, and I really think, despite the heat, they were all enamored with the city."

In a follow-up phone conversation with Judge Duffy a week later, Duffy thanked Mendelsohn for the tour on what he knew was a "scorcher day." He described the tour as "the visiting judges all going on the Bataan Death March. Every group asks how cold or how hot it gets, as if Charleston were different than other southern cities. And there are terms we use here and assume are used elsewhere the same way. But that's not so. I remember taking a Texas group of World War II veterans into the Heyward Washington House. As they began to look around, I told them that I'd meet them back in the garden area. One asked, 'What garden? I don't see corn or tomatoes.' Here a garden represents a floral planting. In Texas, it represents vegetables.

"Another term we have used here since I can remember is the 'necessary house.' If you're not from Charleston, they think you're talking about where the electrical box is—not the bathroom," Mendelsohn reflected. "It is our way of saying something with the utmost politeness."

Some of the tourists are better known than others. Mendelsohn had a few celebrities she entertained: "A number of years back, Michael Douglas came, and I took him and his date on a tour. His date was the columnist Maureen Dowd. They were here with his college-age son, Cameron, and his girlfriend. We went out in a chauffeured station wagon on a city tour. It was a nice day in February. They wanted to sit outside to eat lunch. I took them to Blossom Café. Blossom was full. and while they waited at the bar, I took it upon myself to make sure that the host saw who was waiting. A table was ready right away! They insisted that I join them. I was working and just had a salad. No drinks. They had a sumptuous meal and plenty of champagne.

"I also had other well-known personalities like Sandra Day O'Connor, Antonin Scalia and Dee Dee Myers. Charleston is on everybody's travel wish list!

"The silliest questions I get are sometimes things that I answer while trying not to laugh. From the High Battery, someone asked me, 'Where's the ocean?' At that same location, someone asked, 'Is this salt water?' And I don't know how many times I was asked, 'What does Lowcountry mean?' But maybe the most memorable circumstance that made me laugh was on a joint bus tour to the gardens I shared with a lovely friend and fellow tour guide, Butler Mappus. We stood facing the seated passengers as the tour bus got started. I took the microphone and introduced us as their guides for the day. 'I'm Rhetta, this is Butler.' Somebody up front immediately said, 'No way!' Butler and I never realized that we really had that *Gone With the Wind* name when we worked together."

Mendelsohn laughed. "You know, you concentrate on what to say, not what they hear!"

Fran Bennett began giving tours at the insistence of her sister-in-law, Linda Wohlfeil Jones, an already established guide. She's never looked back on the experience as anything but interesting and fun.

"It's because you meet new people every time," Bennett confided. "People who come here cannot believe the beauty. We've been here all of our lives and never think about how special it is. The tourists get genuinely excited.

Fran Bennett became a tour guide through the prompting of her sister-in-law. She is passionate about Charleston. *Courtesy of the Hibernian Society of Charleston.*

"And there are moments. A young man in a group tour once asked me while I was pointing to Fort Sumter from the High Battery if it would be possible to ride his bicycle to the fort?

"Once at one of the plantation gardens on tour, I pointed out an alligator resting on the bank. I was asked if it was real. Of course, I couldn't resist! I told the group that the fake alligators were too expensive to maintain!

"People from other places rarely see things that we take for granted. For instance, they rarely see boiled peanuts. They never see pecans in the shell or Spanish moss. When I tell them that our palmetto bugs are like airborne roaches that can fly down but not up, they think I'm joking with them. Our state vegetable is the collard green. They have no idea what that is. I dare not mention Hoppin' John.

"On the educational side, the professional guides are really teachers that leave impressions. We have an opportunity and an obligation to set the record straight. We emphasize the importance of the Battle of Fort Sullivan [now Fort Moultrie] during the Revolution. History books forgot us for a hundred years after the Civil War—which is correctly named the 'War Between the States.' The 'War of Northern Aggression' and 'That Late Unpleasantness' always get a chuckle. But we are responsible for getting the facts right. The narrow single houses were incorrectly thought to be built in that style because of a tax on the width of the frontage. That sounds good, but it's wrong. I mention the history of the wealthy in Charleston. Several compelling sources of study show that nine of the ten wealthiest people in America lived in Charleston area near the time of the American Revolution. That's astonishing. So, it is no wonder that these large mansions are breathtaking to the tourists. We look at them here as if every city had these exquisite homes."

Bennett continued: "The one thing that I tell people that is overlooked that changed Charleston and the entire South is air conditioning. I cannot imagine how the people of the past dealt with the high summer season and the humidity here. We at least had electric fans when I grew up. The sweltering heat had to be a major disadvantage of living here hundreds of years ago.

"There are two other things that I noticed from the reaction of tourists that we, as Charlestonians, take for granted. We dress for church here. The tourists see us coming out of St. Michael's or St. Philip's and they gawk at the formality. They do not wear suits and pretty dresses to church like we do. We still hold to the more formal dress as a tradition of church attendance. Nobody else does that. To me, that makes us the Holy City, though I know that is not why we are called the Holy City."

She added: "Other things we take for granted include what we don't hear. I never really noticed it until tourists started asking me if we had outlawed car horns in the downtown area. Of course, we haven't. The big cities have that as a constant noise. In Charleston, blowing your horn is considered quite impolite. So we don't do it. We just wait patiently. That's our reflex—to be patient. Now I notice that when others from away have moved here, they have adopted our more genteel approach to traffic. It is rare to hear a car horn blown downtown. But really, I never thought about it until the tourists asked the question.

"And you know that when you leave Charleston to travel anywhere else, you have to adjust your use of meal language. Ours comes from the plantation traditions that had the largest meal served in the heat of the day. It was 'dinner.' As a result, we have breakfast, dinner and supper. Outside of Charleston, it's breakfast, lunch and dinner. I grew up on those terms. So I tell the tourists that there is no such thing as 'lunch' here."

The tourist industry has grown substantially. There are more and more restrictions on the carriage tours. All walking tour guides, as well as the carriage and drive-tour operators, must be licensed, to include testing given for historical accuracy. There are ghost tours and wine and cheese tours, garden tours and private home tours. There's an occasional pub-crawl. There are even rickshaws now, operated mostly by college students. They are a non-licensed exception, though that may change. There are cruise ships stirring some heated controversy for myriad reasons. All of these conveniences to the world of Charleston tourism lift this as the number one industry of America's number one travel destination city (cited by the Conde Nast Readers' Choice Awards of 2011).

Our tour guides are our frontline ambassadors. They edify each of us. So they can be excused for enjoying the humor of a comical question.

"Where do the homeless people live? In which direction do you have your sunsets? What was the Morris Island lighthouse used for? How long is the one-day bus pass good for?"

It is the Charleston tour guide, ostensibly, who makes a visitor's stay in Charleston memorable. Finding the pace of others' happiness on a vacation to the Holy City includes a genuine smile, an agreeable nod and the professionalism that being the prominent "host" of our magnificent peninsular home demands. They make our community a better place to visit. They represent an insight to our way of life through their kindness, their historical knowledge and their sincere congeniality.

Ken Burger from the Hip

R etirement is a swinging door for most. It moves you forward to the true rhythms of your soul and the actual pace of your slumber. It takes you back to the kaleidoscope of possibilities you dreamed about in your youth. It feigns the completion of something that is incomplete after all: a life. It comes as earned respite and leaves as nostalgia. Ken Burger knew this before he sent in his resignation letter to Charleston's *Post and Courier*, the South's oldest daily newspaper (established in 1803). With the pressure of deadlines lurking, columns of five hundred words trimmed and the smell of paper chemicals and ink pervading the sounds of production, the newspaper business seems to have more deaths and disabilities than retirees. Retiring is the ultimate desired outcome.

"When I started, the noise at a newspaper was really loud and different. The constant typing—on old typewriters—the phones ringing and the thick smoke that filled the large rooms was a daily atmosphere that you dealt with. Now it's keyboards and cellphones, 'no smoking' and sterile. You can hear someone talking way across the room," Burger noted. "The world of newspapers has changed."

The metamorphosis of newspapers has nothing on Burger. His story is worthy of a news desk headline covered by a features writer with a sidebar of victory mindful of the best comeback of the sports pages. He would not likely impose on the society pages.

It seems the ink ran in his blood. As a native of the small town of Allendale, he was encouraged as a schoolboy. There, something rusty could also count as rustic. For Burger, Allendale would serve as a perfect incubation for his life's work.

Burger recalled the beginnings: "An English teacher first encouraged me. I was told that I should write. I found myself retyping articles I read in the paper just to try and get a feel of what the writer was thinking when he wrote them. In my educational training, as well as in practice, I measured punctuation as 50 percent of writing. I'm not a big fan of the semi-colon, but I love the comma. They're traffic signs. Slow down and stop. And equally, they can destroy a story. Too much is just too much. I became the king of the fragment. I learned to use rhetorical devices. Writing came easy."

Burger never met a metaphor that couldn't be turned into a five or an onomatopoeia that didn't make him envision an ATM in Tokyo.

Burger is his own man. He is like a stray wolf who has gnawed on depravity long enough to recognize a whiff of something else beyond the next hill. He's a survivor. He tells it like it is because he knows exactly how it has been. Only his closest friends "get" him. If you're seeking a truth, nothing with frills and icing, he's your man. He would have been a fine Sergeant Joe Friday. He is more honest than he is brutally honest, but sometimes the distinction disappears. And he can do it with the most casual of down-home smiles.

"I graduated at the very bottom of my class at the University of Georgia," Burger proudly relates. "I know this because I had exactly a 2.0, and you had to have that as a minimum to graduate."

As a journalism major, Burger was quick to find work. He was hired by the *State* newspaper in Columbia, South Carolina. For the next ten years, he had regular paychecks, a struggling marriage, a growing reputation and a demon. The demon tried to gobble it all.

"There was no challenge I have ever faced in my life to compare with alcohol. It takes over. It destroys families, friendships, careers, and ultimately, it will destroy the alcoholic. I was the alcoholic being destroyed," Burger recounted. "I could continue and die or do the hardest thing you can ever imagine: quit. I have not had a drink since 1980, and I will never drink again."

To be sure, Burger has had challenges that would fill other lifetimes. To point to alcohol as his biggest challenge intimates something other than what would be expected. Burger has also beaten deadly prostate cancer.

"Cancer's different. It is a very personal challenge, but in simpler terms, it's in the hands of professionals—the oncologists, surgeons and even nurses. The patient has very little control. You go through a lot of physical changes, and some days are just terrible. You're going to make it or you're going to die. That's all based on the cancer and the treatment,"

Burger stated. "With alcohol, there are no professional control mechanisms. You are the control. You are the only one who can beat alcoholism. Nobody can do it for you. You're on your own. And for me, that battle was the greatest battle of all time. I should say battles because you battle it every day. And the war is never over. Beating alcohol when you feel helpless and alone is the greatest personal triumph there is…or at least, the greatest I've experienced in my lifetime.

"I was thirty years old. I was spiraling to death. I was on a progressive and unrelenting train to the grave with only a small hope of jumping off. I got lucky. I was able to jump off. Now, I've been not drinking longer than I was drinking. My life changed. My writing got better. There are two truths about alcoholism. It makes you a liar and it makes you a thief. You can survive a divorce, a bankruptcy, even cancer. You cannot survive as an alcoholic. You have to quit or die."

A change of scenery helped. Burger moved to Charleston in 1984 to work for the *News & Courier*, and by 1985, he was dispatched to Washington, D.C., to cover Congress for the paper. After two years on the Hill, he returned to Charleston to begin a twenty-one-year stint writing a well-read and often controversial sports column. He moved back to the news department to cap his sterling career with a popular metro column about everyday life in Charleston.

"I came here in a $500 car I paid too much for," Burger quipped. "I came to work for the worst newspaper in the state at that time. Charleston was an old, gray Confederate relic. You could get in any bar here under-aged, I remember. Charleston was not a destination; it was the place I landed. I needed a job. It turned out to be the right place at the right time with the right stuff. The paper and the city went from worst to best in twenty years. Once you come, you never leave. So it's not only a world-class city for those visiting, it's a wonderful place to live."

In 1991, the *News & Courier* absorbed the *Evening Post* to become the *Post and Courier*. Burger's first marriage had ended in Columbia. A second ensued, then ended and sued. Living the hours required to maintain a career in newspapers has never been conducive to matrimonial bliss. There are sixteen-hour days, weekends set for clashes of titans with the accompanying intense readership interest. There are meetings and press conferences and interviews and research. Not all sporting events come to you. There is a prerequisite of frequent travel. There's nothing like a Masters golf tournament or an NCAA Final Four to distance a relationship. Even a third marriage came as a seemingly natural progression. By the time Hurricane

Ken Burger has punctuated his brilliant newspaper career with his newfound joy as an engaging southern novelist. *Courtesy of the* Post & Courier.

Hugo struck Charleston in 1989, it was blown away as well.

Indeed, Burger moved into and out of relationships before the happy circumstance of meeting his wife, Bonnie Grossman, an adjunct professor in the School of Business at the College of Charleston. She has been an inspirational catalyst to Burger for that other career he always desired. He's a novelist.

Burger's well-earned and resolute following through his lengthy prowess as a witty and insightful columnist has been its own reward. In addition to published collections of his columns, Burger has embarked on a literary career that has been lauded by others. His first two novels, *Swallow Savannah* and *Sister Santee*, have established him as a viable and charismatic southern writer. His easy pace, flow of thought and simple articulation would place him in the unique company of those we cling to by the breezy Spanish moss–adorned oaken avenues. We recount them as William Faulkner, Harper Lee, Tennessee Williams, Flannery O'Connor, Margaret Mitchell and Robert Penn Warren. They have resurfaced in our generation as John Grisham and Pat Conroy. They are one with the southern sentiment of place and time. It is what sustains us all.

Burger's wit is best styled in a light and hilarious collection of tales from his southern experiences titled *Baptized in Sweet Tea*. It has become a favorite for Charleston sitting rooms and parlors. Burger's third novel, *Salkehatchie Soup*, is a 2012 publication, extending not only his lifelong romance for the written word but also his alliterative creativity in the art of book titles.

Citadel associate athletic director Andy Solomon knows Burger well. He presented his observations of personal insight to Burger's personality and skill as a writer: "Ken Burger, who was a post–Hurricane Hugo roommate more than a quarter century ago, remains my best friend today. He possesses that uncanny knack for meeting a stranger on the street and, within minutes, departs with a new acquaintance. And as a writer, he's like the Cooper River in that he can make words flow like a strong current, and in several spots, he can be surprisingly deep."

The expectation of Burger's post-retirement journalistic accomplishment would be, by readership accounts, a given. His awards from every imaginable press association announce him as one with a natural ability and deft timing. Being honest with himself, he never hung the awards. His office walls were always devoid of the plaques and citations. He never needed anyone to tell him he had reached a pinnacle or was lauded by a panel of experts. The really special ones are kept in a box under his desk.

"Those things get in the way," Burger deadpanned. "Maybe it would impress someone coming in, but being an award recipient never really was a goal. Writing is my goal. I don't need to wait for a mood or have just the right circumstances fall into place like some of the famous authors you read about. I just get my computer and write. It is what I've done for so long. I can smoke a keyboard with anyone. I'm fast. I may be the fastest typist in the history of sports. I think of what I want to say and type it in as my thoughts move me. My thoughts go to my fingers. I don't need it to be raining or to have a seat with a view. I just need to sit and start writing. Write for a newspaper for a year. They pay you to be in the mood. They fire you if you're not."

Burger's routine now has no curfew. The delivery trucks are not waiting on his next paragraph or headline-grabber. He has the retreat of a wide beach at Seabrook Island to walk and dream up characters and plots. The names are in his catalogue.

For years, Burger has been tuned into unique names. Some he found on airport luggage, others in the obituaries, on player rosters and in press guides. The modest appraisal of a good name is a science to Burger. The good ones make it; the forgetful ones are forgotten. Try finding another Atticus Finch or Rhett Butler. They're not easy. The crafting of characters and the articulation of words into sentences and paragraphs is an art form he appreciates profoundly.

"I could make you mad, sad, cry or laugh with words. There are 988,868 of them. The English language is a buffet. The secret is to choose the right word," Burger detailed. "Mark Twain once remarked that he 'would have written a shorter letter, but he didn't have the time.' It's harder to write with brevity. I had 500 words to write to encourage a fifty-cent purchase. The art, skill, craft and ability to connect with other people is much harder with words. In person, it's easy. Can you do it from a distance with words?

"Writing is music to me. You translate sights, sounds and smells. You package excitement. You evoke an emotion. I am happiest when I write. Making sentences to me is the same as connecting trains. They are a part of something going somewhere magical," Burger expressed. "I especially like speaking about it to young schoolchildren. They are so impressionable. School is an elimination program to find out what you're not good at—band, sports, math, et cetera.

"Kids today are concerned that newspapers will go away and there will not be writers in the future. There will always be writers. Where they write and in what type of media will continue to change. But writers will write."

Burger is at home in Charleston. He loves the excellent golf courses and the splendidly small events. He is genuinely excited about his favorite "retired" activity: walking the beach at Seabrook Island. The area that has given him personal growth has also grown on him: "I lived just about everywhere. I lived at Folly Beach, downtown, Mount Pleasant, Isle of Palms, West Ashley, John's Island and on Seabrook. I guess you could say that I'm here for the duration. Is there any place better?"

His career is over and just starting at the same time.

"I tried to stay objective during my career—to cover all sides of a story and not to become biased. You sometimes find yourself thinking as a skeptic, but it is part of what you do as a good newspaper reporter," Burger explained. "The lines are more blurred now because of the Internet. It invites commentary and bias. The public has lost its ability to discern news reporting from editorializing. A column is, by nature, biased.

"In my career as a sportswriter, people may have gotten an impression that I had a leaning one way or another. What they never understood was that I am not a sports fan. I didn't care. I didn't give a damn who won."

He is refreshingly honest. Time and place were always deeply important to him. Reaching through the window dressing to get to the center of a story or to prompt the proper emotion is what he strived to accomplish. To do so sometimes brought on controversy.

"You have to be fearless to be a writer. I couldn't write some of my columns in another city. In Charleston, there was always great latitude. There are no major-league sports teams. It is not a truly large-market city," Burger noted.

"So I was a person who was a writer that reported events. My events happened to be sports. My training and objectivity was to write on any and all subjects. Sports in Charleston had to be no different than any other news subject.

"There is also the aspect of being a good reporter. Early on, I found that the only bad question is the one you forgot to ask."

There is not much he has forgotten in any arena. Burger has a deck full of stories. Pick a card, any card. He has even kept the jokers: "All reporters see and hear about things that may or may not belong in the newspapers. There is a great deal of discretion behind the scenes. There is a hand-in-glove relationship between sportswriters and sports. Many things go unreported. Yet less gets by now than before. Years ago, in the days of Babe Ruth and Ty Cobb, there was an unwritten rule. The sportswriters traveled with the teams. Nothing outside the chalk lines of the field ever got into the paper. The reader only saw the player as what his playing ability allowed the writer to report. The bar brawls, the women, the gambling and the drunkenness were things seen but accepted as not part of the assignment. The reporter's stories were submitted only on the narrow and thin surface of sports."

"Surface" is a defining word that invites more detail. That's where Burger excels.

It's the thick surface of the sand that Burger now walks daily, conjuring the right word and the perfect alliterative phrase. He will return to his keyboard and dance his fingers into a story for the ages on the vagaries of life, the scent of the ocean and the warmth of the winter sun in Charleston. He will do what he has done with a poignant passion for a lifetime. He will write.

Martha Rivers Ingram
and the Art of Living

Simultaneously, she is both a Shakespearean sonnet and Dickens classic. Alas, poor Yorick, Sonnet 55, knows her well:

> *Not marble, nor the gilded monuments*
> *Of princes shall outlive this powerful rhyme,*
> *But you shall shine more bright in these contents…*
> *…Shall you pace forth, your praise shall still find room,*
> *Even in the eyes of all posterity*
> *That wear this world out to the ending doom.*
> *So till the judgment that your self arise,*
> *You live in this, and dwell in lovers' eye.*[1]

Martha Robinson Rivers Ingram likes to be called "Martha," even by those she first meets. That's ironic. One's first tendency would be to bow or genuflect. She has been recorded as among the greatest private donor-advocates of higher education in the nation's history. She may likely exceed even that impressive accolade in her passion for the arts, especially the performing arts. She has heightened all the perceptions of Nashville, Tennessee, by her encouragement within all manners of art. In doing so, she introduced a cultural Music City revival, building the next generation of Old World nuances for an already great metropolis that boasted the Grand Ole Opry, Vanderbilt University and Old Hickory himself, Andrew Jackson. It is bettered by better yet, thanks to Martha.

The sonnet sings of her joy, her majesty and her timelessness. It even laments the love of her life, the late E. Bronson Ingram II. He was the iconic microcosm of American ingenuity. But the sonnet is Martha. It captures her foresight and her formidable impact on the world around her. Generations forward will know her, indubitably.

But what about the Dickens classic?

Try *A Tale of Two Cities*. Ingram is from Charleston. She went to Ashley Hall School before obtaining her undergraduate degree at Vassar in Poughkeepsie, New York, and later returning to Charleston. Her father, John Minott Rivers, a graduate of the famed Wharton School at the University of Pennsylvania, was an astute banker who took a leap of faith and bought WCSC radio. The synergy between John Minott Rivers and the previous owner, Francis Hipp, had been inlaid from the trust of Mr. Rivers's commitment to assist Mr. Hipp in making a profit from the station. In time, Hipp sold the radio station to Rivers on a handshake. Prior to its legal transfer, Hipp suddenly died. Hipp's children, knowing the reputation of Rivers's integrity in the community, honored the handshake agreement. Rivers was the father of South Carolina's first television broadcast network, WCSC-TV Channel 5, which went on the air in 1953.[2] Martha joined her father's company after graduation, in training to take her father's place. As part of the effort, she became a "disc jockey, aka Elizabeth Crawford."

Ingram enjoys the benefit of other family—a younger sister, Elizabeth Craig (Mrs. Richard Lewine), and a younger brother, John Minott Rivers Jr. Elizabeth lives in Charleston. Her late husband was a New York Broadway producer. After his death in 2006, Elizabeth moved back to Charleston and has become an enthusiastic volunteer for Ashley Hall and other educational institutions. Her brother, John, remained in Charleston and is the owner of the upscale Gateway Center offices, among other holdings, at the corner of Calhoun and East Bay Streets.

Daughter Martha attributes her passion for her home city to the profound lessons and community spirit of her parents.

"My parents were my inspiration for so much I have had the opportunity to pursue and participate in," Ingram recalled. "My father was a forward-thinking person who often told me, 'Get the best education you can but also learn how to type—if you want to get a job.' I took a typing course at Rice Business School on his advice, although lamenting the missed boating and beach activities with my friends that summer as I was learning to type. After I completed the course and became a much better typist, he said, 'See, that didn't hurt you a bit.' And he was right. I've used that skill ever since. He

There may be no historical comparison to the benificence of native Charlestonian Martha Rivers Ingram. *Courtesy of Ingram Publishing.*

never told me that it was a handicap to be a girl. He, in fact, told me I was smart enough to succeed him. (My sister wanted to be a teacher and my brother was [is] ten years younger.)

"My mother was also a person of great encouragement. She took great interest in us and was equally set on our education potential. There is one story of my sister and me that emphasizes my parents' intention of teaching responsibility. At our church, St. Philip's, we were supposed to be saving money to put in a 'Mite Box'—i.e., 'little box'—for those who needed food and medical care elsewhere in the world. Well, we did not follow through, and the time to finalize the collection of the money at Easter approached. So my sister and I had this idea to raise money. We sponsored a flower show in our backyard at ten cents per entry. Arrangements were submitted for judging; parents came to see our show. We had plenty of entries and took the money we had earned and put this into the 'Mite Box.' Our parents had refused to bail us out so that we had to find a way to generate money on our own. We did so, and in getting the money, we had 'saved face.' Both my sister and I had enjoyed earning the money that we gave away and have been doing this ever since."

It is not enough that she incited a renewal of classical culture in the American South. It is that she did it with vision, confidence and panache. She has been there before.

"Charitable giving is a wonderful feeling," Ingram intoned. "There are so many others that experience this surge of feelings and understand the good feeling and the profound benefit you are able to bestow upon current generations as well as those to come. I have now had quite an opportunity to be part of the process of planning, fundraising and designing some of Nashville's cultural buildings—and now one in Charleston.

"When I grew up in Charleston, there was little in the way of the arts. We had a modest symphony, and I learned to play classical piano and to be a beginning ballerina but had never seen a professional ballet or heard a fine orchestra. When I entered Vassar, my friends there had come from richer cultural cities that had opera, accomplished symphonies and classical ballet. Charleston had been deprived of this owing to the calamitous aftermath of that 'recent unpleasantness,' as my grandmother called it—the Civil War. Nashville, same as Charleston, experienced a complete artistic decline. The Yankees occupied Nashville for three full years! It recovered quicker than Charleston. So when we started down this path for artistic excellence in Nashville, we built a coalition with government and the private sector.

Everybody wanted something for which to be proud. I was convinced we would be able to do just that in Nashville. Now, we are doing it in Charleston."

Ingram was a history major with an emphasis on cultural arts while at Vassar. She has now been to many venues across the globe and experienced the gradations of tone, form and style. She knows people. She understands community. She exhibits an acute business mind. She can inspire others. Her leadership skills are only exceeded by her exemplary generosity. So, when a Spoleto conversation in 2008 with Charleston mayor Joseph P. Riley Jr. led to the City of Charleston's most pressing facility need, Ingram offered a solution: "The architecture of the 1960s was an unfortunate period for America. The J. Palmer Gaillard Municipal Auditorium was a good product of that time. But now, it looks like a cross between a factory and a delicatessen, and the acoustics are not good. It is so un-Charleston. My parents were friends with its namesake, Mayor Gaillard (Charleston's mayor 1959–74),[3] and my father was active in St. Philip's Church vestry along with Palmer Gaillard. He certainly deserves to have the naming rights, and I would be opposed to any change of that wonderful name. But that building needs to be redone and brought into the new science of acoustics and multiuse cultural centers. Everybody wants to see a state-of-the-art upgrade of this old facility. I do too! There is a very personal family history there. My mother and father attended an event at the Gaillard the night that my father passed away in 1988. They had a nice evening with so many Charleston friends at the symphony. It was a special evening. He came home, went to bed and died in his sleep. He was only two months shy of his eighty-fifth birthday."

It was a painful, yet prideful, memory. "The Gaillard site is well situated and is walkable from many places downtown, very near the College of Charleston. That is so essential to buildings like this. The City of Charleston also needs office space. They're currently paying nearly $1 million a year to rent space. The rendering of a new Gaillard would move city offices to the Gaillard perimeter to give it daytime activity, share security and operational expenses. It would be open in the evenings for the performing arts, as well as other uses; schoolchildren can see performances from 10:00 a.m. to noon. It can give downtown Charleston the largest banquet hall in the area by seating 1,800 people (formerly in the plain exhibition hall constructed of 'bricko-block').There would be an enlarged and enhanced catering kitchen. The concert hall would have modern and comfortable seating for 1,800, in addition to tremendous improvement to the acoustics. Acoustics define an auditorium. The best acoustics make the best auditoriums. And auditoriums are the most prominent place in a city and create the warm feeling of community."

There are opera houses in many great cities. None is better than Nashville's Schermerhorn Symphony Center. Its cost was $125 million. Its local project chair? Martha Rivers Ingram. The Schermerhorn is known for its precise sound clarity. The same technology will be in place at the Gaillard. The same team of architects and acousticians are on the job for the Gaillard.

Getting the sound right is not a given but is *the* essential element in the project.

The Sydney Opera House? The acoustics are said to have boomeranged. It's a beautiful and iconic building that fails its musical mission. It's considered Australia's most successful failure this side of Mel Gibson. The *Alte Oper*, "Old Opera House," in Frankfurt, Germany, is heralded as among the prettiest buildings in all of Allemagne. But the rebuilt icon is thought of as the sauerkraut of acoustics.[4] Yet perhaps the worst of all is the Hong Kong Cultural Centre (HKCC), which, according to artists, "throws piano notes back at the pianists and makes it impossible to concentrate or even to record."[5] They are building its replacement. The banging of pilings and constant jackhammers has not been a deterrence to the acoustic-deprived HKCC's continued use.

If getting the acoustics right is essential, bet on Ingram. Ingram is betting on Ingram. Her financial commitment to this project will mean she will be responsible for perhaps the largest private donation ever given to the City of Charleston. She'll likely pass pre-Revolutionary Patriot Charles Pinckney and antebellum shipping magnate James Adger. Her largesse is intended for the future of Charleston's previously proclaimed romance of culture. That was in 1860. A century and a half has passed. The Gaillard will rate among the world's finest staging and acoustical venues for the performing arts, especially for the Charleston Symphony. Yes, our Gaillard! They'll strip it to the steel and dress it in most deserving attire. You'll see marble and crystal, mahogany and polished brass. Fortuitously, Ingram's bonus of expertise in these matters is indispensable. She's "been there, done that." She understands every detail. The great news for those in Charleston is that Ingram will be available to personally assist. There is no one more qualified, more passionate or more driven.

If this sounds too good to be true, then you, dear reader, have not been following the career of Martha Rivers Ingram. Timely background assistance follows. She has already been the person most responsible for the three-theater

Tennessee Performing Arts Center. It was an eight-year mission. She was up to the task. The aforementioned Kenneth Schermerhorn Symphony Center effort was Ingram's idea. She chaired the Nashville Symphony Association. The Martha Rivers Ingram Center for the Performing Arts is on the campus of Vanderbilt University, where she and her family donated $300 million for the university. She recently stepped down after twelve years as chair of the Vanderbilt University Board of Trust. Need there be more evidence?

The Ingram family endows a total of fifty full undergraduate academic scholarships at Vanderbilt each year. Yes, fifty! They are the Ingram Scholars. Nobody does that. Vanderbilt has an average class size of nineteen students. There are theoretically two and a half classes of Ingram Scholars enjoying the benefits of perhaps one of the finest academic institutions in the country. Every day is astonishing. They hail from every walk of life, from multiple countries, from every race, creed and socioeconomic background. The Ingram family endows every year; there are always fifty Ingram Scholars on campus. In time, those scholarships will total five thousand. Ingram Scholars are essentially a small college within a big college. Several have become student government leaders, and many graduates are making their way in the wide world of government, business and education. They are becoming leaders, fulfilling Vanderbilt's main mission: to create "world leaders."

In addition, Ingram has chaired several other major business and community boards. A person of her expertise, generosity, foresight and pure community spirit is quite rare.

Tandy Rice and Martha Rivers Ingram have much in common. Rice is among the most recognizable personalities in the Music City. His career includes roles as agent to the top talents of Nashville, from entertainer Dolly Parton to the late comedian Jerry Clower. His aunt was none other than the late Minnie Pearl. (Howdy!) This highly enthused white-haired icon has hosted radio and television shows ranging in subjects from the Grand Ole Opry to Nashville happenings, with the biggest among them being Martha Rivers Ingram. He has interviewed her multiple times, and they are the best of friends. That "other" city for which they both hold much fondness is Charleston. Rice spent four years at The Citadel as an English major. He graduated in 1961. He and Ingram both hold honorary degrees from The Citadel. There are two people in Nashville everybody knows: Ingram and Rice.

Rice attributed the sentiment of the Nashville community to Ingram: "Nashville's acknowledged 'greatness' of many dimensions is due in very large part to Martha Ingram's leadership and support by example.

Vanderbilt's pace-setting greatness owes much to the entire Ingram family. If you were to remove the Ingram influence from the composition of this city, I'm afraid we would be a barren non-event, city-wise. All hail to the Ingrams, children and all, totally class citizens of this amazing city. Consider this your Diamond Jubilee, Martha! I bow deeply, unhesitatingly, thankfully and proudly."

Ingram has lived in Nashville for five decades. So her affinity for Charleston is especially significant and timely.

The rebuilt Gaillard, with all the city offices and the banquet hall, will cost $142 million. Ingram will chair the project to raise private funds. The enterprise is expected to become one of the most successful public-private partnerships for cultural arts renovation ever attempted. The commitment of the public sector is only 50 percent. Ingram and her volunteers will raise $71 million; the City of Charleston has already identified its $71 million. The approved project will be completed by 2014.

If you toss around a million here and a million there, it begins to add up to real money. Ingram might have lost count, but *Business Week* magazine once ran a story on charitable giving that cited her as among the top fifty most generous philanthropists around.[6] Ingram is not a hoarder; she's a sorter. There are passions important to posterity that she feels responsible to endow. There is but one of her, unfortunately. She gets tugged, pulled and entangled. Yet she does not complain. She simply applies herself to the focus before her green-eyed vision.

The 2012 version of this fine lady is quite impressive. She is thin and petite and exudes energy, confidence and insight into how to achieve the otherwise unachievable.

So Charleston came into her view. She has been active with the Spoleto Festival, USA, nearly since its inception. She serves on the Spoleto Board and in fact chaired the board for three years. She coddles the memories of her birth city. To her, there is no experience quite like growing up in Charleston.

"There are so many bittersweet moments I recall," Ingram detailed. "I had such happiness here. There are sad memories, too. There is much I wish I could do again. I remember wanting something as simple as a kickball, and my mother told me I could only earn it with my academic work. She agreed to give me a quarter for each A. I worked hard to get the As and eventually bought that kickball. It was the pursuit and hard work that made that prize so special. I will always remember that.

"And I can remember being such a tomboy. My friend Lavinia Maybank and I used to climb up the neighborhood brick walls and shimmy across from one yard to the next. I remember Miss Poppenheim at 29 Meeting Street, who would beg us to get down and invite us in for tea. She had graduated from Vassar. She seemed like such a sad old woman with her black velvet choker-style necklace. She was properly spoken. We were only eleven or twelve, and she would tell us that we needed to act more ladylike and go to Vassar. We said we would try. We had teachers like Mary Vardrine McBee, a graduate of Smith College, and her sister, Estelle McBee. They founded Ashley Hall in 1909.

"It was such a simple time, and people in the neighborhood looked out for you. We seemed to all know each other. It was Ms. Caroline Pardue, headmistress of Ashley Hall, who told me I was 'good enough' to make it to Vassar. So I applied and 'made it.'

"The obvious driving force behind Charleston's rise to prominence is Mayor Joe Riley. He really is a visionary. He is such a steady influence and the best government official I have ever worked with on any project. Some politicians wiggle all over the place. Not Joe. He's a stalwart. Some may become angry about this or that position, but just look around. Joe Riley has changed Charleston for the better. Now there are factions making a fuss about the cruise ships docking here. Why would they not want to come here? It's an incredible city, and Charleston needs more revenue. There is so much that is positive about Charleston. The city is a walking city with more charm than anyplace else in the United States. You can thank the late Frances Edmunds, who insisted that we keep its charm by keeping the old houses original, and people like Liz Young, who had such an enthusiasm for preservation. She noticed what others from away noticed. Charleston is special.

"When I got married in 1958, I went away as one person," Ingram noted. "I had four children between 1960 and 1965. With twelve grandchildren now, I can come back as twenty-one people. There are twenty-one when we are all here. That's amazing. It is more and more difficult to get everyone together in Charleston as we used to do every Thanksgiving. But I come here as much as I can. What I miss the most is the Charleston harbor. I love the view from the Battery. You really do not realize how much it means to you unless you are away. I love putting on my walking shoes when I get here and going out to make sure 'my harbor' is still there. I have not figured out yet how to get the ocean to Nashville! When in Charleston, I walk every morning for an hour—rain or shine. I love it so."

Ingram's wide interests exceed even the arts. She also authored *E. Bronson Ingram: Complete These Unfinished Tasks of Mine*, a biographical and compelling view of her late and beloved husband. She wrote it to retell the incredible Ingram family history for their grandchildren and those beyond. A tender tribute, the book inspired a much larger readership with its dedication to the American entrepreneurial spirit. In it one will find a brilliant emanation of a small family business from an Eau Claire, Wisconsin lumber mill to the invention of ISBN codes, oil derricks, river barges and book warehouses. Each generation of Ingram beneficiaries seemed to take the foundation of greatness further yet. Martha Ingram is the matriarch. Her business acumen became the next line in the famed progression.

Ingram also dedicated a book to the history and rise of the arts in Nashville, the city that is accorded the title of the "Athens of the South." After all, can you name a place other than Nashville that has a Parthenon housing a beautiful, enormous statue of Athena? Truly, art flourishes in Nashville. Ingram's much-researched *Apollo's Struggle* reveals stories of Nashville's long history of the arts. Somebody needed to research Nashville's rich genealogy of the theater. Ingram did it for the benefit of the coming generations. No surprise there! Local fundraising groups occasionally use the landmark Parthenon edifice. The Parthenon was built for the Nashville Centennial in 1897.[7] Ancient Athens thrives in America. In Nashville, you can even find a summer production of *Antigone* or the *Medea*[8] outdoors in Centennial Park, near the Parthenon.

There are other books. Nearly ten million titles exist in only one distribution point globally. Ingram Content Group (Nashville area) is the largest book wholesale distributor on the planet. They provide for some seventy-one thousand[9] retail and library customers from Afghanistan to Zimbabwe. In addition, Ingram Content (Lightning Source) prints things that may seem innocuous but are necessary, like owner's manuals and assembly references and guidebooks for manufacturers. Their state-of-the-art digital production can "take an order from Amazon before noon and have it digitally printed and shipped out by 5:00 p.m.," according to Ingram.

The book that is not written is whispered from generation to generation. It is the height of reality that meets the depths of the surreal. The endowed beneficiaries are Nashville, Charleston and America. They are the Ingrams. They have enhanced education, the performing arts and the economic landscape of America. There are Ingrams coming of age for the future of other American passions. There is but one Martha Rivers Ingram. There exists the propitious among us, the lucky ones who will ever climb the Acropolis and have the exalted privilege of calling her "Martha."

Lonnie Hamilton...and All That Jazz!

S ome days Lonnie Hamilton just laughs. It's his natural way. He's quite alive for a man honored by the area's most utilized junction of roads: the "Lonnie Hamilton III Interchange." It was accorded, and then dedicated, in 1995 by a joint session of the South Carolina legislature. He simply smiled when they unveiled the signage and then spoke about others he had met along life's path.

Being gregarious is Hamilton's strongest suit. There is always a twinkle in his eye and a serenade of music in his soul. He may have played show tunes and jazz hits a thousand times in his head. He played them even more in person. Hamilton is one of the more accomplished jazz musicians ever to grace the Holy City.

But there is a lot more to this venerable man than music. Hamilton took his love of people into his vision to build a better community— and he got involved. He was elected to the Charleston County Council five times. He became the chairman. Hamilton was a stalwart for the development of the Spoleto Arts Festival in Charleston and several other multicultural attraction events. He saw the future of Charleston as it related to the arts.

Hamilton wore four hats. He was a band director, a teacher, an entertainer and a county councilman. Which defined his career?

"One thing has defined me more than any one thing I have done," announced the spry eighty-four-year-old gentleman. "I have always loved people. So whatever I did, it was part of that, whether it was teaching a young musician or working within the political realm to make Charleston a better place to live. People have always been the reason of any motivation I have had."

Hamilton is small framed and youthful in appearance, despite his full endowment of white hair. He never hides the assets of his warmth shown within his deep brown eyes and brilliant alabaster grin. His friendship has a chemistry of immediacy. You know you've met a fine man of great experience and insight. That grin won a following. It is genuine. It introduces a friendship invitation and a capture of golden memories in concert.

Lonnie Hamilton III is a native Charlestonian. He was born in an area called Silver Hill near Accabee, where he spent his youth. "Individuals in these and other similar communities had very little wealth; however, they shared whatever resources they had among them, and no one lost a meal. There were outhouses instead of bathrooms, but no one was considered poor. Everyone knew each other, and adults were heavy-handed with discipline. It was on the 'neck' of the peninsula and eventually absorbed into North Charleston."

Hamilton noted, "There wasn't much there at that time. We moved a few times. Nobody had anything. Everything we had was shared. We were all in the same shape. I became interested in music in the ninth grade, trying to get to Grants Park, where there was an outdoor music pavilion."

Grants Park, near Rosemount at Four Mile, hosted outdoor musical concerts and was famous for the showcasing of young talent from across the Lowcountry.

"I was very much an introvert. I never said much. But I listened. It was rare to see the expression of joy in people I remember, though I was a happy young man," Hamilton recalled. "People who played music at Grants Park seemed so happy. This appeared so special to me at that time. I wanted to smile and be happy like them. Music seemed to make them happy, and I saw it as a key for me to be the same. So I told my grandfather that I wanted a saxophone for $135. I was only thirteen. My grandfather helped me to get the saxophone. I enrolled at Burke School for their music program under the direction of Holland W. Daniel, the band director. That really started me into the music career.

"After one year at Burke, I was good enough to join the Jenkins Orphanage Band. Now that was a big leap. They were the best band going. We had a raggedy old bus and 'May Pop' tires. We went everywhere. We had twenty band members, and they were all fine musicians taught by

Vibrant and witty, Lonnie Hamilton understands the rhythm of music and politics. *Courtesy of Tommy McQueeney*.

the best. Now, there are only two of us left: James Tolbert and me. That old bus finally gave way, and we toured in that second year with cars."

A Charleston legend, Reverend Daniel Jenkins passed away in 1937.[10] The band continued in his tradition: "We became popular and were requested to special events. We played ragtime, dance and just about everything you could think of while going up and down the seaboard in 1943 and 1944. Man, those were some special times during the war years. We made people happy, and that made us feel like we were important to the war effort. We were still too young to join the service—and when the war ended, we were still too young."

One would certainly gain the sense that Hamilton would have been a fine soldier for a cause. Hamilton stayed on key with his music as the war ended and the "baby boom" ensued. As he intimated, it became his lifelong passion.

"Music is not a gift, it's a study. To be good in the music business you have to study it to the level that would be a master's program. It has to be a part of you," Hamilton noted. "And there are all kinds of music for everyone to enjoy. There's pop and country, jazz, classical and blues. I always liked to play the blues. Blues comes from everyday life. There are rhythms of deep meaning that you have to feel in your bones. There are notes that give the sense of a bad feeling. The blues is like a therapy. You have to feel your way through the rhythm of the blues.

"I played for years with the Diplomats. We played all of the jazz tunes. We played for nine years at Henry's on the Market. We played tunes from the movie *Rich in Love*, from the novel of the same name by Josephine Humphreys. One of the tunes we play, the 'Ugly Ways Blues,' always seemed to be a favorite."

The novelist Josephine Humphreys is from Charleston and a graduate of Ashley Hall School. The movie, starring Albert Finney and Jill Clayburgh, was shot in Charleston.

"The music was part of what I did. It was always in my heart," Hamilton continued. "But there were other areas that had my attention. I had great mentoring influences that gave me the desire and confidence to get into the political arena. There was Malcolm C. 'Doc' Hursey. He inspired me to get involved. Dr. Charlie Wallace was another one. He has been a fine friend over many years."

In twenty years as the band director at Bonds Wilson High School, Hamilton taught nearly 3,600 students. He gained many friendships as these young people attained adulthood. His personality was encompassing. It circumnavigated the sphere of those he taught. When Hamilton thought about going into politics, it was the band members he taught who came forward to lend him support. He still maintains many of those relationships.

Hamilton ran for a Charleston County Council seat in 1970. He won. In doing so, he became the first African American to be elected to that body.[11] Later, he was twice elected chairman. It was under his watch that the marriage of the Charleston community and Maestro Gian Carlo Menotti's Spoleto event occurred (1977). Hamilton was a major player in Spoleto's arrival.

"I worked with Mayor Joe Riley to get his support and approval for the proposed Spoleto event. Mayor Riley was not particularly involved in music and probably had no idea just how popular this event could be. But he was excited to bring people in for anything that had a heightened cultural side to it. It fit what the community needed. Menotti had met with Riley and myself on several occasions. The county was interested in providing not only financial support but also other direction as

Menotti needed. I went to New York a few times to meet with Mr. Menotti. I got to know the man. Spoleto Festival, USA, became a reality for Charleston.

"We opened with Dizzy Gillespie—from Cheraw, South Carolina—at the Gaillard Municipal Auditorium. Gillespie was happy to be in Charleston, and he really enjoyed the food. Doc Severinsen from the *Tonight Show* came. He was another one that liked our southern cuisine. He liked collard greens and Hoppin' John. I brought in Count Basie and the entire Duke Ellington Band. We were able to get Lionel Hampton. B.B. King's bus broke down on the way here. And the county council that was hesitant at first was simply amazed. I can remember J. Mitchell Graham, one of the council members, who was the last person you'd figure to support the Spoleto initiatives or even take a liking to me. He was impressed with the results."

Indeed, it was Hamilton's reputation in the craft that brought in the great musical artists. He knew them all.

"I even had a 'jam session' with the chairman of the National Republican Party, Lee Atwater. Now, I'm a Democrat, but music has no allegiance. It is universal," Hamilton noted.

Atwater, a South Carolinian, died tragically from a brain tumor in 1991. He was an advisor to both President Ronald Reagan and President George H.W. Bush. Atwater had played backup guitar for fun with others like Percy Sledge and B.B. King. He knew of Hamilton's noble legacy and contacted this musically famous Charlestonian. Atwater asked to join Hamilton at an arranged musical session. The experience left them both friends through music, which Atwater noted "had no color and no politics."

"Lee Atwater was a fine man and a really good guitarist. We had the common interest of music. Sometimes that's all you need," Hamilton reminisced.

Hamilton accomplished much more than leading the team to get Spoleto to Charleston. His community dialogue led to greater understandings and more peripheral benefits. For instance, it was Hamilton who first championed the idea of recycling waste. He saw it as he studied other communities smaller than Charleston. He pushed for a county waste recycling plant. He noted the many nations that had already begun recycling—like Italy, France, Japan and Great Britain. Hamilton went to Washington for guidance and federal financial support. He met with Senator Fritz Hollings, who was enthusiastically supportive of the plan. Charleston invested in a recycling plant. He also worked for positive results from Senator Strom Thurmond's office. A recycling plant became a reality for Charleston through Hamilton's efforts.

"Is it revenue neutral? No. But it saves the planet," Hamilton explained. "Look back now and understand the plastic, paper and aluminum that would otherwise be wasted. Those items were incentivized for recycling. They are no longer a part of the countryside where people throw them out. They are viable revenue streams for some, and they really do cut the costs of manufacturing those products."

Hamilton later served on a statewide commission for Governor David Beasley that focused on recyclable waste materials. For these efforts, his service to his community and his contributions to the world of Lowcountry music, Hamilton was awarded the state's highest honor to be bestowed on a private citizen: the Order of the Palmetto.

Though Hamilton spent his undergraduate years at South Carolina State University,[12] there were other institutions of higher learning that benefited from his appreciation of formal education. He was the director of the Burke High School Band and the Bonds Wilson Band. He supported much, especially as county council chairman, for the benefit of the College of Charleston's growth and impact.

Through it all, Hamilton followed his music. He hosted the *Lonnie Hamilton Show* in 1963. He was the director of the newest version of the Jenkins Orphanage Band from 1977 to 1990. He formed Lonnie Hamilton and the Diplomats in 1979 and played in that group for twenty years, with brief intermissions with the Lonnie Hamilton Quintet. Then there was the Ambassadors Band. The Diplomats remained the standby group for which Hamilton was characteristically recognized. One would only need to venture to the second floor of Henry's on the Market to find the deepest, sweetest melodies of the foremost man in Charleston music. Hamilton's saxophone interludes would bring a crowd. He was within himself while playing, but the sounds wafted across the market as an invitation to anyone looking for the mood that only the blues could capture.

Hamilton's days are still full. He has projects, correspondence and friends to call. He lovingly accepts the care of his wife, Clarissa—who suffers from kidney ailments and requires dialysis treatments. They married in 1958 and have one daughter, Kendra. Hamilton stays involved in community and spends much of his available time helping others. Helping others has always been the theme song of his heart. It is best when he plays it out loud.

The notes of community have reverberated across the Holy City. Lonnie Hamilton III has the mind, the heart and the soul of an emerging world city paced within the stanzas of his life.

Hey, We Are Number One!

HELEN HILL

B eing first is a tradition in Charleston. Of pugilistic interest, Charlestonians won the first large-scale military battle of the American Revolution and fired the first shots of the War Between the States. The more genteel history denotes several American firsts from Charleston: the first public library, the first opera, the first public museum, the first golf "country" club, the first formal gardens, the first tea planted, the first artificial ice (but not the first iced tea), the first passenger train service and the first fire insurance company. The list of American and international firsts is seemingly endless. But that's the past. The firsts of Charleston are now citations, plaques and trophies. They are available for viewing at the Charleston Area Convention and Visitor's Bureau (CVB). It's good that it has plenty of wall space.

For the last twenty-five years, the CVB has been enhanced by the personable and brilliant Helen Hill. She is the executive director. If you have not met her, you have not been around Charleston long enough. You will. She's vivacious, energetic and—aptly—Charleston's number one fan.

Hill was in New York City during the October 2011 announcement of the Readers' Choice Awards of *Conde Nast Traveler*, considered the ultimate authority on the topics of world travel, luxury hoteliers, top cruise lines and signature events. There, presenting the award to her as America's #1 Travel Destination, was Charleston's very own comedic son, Stephen Colbert. Charleston first appeared in the top ten of American cities in 1993. San Francisco had been perched atop this list for more than a decade. Those avid travel connoisseurs who trot the globe—not the advertisers, publishers or editors—establish the rating system. So, it's a fair tally. As more travelers amassed more travel to see Charleston, our city vaulted even further in 2012—to the number one world travel destination!

There was wall space left at the CVB after eleven consecutive years as being deemed America's most mannerly city by Marjabelle Stewart, America's renowned expert on etiquette. At Mrs. Stewart's passing in 2007, her widower husband proclaimed the permanent award to be Charleston's by noting that the most mannerly city in America is always Charleston and that future awards should go to that city that raises itself closest to Charleston's standards.

Hill has seen the other accoutrements, as well—Charleston firsts, all! The Holy City and surrounding community has been at the top of magazine and journal poll lists as America's most livable city, America's best city for tennis, America's best beach resort, America's friendliest city and a plethora of other firsts, finests and bests. These have not happened by default or accident. It took great strategy. It seems we had to decide not to be everything for everybody. That's where Helen Hill became the savvy liaison to the rest of the world. She and her stellar staff did it with style and aplomb.

"It has been critical in the market that we have been able to advertise and sell Charleston when others have pulled back. It's because we have sewn together nine funding governments from Kiawah to North Charleston with other corporate and private interests," Hill explained, "and they work cohesively. Our leadership has been willing to go under the banner of 'Charleston.' We at the CVB are the protector of the brand."

That brand has also moved to the world stage as the number three travel destination on the globe in 2011, then "numero uno" in 2012. *Conde Nast Traveler* readers found a place for Charleston that reflected what all Charlestonians already knew.

This first high honor of 2011 was reported by the United Press International. "The upscale travel magazine tallied eight million votes as part of its annual Readers' Choice survey, which ranked cities around the world based on their ambiance, friendliness, lodging, restaurants, culture, sightseeing and shopping."

That's right. Number one worldwide—ahead of Paris, London, Cape Town and Vancouver. Step aside, Barcelona, Rome, Quebec and Buenos Aires. Vienna, Bangkok…ha! Back of the line! With the awards come the responsibilities. We have to maintain our standing and even look to improve.

Helen Hill is the face of Charleston. She traveled to New York to accept the award for America's #1 City. *Courtesy of Charleston Convention and Visitors Bureau.*

"Funding is essential. We also have a true sense of community on tough issues in Charleston. We seem to have a disposition to agree or disagree agreeably," Hill detailed. "It is important in Charleston to not lose what is special. We cannot be everything to everybody. We can't forget how we got to number one. We have to stay true to who we are. Here, you get that old city market experience, the carriage tours and the beautiful living history seen in our old homes, the beaches, the unique Charleston events, the friendly people and more. When you walk out on King Street, you may see something you know and then something you don't know that's authentic. There are a few national chains like the Gap or Banana Republic, but you also see the unique Charleston retailers like Christian Michi, Croghan's Jewelers or Bob Ellis Shoes. They say 'Charleston.'

"We cannot become something outside of our identity. Maybe that's why the theme park ideas don't fit. They do not meet our brand as 'Charleston.' We recognize the expectation of who we are to others."

Hill has been integral to Charleston's historic emergence. She has assisted the city in orchestrating the community by pointing her baton in the rhythms of rapture. The city was devoid of everything necessary for its phoenix-like rise just fifty years ago. It has everything now. The people who were there then are astonished now. They have praised Hill for her magnificent role.

"Helen Hill has been ahead of the curve and has kept ahead while others have fallen back," expressed Kathleen Cartland of the Charleston Metro Sports Council. "She is so very adept at combining our resources and targeting the things that fit the community as a whole. Her personality is a perfect fit for what she does."

David Jennings, the chairman of the CVB board, concurs: "Helen Hill's time as executive director mirrors the emergence of Charleston as the premier travel destination in the United States and the growth of the CVB as perhaps the best tourism marketing organization in the country. When she stepped in as our director in 1989, Charleston was a sleepy tourism spot known to a few in the country and no one internationally. The entire budget was less than $1 million. Due to her leadership and the excellent team she has hired, we have a budget of $11 million, and we were named the number one travel destination by *Conde Nast Traveler*. In addition, I hear many foreign accents on the streets of Charleston. The confluence of these events is not a coincidence. Leadership and the desire for excellence matters. Helen Hill has given these qualities to Charleston, and we are better for it."

Our Eden has it all. Outdoor activities like golf, sailing and tennis? Check. Cuisine? Among the best. Events? Something for everybody. History? Well, yes! Architecture? Preserved and timeless. Gardens? Stop and smell the camellias. Ambiance? Take a sip. The people? Are you kidding me? The best. Period.

As in Eden, there is this tree with apples. Those forbidden apples have sometimes led to a lot of public conversation. Our normally civil deportment has been more audible recently than we are accustomed to. There was the Boeing debate that has surfaced as the airline giant has built a modern plant in North Charleston. The controversy was brought on by the U.S. Justice Department in the inherent grievances of union states (Washington) versus right-to-work states (South Carolina). It was resolved.

There is also another forbidden apple: the controversy of port dredging. It has split our politicians. The super-container ships will need a deeper harbor. The 2005 Arthur Ravenel Jr. Bridge was built with those ships in mind. But the federal funding that supports international commerce has been difficult, and other cities—like our neighbors in Savannah—have been in competition for available dredge funding. The viability of the port is at risk.

But the most sinister "apple of upheaval" would—on the surface—seem to be quite innocuous. Lucifer himself must have pointed it out. You see, the world has discovered Charleston. The people who own cruise ship lines have read the magazines. The famously low skyline of the historic peninsula makes a docked cruise ship become a delightful vantage point to survey the city. Unfortunately, those ships cast a monumental shadow. The other obtrusiveness has been chronicled and detailed ad nauseum. There's the vehicular loading and unloading traffic, the blocked water views, the concerns of air and water pollution and even—*egads!*—people without collared shirts or proper footwear walking into our market area. This is an affront to proper Charleston sensibilities! They should issue seersucker suits and Weejuns at the gangplank.

On the other hand, Charleston is a visitor's dream. You can't keep people out. Cruise ships bring people. They spend money here in varying amounts—according to what side of the argument is auditing. The suppliers, like dairies and groceries, are thrilled. There are other fees the port collects. Cruisers spread the good word, and so many of them come back by other means on follow-up visits. In addition, the city is planning a major upgrade of its only cruise terminal. This can mitigate some of the negative issues but will certainly be a catalyst for other cruise lines.

"Ninety-eight point nine percent of all first-time visitors to Charleston give a positive satisfaction report," Hill noted, "and so, many of these folks will likely come back and stay in our hotels and eat in our restaurants. So there has to be a balance of what's good and what's not concerning the cruise industry."

Hill has been a pivotal voice in the current debate. The bureau has even submitted a balanced view to the local newspaper. The CVB plan calls for no more than 2 ships to visit per week, or a maximum of 104 cruise ship visits per year. In this way, the terminal slip is vacant and the sightline open at least five days a week. It's a way to have the upside advantage but not the overdose. By way of comparison, it's the two glasses of wine the doctor advised that made you healthier, not the three bottles you drank that gave you a hangover for the ages. Too much of anything has rarely been beneficial.

The debate has made headlines outside Charleston. That's normally not our way. Factions are making frictions into fractions. Mayor Joe Riley, a downtown resident, has been mostly supportive of a controlled cruise industry with a new and better terminal. But the normal "give and take" has been given and taken, as Hill notes: "Historically, Charleston has been an amazing melting pot of cultures, ideas and values. When you look at the three-plus centuries of interaction between all of the groups, you see a very genuine appetite for harmony. People have worked together here for the common good. It has been a positive indication of our self-identity—who we are and what we expect of ourselves. If anything, this has been a place where respectful people disagree in a most respectful manner. I'm not sure our cruise ship debate always shows us in that light. That's why we, the CVB, have offered a reasonable and effective solution that the highest majority can appreciate as the best solution. Cruise ships will not be going away. But they can be reasonably scheduled to everyone's benefit."

So being Number One is always tenuous. Things can change. Factors such as the world economic swoon and some relevant safety concerns have reduced travel. The ability to experience Charleston in the most meaningful ways has been extolled by those who do it best: those who travel. They like our weather, our ambiance and our events. By most standards worldwide, we are a deal. It's up to those conduit-like organizations to "keep 'em comin." The CVB and Helen Hill know how to stay on top. Even as the world Number One, there is always room for improvement!

Local Operatives of "Locally Owned"

Bobby Molony, Frank Lucas, Sonny Mevers, Ronnie Banks and Edwin Pearlstine

A road construction foreman and his buddy stop in a uniquely designed, locally owned Charleston restaurant. An undertone of music is playing in the background. The waiter brings a menu, and the foreman orders two Bud Lights. He tells his buddy about just getting a lower mortgage rate on his home. The friend mentions that he just remodeled his home. A conversation is started that permeates much of old Charleston.

A simple setting? For more than forty years in Charleston, that conversation might have touched five iconic local figures. Ronnie Banks has been a part of the Charleston road system and beyond since 1948. Sonny Mevers has been remodeling homes and small businesses since 1955. Bud Light, a product distributed by Edwin Pearlstine's family, recounts a business back to 1865. Bobby Molony took control of the Credit Bureau of Greater Charleston in 1946. Frank Lucas founded the architectural firm we know as LS3P in 1963.

The nature of local business may have changed in rapid order from Seattle to Miami, but not so much in Charleston. It is the locally owned businesses that have preserved much of the community's character. You see it especially in any view of King Street, where locally owned shops—dress stores, eateries and haberdasheries—have attracted tourists from across the globe. It is not unusual to hear the stories families tell of dealing with old Charleston establishments and long-term Charleston merchants from several generations in the past.

Sonny Mevers has restored nearly two hundred homes on the peninsula of Charleston over a career spanning nearly six decades. He exudes the disposition of Charleston's reverence for the distinctive and the simple. Porches are piazzas. Napkins are doilies. Tea only comes with ice cubes. Mevers never writes out a contract; he just accepts the personalization of a handshake on a proposal, and then he'll start on Monday. He'll send you a bill with a stamped return envelope when he needs a payment for services rendered. That's the way he has always done business.

Roy E. "Sonny" Mevers has made a career of preserving old cars and old Charleston. *Courtesy of Billy Mevers.*

"The people that call me usually do so because I did the work on a neighbor's house or for someone else in their family a few years ago," Mevers offered. "I never needed a brochure or a letter of recommendation to do the work I've done. I just needed to show up and do the excellent work they hired me to do."

Mevers exemplifies historic preservation in other astonishing ways. He has the same 1955 Ford F-100 pickup truck he started with—in the garage he restored at the house he has lived in for seventy-six years. Hr summers at his Station 25 beach house, which he's had since 1966 on Sullivan's Island. He also owns a Model T. Everything old ought to look new is the Mevers cred: "I started out of the trunk of my car, a four-door Chevrolet. In a few months, I went to Arthur Swanson at the bank and convinced him that I needed a loan for a pickup truck. He advanced me $750 to buy a used one. I went to Darlington to find one at an auction but had no luck. I came back and bought the one I have now for $1,500, or $50 over the invoice. I went back to Arthur and told him about the new truck. He asked how much more money I would need. I said, 'The rest of it. I don't have a dime.' You know, he gave me the loan." Mevers raised his voice, as if surprised by the old way people did business in Charleston.

The bank probably did not check with the local Charleston Credit Bureau, especially on people it had known in the community. That credit-reporting agency it might have used had it been a questionable credit proposal was essentially the Molony family. They were the only game in town.

"Credit bureaus were becoming a useful way to qualify borrowers and inform lenders but were only operated on a regional basis. In 1931, my father, Harry Molony, was in the fertilizer business and shared offices with the Charleston Board of Trade," Bobby Molony recalled. "Dad bought the board of trade in 1938. That became the Credit Bureau. I was a senior in high school, and he only had two employees. I took over in 1946, and we made two interim moves before coming to the 57 Hasell Street location in 1963. We were once in the People's Building.

"Looking back, it was a great business and touched all of Charleston," the ninety-one-year-old Molony recounted. "And it was one of the few private companies with a lot of phones. We had twenty-five desks with dedicated phone lines in one room. So the Credit Bureau served another important after-hours function: we became an important resource for political candidates."

Molony's wife of seventy-one years, Sadie, added, "We knew Joe Riley Sr., a fine gentleman, and helped young Joe with his initial campaign in 1975."

"We helped the mayor every election cycle, and he never needed to ask. He's our friend, and he's a great man that changed this entire community for the good," Mr. Molony interjected.

"Mrs. Sadie" continued: "Some changes were good, but some places I miss. Just look at the restaurants now. They're wonderful. But years back, we went to LaBrasca's with the kids every Saturday night. There wasn't much

As they both reach their ninetieth years, Sadie and Bobby Molony have much on which to look back and be proud. *Courtesy of Cindy Molony Masters.*

else here. There was Bill's Holly House across the river and Henry's on the Market. We used to buy from Carl Harley's Meat Market at Spring and President Streets. That's gone now, too. It was easy to be pleased because there were not that many choices, and the people that ran the places were people you and your parents knew from way back when."

The Molonys raised seven children. There was always plenty of activity at home. The holidays with bigger families were always special. Bobby Molony stated that he always knew "Mrs. Sadie's" favorite gift at every Christmas— and her birthdays and their anniversaries.

"The green stuff. Cash. She knew I had no taste in anything nice to buy, so cash has always been my most thoughtful gift," he winked.

After working at the Charleston Credit Bureau for a half century, Molony retired in 1987 and sold the company to Equifax Services, a major national credit-reporting service.

Molony, a gentleman of the highest order, was always affable but astute. As a profoundly involved businessman, he gave back to the community mightily. The Credit Bureau found ways to assist other area efforts to make Charleston better and to assist those who could not assist themselves.

There is a long road back to the old ways. But those ways deserve the pang of nostalgia. Other roads were being built.

Ronnie Banks had the benefit of his company's local legacy when he retired and encouraged his two sons to continue the tradition. Their paving company grew with Charleston. Many of the major projects that have extended and widened Charleston for safer, better access are on the Bankses' résumé. The 2012–13 widening of Highway 17N (Johnnie Dodds Boulevard) in Mount Pleasant showed Banks Construction expertise. More than $1.5 million in landscaping after the project meant the aesthetics of the massive project would heighten the experience of the new roads. And they made the commute for the growing bedroom community less time-consuming and more pastoral. It's an eye-pleasing improvement.

Ronnie Banks shared the insight: "We wanted to be a part of improving our community. Pretty much everything we do is by a bid process. But we feel that our experience, local reputation and ability to perform these intricate projects within the time frames allowed has helped us to compete and to put out the best product available, one that motorists and even bike riders will enjoy for many years. Heck, my children and grandchildren will drive on these roads. They have to be safe and of the highest quality.

"My best friends will remind me if they are inconvenienced or if any little detail needs attention. Living in the community you serve as a local

Going somewhere? There's a good chance that Ronnie Banks has something to do with your safe arrival. *Courtesy of Tommy McQueeney.*

businessman by its nature keeps you humble but responsible."

Banks Construction performs grading work, paving and drainage. It has built runways and parking lots in addition to major area road projects: "As a Charlestonian, we learn that doing something worthwhile means that it has to be right and something that gives you pride. We live here, and we are responsive to anything that may be of concern in the road construction business. The technology has advanced, and safety systems for modern roads are the best they have ever been. We have no other option than to do the job with the best materials, on time and with the utmost safety in mind."

The Banks family has been a part of Charleston's premier road builders for seventy-four years. They continue to be a locally owned and operated fixture of the community.

Frank Lucas graduated from Clemson University in 1959. He had pursued his childhood goal to become a certified licensed architect: "I grew up at the Mitchell Playground area and wanted to be an architect since I was eleven. I attended Mitchell School and Charleston High. After Clemson and a stint of serving in the army, I came back to Charleston. I passed the exam and started a firm, with Sidney Stubbs, in 1963."

Lucas and Stubbs Architects morphed through mergers, buyouts and expansion to become LS3P, one of the leading architectural and engineering firms in the region, with offices in Charlotte, Columbia, Greenville, Raleigh and Wilmington. Their home office is Charleston. The "three P's" were added in the process—Vito Pascullis, Thom Penney and Richard Powell.

"Thom Penney started as a high school intern here who did everything from copying blueprints to deliveries to sweeping. He continued to Clemson, got his degree, came back and went to work. Through hard work, he later became a full partner, then the president of the Chamber of Commerce and, eventually, the national president of the American Institute of Architects. Now, that's a proud story!" Lucas beamed.

Founder Frank Lucas can scarcely drive downtown without seeing LS3P's work on the left and the right. *Courtesy of LS3P Architects.*

LS3P has had an exceptionally visible role in Charleston's surge to prominence. Its work can be seen daily—from the Gaillard Municipal Auditorium to the Commissioners of Public Works Building to the Charleston International Airport. It designed the corporate office for Piggly Wiggly Carolina and dozens of other locally owned businesses, including designs for the Pearlstines, for Sonny Mevers and for Ronnie Banks, as well.

In a way, it was Frank Lucas, and later partner Sydney Stubbs, who took the old dilapidated city market and turned it into a tourist mecca. It was in the mid-1970s that Mayor J. Palmer Gaillard took a group of businessmen to Bermuda. Out of the event came a consortium idea to transform the market. The group formed, and in time, a plan was put forth with a lease from the city. The Christopher Company leased the old market, and LS3P redesigned it. It became a major part of Charleston's transition. It was remodeled again in 2011. Lucas enjoyed the experience: "It was the names you knew—great minds like Bobby Scarborough, Falcon Hawkins, Dr. Gordon Stine, Leonard Fulghum and a few others—all fine Charleston businesspeople. So the market was a private enterprise that benefited the city, both aesthetically and financially. That change also benefited the tourism industry, the local merchants, hotels, restaurants and the original people who put the plan together.

"Charlestonians have their stake in Charleston. You can see that when the United Way and chamber of commerce cranks up. Lucas and Penney both served as president of the chamber. The national or regional companies don't necessarily have their heart in it like the locals do. We are able to put not only our money but [also] the resources of our time and our service. Some of these architectural bid firms come in and do a job, then leave. We've seen it time and again. We're here to take care of our work. We work, live, play and pray here."

Frank Lucas will retire in the coming months: "I'm staying on until May 1, 2013. That's the fifty-year anniversary of our founding. I am proud to be a part of this community and to have gained so many true friends along the way. But LS3P will carry on, serving the community for many years to come."

It would be difficult to find a pedigree in Charleston as long as that of the Pearlstines'. The Pearlstine name extends back in time more than a century and a half. Edwin Pearlstine explained: "My great-great-grandfather I.M. Pearlstine was a Confederate sympathizer in 1865. He and his brother were German immigrants. They had a small business that made buttons, caps and belt buckles for Confederate soldiers. After the war's end, they had a small dry goods business. They expanded into groceries by the 1880s, and the business grew when the navy yard came at the turn of the century [1903]. We hung in there during the Depression, when I was born [1935], but nearly went broke. The war saved us. The navy yard had twenty thousand workers operating around the clock. We could feed them and still had other wares that people purchased. We sold every kind of beverage, and we learned of an opportunity the August Busch family, other German immigrants, had to

Edwin Pearlstine's family lineage in Charleston goes back to the War Between the States. Now, the family is a major community donor. *Courtesy of Pearlstine Distributiong Company.*

distribute Budweiser in the local region. My father, Edwin Sr., and his father, Hyman, thought it was a good idea. Eventually, the beer business took over everything else."

The Pearlstines never got a hangover from the beer business. It allowed the family to become even better stewards of the community. The Pearlstine Foundation was established. Each member of the foundation receives one full vote to assess and contribute to the myriad local causes presented each year.

"When the children and grandchildren reach the age of eighteen, they each get that one vote in the Pearlstine Foundation. They have an equal voice, and we require that they research every donation. We want to know that the money invested in each and every cause is well spent. We operate through the Coastal Community Foundation and have given, just through that entity, $1.6 million to local charities."

They have been able to do so because of their dedication to a fine business model. "In 1957, we only had eleven products to sell. We grew with the industry, trying to make decisions about products that made sense. In 1971, we sold a total of 300,000 cases for the year. In 2011, there were more than seven hundred products available for us to distribute. In those forty years since, we found better and safer ways to get product out. By comparison, in 2011, we distributed 7 million cases of beer."

The Pearlstine distribution center on Daniel Island is state-of-the-art. "PDI" is recognized as one of the great pedigreed Charleston businesses. Yet Pearlstine looks at the future of his industry with some stark considerations: "The Busch empire has been bought and sold by multi-national firms. InBev is a Brazilian and Belgian group. Miller and Coors have been bought out and is now SAB Miller. SAB stands for South African Breeze—a company out of Cape Town, South Africa. So the major world breweries are no longer in the United States. There are other concerns. Major city mega-distributors are out buying the local distributors. That's a growing anxiety. For instance, Reyes Holdings out of Chicago is five brothers who have bought up the large markets. They just paid over $200 million to buy out the Orlando market. So where will the smaller distributors be in a few years? Will the mega-distributors buy them out as well? The next thought should be: 'Where will the charity go?' They'll donate, but those donations will be in places like Chicago."

"We are a Charleston family and proud to be a part of the community. The people here are so rich in culture—and everyone is welcome here," Pearlstine expounded. "Our little arguments are over silly things, like how many cruise ships? Cruise ships don't bother anybody. That ought to be a compliment to everyone here that so many others want to come here.

"But we're becoming a bigger part of the world market for everything. You're seeing Boeing here, and I'm sure others will follow. We need to be certain not to lose that smaller market charm, the strength we have amongst us to assist the local causes. You look at the College of Charleston basketball. That support is not from people who graduated from the college. It's from locally owned businesses that want to see every part of our city succeed. It's the local operators who step forward, like the Darby family, George Fennell, the Zuckers and so many others, that make Charleston such a special city. We just can't lose that."

Indeed, the local establishments have the local ties. They know the local market, the local appetite and the local needs to be addressed. In the difficult economies that have rolled through the decades, the identifiable Charleston establishments have persevered with a sense of empathy with others. Purchase-order billing times might have expanded a bit with wider understandings and price margins might have shrunk. The person who knows you knows Charleston. They've all been here for the long run. And they've had a long run here.

It's the long run that has built these five Charleston business personalities into Lowcountry legacies.

Commanding the Sun, the Wind and the Water

ELIZABETH COLBERT-BUSCH

There is a dichotomy in the things of the earth—and its people. It is the yin and the yang, the static state of continual movement—the hot and cold, black and white, open and closed. All is science wrapped in the mystery of the unexplained, the spiritual and the theoretical. Most of us accept all that is before us; others accept that there is more. We've only just begun.

We all wondered what would come after the navy left the shipyard nearly twenty years ago. South Carolina leaders knew technology and innovation supported with a solid educational foundation would bring opportunity for industrial commercial growth, a driving force for economic recovery and development. Clemson University's Restoration Institute (CURI) is part of that plan. As part of Thomas Green Clemson's will—which established Clemson's land grant mission requiring service to our state in economic development—and a gift from the State of South Carolina and the City of North Charleston, CURI came to rest on deep water at the Old Charleston Navy Base. Its mission? Create opportunity. Ready South Carolina with the next-generation workforce. Accelerate technology and drive it to the market. Elizabeth "Lulu" Colbert-Busch, as the director of business development working with a unique team of brilliant scientific minds and scholars, is part of that mission.

It's about the next industrial revolution: energy. It's about independence and sustainability. It's about environmental economics and protecting your natural resources principal. It's about science, math, engineering, technology—and that's cool. It's about lifting us up and bringing our jobs

Elizabeth "LuLu" Colbert-Busch has overseen much in her career but has more excitement on the horizon. *Courtesy of the Colbert-Busch family archive.*

back to us. It's where the world is taking us and where we will take the world.

Colbert-Busch detailed the concept: "We understand that knowledge really is power and power brings opportunity. It is the greatest gift you can give yourself. No one can ever take it away from you. It lifts us up."

Power at CURI is like no other in the world. It's a place of wonder, discovery, possibilities and change. It is the home of modern marvel—the turbine drivetrain testing facility and the world's only multi-megawatt grid simulator—unique in the ability to test mechanical and electrical compatibility for any electricity grid for any city, state or country in the world.

Offshore wind and other alternative energies are part of the power future of the world. Nothing this big has ever been done before anywhere. Our old navy base is the nexus of the new energy systems research and technology.

The first Industrial Revolution began in Europe and crossed the Atlantic to the United States. "History repeats itself. We've looked at Denmark as a benchmark when we were assessing job creation potential for the wind industry. Denmark is the home of Vestas, one of the top three manufacturers in the market. Denmark is estimated to have forty thousand jobs in the industry. In comparison, a Department of Energy report indicates there is a potential of twenty thousand jobs for South Carolina in the industry. We have coastal demand, shallow waters, sustainable winds in state and federal waters, top-rank port infrastructure for deployment and industry cluster already established."

Colbert-Busch continued, "South Carolina is uniquely positioned. It's a mature and strategic growth market in Europe. It's coming our way. We need to prepare for the opportunity."

Colbert-Busch could explain wind like a breath of fresh air. It made sense. It was when she led the conversation into a mammoth building with goggles, hardhat and earplugs that the wind conversation subsided. The monolithic concrete box had pile drivers on the inside, a retrofit of a former navy base structure. The roofline will change at a juncture once other piles are driven and steel reinforcements tie it together from the ground up. It will rise to nearly ninety feet. Project manager Jim Tuten is aptly proud of this worldwide landmark effort. The drivetrain testing facility will change the world.

Tuten walked the interior: "It's all reinforced and will house a permanent ceiling track for lifting the turbine parts into place. Nothing like this has ever been engineered before. There will be three test beds all with deep-water access, the grid simulator, the fifteen-megawatt test bed and the seven-and-a-half-megawatt test bed. There will be more concrete poured here than anyplace in the area, with the exception of the Arthur Ravenel Jr. Bridge."

If you see anything suspiciously nuclear in a mushroom shape on the horizon, just step inside Tuten's concrete box. Its massive dimensions do not even begin to intimate what work was done in the subsurface. The finely detailed color-coded chronology chart showed the sequence of the construction within the work trailer. It took up two full walls. It's on Supply Street. The name has a broader meaning now.

The energy it is to supply is perhaps only a footnote. The technology it will supply to the world is the real story of the new drivetrain.

The new science has been created because of Charleston's greatest reach back into old science. Across the parking lot is where CURI started in the Warren Lasch Conservation Center. Colbert-Busch's office is there. All that is around the perimeter of the parking area began because of a technology that succeeded and then failed a century and a half prior. The *H.L. Hunley* submarine successfully sank the USS *Housatonic* on February 17, 1864.[13] But the victorious *Hunley* and its crew of eight sank upon its return, not to be found for nearly 136 years. After the magnanimous donation of the heralded submarine for research and posterity, insights into metallurgical sciences were realized. The science is seen daily at the Lasch Center, where the *Hunley* is still suspended in time and submerged in both water and science.

Colbert-Busch explained the dynamic: "Sun, wind and water are sustainable and renewable. They all depend on each other. There is a relationship between what we're discovering with the *Hunley* to an application for success in the field of offshore wind—and especially to understand technological advances affecting corrosive metals in a marine environment. If we can better control the natural process of metal corrosion, we can make advances that will help us with the offshore structures of wind turbines, not to mention road and bridge infrastructures. The *Hunley* started as a new science in the 1860s and is here as an artifact of an old science and a most highly interesting world history. And now it is home within other new sciences. Importantly, this science we continue to develop applies to the future, as well. That makes what we do not only significant but also incredibly exciting."

Colbert-Busch can draw on the lessons she learned growing up in Charleston. She especially recalls her parents. Her father, the first provost and vice-president of the academic department at MUSC, led by example. His passion was education. Both a large James Island family and a medical student population looked up to Dr. James W. Colbert.

But the City of Charleston, MUSC and especially the Colbert family were devastated by tragedy. Eastern Airlines flight 212 crashed short of a Charlotte, North Carolina runway in dense fog and took the life of Colbert-Busch's father, along with two younger brothers, Peter and Paul.[14] It was on a Wednesday morning, September 11, 1974. Seventy-two of the eighty-two passengers and crew perished. Life changed. Young LuLu was only a sophomore at the University of South Carolina. The shattering aftermath reshuffled her objectives and interrupted her academic career. Youngest brother Stephen, ten, was now the only one at home with mother Lorna. It was a sad day in Charleston, where that fateful flight had originated. The city only boasted of sixty-seven thousand inhabitants in 1974.[15] Everyone seemed to know everyone. A local television station lost its anchorman. The local newspaper lost three executives. The local college lost its tennis coach. The local concrete firm lost its president. The navy lost an admiral. And the Colbert family, a mother and the nine remaining children, prepared for the hardships without a loving and accomplished provider, their father. This was compounded by the loss of two young brothers who were flying with their father to start school in Connecticut. The sadness remains for those affected, as well as those whose hearts sank with the news.

Young LuLu rallied around her family. Her mother, Lorna Tuck Colbert, age ninety-one in 2012, exhibited the strength of her faith, and with her guiding hands, the family held strong to one another and persevered. Being a Colbert is not for sissies.

"My mother is my best friend. I am so proud to be her daughter. She inspires me. I learned from her that life is good, and you never ever give up," Colbert-Busch smiled. "I hope to be a fraction of the woman she is. Incredible."

Colbert-Busch began her search for a career in the continuance of a liberal arts education at the College of Charleston, a much smaller institution than today's sprawl across the Charleston peninsula. "I was lucky. I found Paul Nelson, a professor at the College of Charleston, who was beginning a new program called intermodal transportation and logistics management. He and that program gave me a direction after graduation and opened the door of the world for me."

Colbert-Busch received her degree from the College of Charleston. She then completed an internship with the South Carolina State Ports Authority. She had also worked in Washington, D.C., in order to complete her academic work on government maritime relations:[16] "I found a job in a male-dominant industry with an ocean carrier. I had made it! I was on the waterfront. I worked with a great man named Rick Wen, whose family owned and operated Orient Overseas Container Line. I found the job because Rick was connected with the college. I worked hard. He saw this. He believed in me and challenged me. I took each challenge and thrived in the process. One day, it happened. Rick 'dragged me through the glass ceiling.' He promoted me to become the first female sales manager in North America and then to director of marketing and sales."

Colbert-Busch had other role models.

"I never met Jackie Kennedy, late president John F. Kennedy's widow. But I always admired her. I read all that I could about her. It is especially meaningful to me even more now, how she fiercely protected her children after the tragedy," Colbert-Busch reflected. "She was so very dignified throughout her life—very much like my mother."

Though her celebrity younger brother, Stephen, left the Holy City and made a fine career for himself in the field of comedic entertainment, Colbert-Busch remained rooted in Charleston. There is no place she would rather be. "It's home base. There is such a great feeling of community here. It's a truly caring city. There exists a feeling of responsibility for each other you wouldn't likely find elsewhere. There is pride, uniqueness and beauty all in one place. It's magical. Where else is there that you would find it to be undignified to blow a car horn?

"There are things I miss from growing up here. I miss Friday night football games and the great friends I had in high school. Mom says, 'Give it time.' We'll find each other again. I miss twenty-five-cent gasoline and summers on Sullivan's Island. I miss the drive-in movies. They're all gone now. I miss those crazy Citadel senior class parties they had at the Folly Beach Pier. What I miss most is being home with Mom and Dad and my brothers and sisters. Those were really magical days."

And now, Colbert-Busch has the excitement of her career, her marriage to Claus Busch, her three children and three grandchildren. "I believe in miracles. I have a strong faith. I love reading a good book about real people. I believe we can talk without speaking. I think there is nothing stronger than the human element," Colbert-Busch intimated.

"It may seem Utopian, but my perfect day would be able to get a good night's sleep and to wake knowing there is peace everywhere, that no one was hungry, homeless, tired or afraid. It would mean that we were all good to each other. I'd spend time with my husband and my children and my grandchildren. I'd walk out from an imaginary home on the beach. The temperature would cool with a nice slow breeze. I might see offshore wind turbines in the distance. That would be nice. I'd walk for a while and hear laughter of children at play, dancing with a joyful innocence. I'd sit and talk with Mom. I'd sit on the beach and read. That would be a glorious day. Wind and water, with the warmth of the sun. Camelot."

Camelot. That idyllic Arthurian legend of place and time may exist yet. The modern version might have a harbor in place of a moat. Perhaps there would be a low profile of stately mansions and magnificent church spires instead of a castle. It might have a picturesque city hall instead of a round table and an executive director of the future, LuLu Colbert-Busch, instead of a Merlin. The potions are being conjured. Colbert-Busch is at home.

Emergence as Emergency

MAYOR KEITH SUMMEY

A t the top, one man is in charge. He is outgoing, nonjudgmental and excited about the day. He had just been sworn in the night before for another term of office—his sixth. It is good that most ceremonies are in the evening so that he does not have to divide his attention from his daytime passion.

Meet the mayor of North Charleston, the honorable Keith Summey.

Summey is a realist. He's a burly man filled with bravado. He knows from whence he came and how the city of North Charleston, the third-largest city in South Carolina, has emerged as the center of something even more magnificent than he ever considered growing up. He commanded that transformation.

"I consider myself a pleaser. I try to work with everybody to get a positive solution that is better than the status quo," Summey noted. "I like to build a consensus with others that can also benefit, whether it's the town of Ravenel, Summerville or the city of Charleston."

North Charleston, once the far end of a shortsighted joke, has recently arrived. It is the pulse and heartbeat of a metropolitan area designated on a world map as "Charleston proper." That's a nearly unfair assessment. The city of North Charleston has 100,000 citizens and the lion's share of the tri-county industry, and it commands the geographic center of the area's traffic patterns. It is the railroad center, the location of the Charleston International Airport and the beneficiary designee of the old Charleston Naval Shipyard. It is the nexus of the three counties that merge within the map lettering also named Charleston. That place is actually North Charleston. It is the new home of Boeing and the long-term home of MeadWestvaco. It has a United States Air Base and borders a United States Naval Weapons Station, now a joint command. A large part of the new retail fire that rages in North Charleston is simply called Centre Pointe. How appropriate! There at that centering site appear major retailers buoyed by a wonderland of major "retail wholesalers"—the new and fresh Tanger Outlet Mall. North Charleston has been *the* major retail center in all of South Carolina for the last nineteen consecutive years.

It wasn't always that way. Originally, the area encompassed the outlying plantations of Charleston proper. There were the Elms, Archdale and Oak Grove Plantations. It was the most prominent "north" known in Charleston's Old South. The four years of the Civil War changed that economy but not the usage. The plantations divided like amoebas. They became tenant agricultural divisions. Families farmed them for primary sustenance and what the market would bear beyond.

Through the insistence of former governor "Pitchfork Ben" Tillman in 1890, the United States Navy designated land six miles up the Cooper River to become a navy ship repair facility.[17] Construction was begun on it in 1901. Repairs were made during and after World War I, there being no new ships constructed. In 1933, North Charleston and the surrounding area got a boost when new shipbuilding was authorized.[18] The navy yard and navy base grew, as did North Charleston. By the time of the navy complex's closing ninety-five years later, the Charleston Naval Base and Charleston Naval Shipyard had grown to seventy thousand direct and indirect jobs for the Charleston area. Both were located inward from McMillan Avenue in North Charleston. Now, that property allows ample room for growth and an inordinate conglomeration of viable, but vacant, waterfront.

There was other industry that made North Charleston arise, to be sure. A lumberyard venture one hundred years ago attracted a handful of investors with an eye to the burgeoning ship repair industry. Park Circle, a large residential gamble, was developed on an English countryside plan. The names Buist, Durant, Hyde, Mixon and O'Hear grace the street signs of that area today.[19] Like the spokes of a wheel, Park Circle reaches out to the North Charleston beyond. By the war years of 1941 to 1945, the shipyard was bustling. In the 1950s and beyond, with the advent of nuclear-powered submarines, Charleston became the home to the premier U.S. fleet ballistic missile submarine base.[20] By the mid-1980s, there were nearly forty thousand daily workers at the shipyard and navy base complex. It is also the recovery

As the mayor of South Carolina's third-largest metroplis, Summey has become a major force in the entire community. *Courtesy of the City of North Charleston.*

and archaeological restoration home of the *H.L. Hunley*, the first submarine in history to sink an opposing ship in wartime.

There were other nuances to North Charleston's past.

"When Pinehaven Shopping Center was built in 1959, it was the largest shopping center in the Southeast," Summey reflected. "It had the benefit of the naval hospital, the navy yard workers by the thousands and, of course, the navy itself. It was the 'happening place' of the 1960s.

"Since then, we have opened fabulous venues for shopping: Northwoods Mall, Festival Center, Centre Pointe and a half dozen more upscale places that attract people from the entire Lowcountry. There are pods for shopping spread throughout North Charleston."

North Charleston has taken on the character of islands in a lake. There are important destinations across the area but no real city center. Summey would eventually like to change that: "I'd really like to create a corridor for a downtown that runs next to the Old Village (East Montague) to Virginia Avenue and to Centre Pointe. It would give more character to the city and build a center for our commerce."

Summey was first elected mayor in October 1994 amid the first-wave reduction of workers at the navy base complex. He filled an unexpired term and then was reelected in January 1995. An estimated loss of seven thousand citizens beckoned. The tax base would shrink considerably. The next year, 1996, the U.S. Navy and the navy yard repair complex left Charleston entirely—a product of budget cutbacks after the end of the Cold War in 1989.[21]

It was not a promising turn of events and, some would say, a most difficult time to be the mayor. "I had already developed relationships with three county governments and their chairs. I realized that we would lose over seven thousand residents almost overnight. Other parts of the community would suffer residential losses as well. We needed to work together. Senator Hollings [Ernest F. "Fritz" Hollings] had already warned me that the base could not be saved. After the weekend announcement, I called a press conference on Monday. In it, I said what everyone knew— that we could no longer expect the government to supply jobs. I went further to the point. North Charleston needed diversification. The navy leaving could be a blessing in that regard. Getting SPAWAR [the Space and Naval Warfare Systems Command] out of that transition was a wonderful benefit. That was twelve thousand jobs with a higher-income workforce. So the closing was a wakeup call for everybody. It was a chance to become something better. Besides, I didn't want to see North Charleston continue in a direction that I didn't want my children and grandchildren to inherit."

Summey was up to the task. He had ideas. He marshaled a vision. He had to change old perceptions. He had to walk a few older council members into the dream and excite other younger people to get involved. As only the third mayor of the city, there was little history—and most of it needed to be forgotten. North Charleston had the reputation of being Charleston's attic. There were things there you wouldn't see anywhere else. Much of what the government took away had a silver lining, and Summey was certain of its promise. With the largest economic engine—the navy complex—on the way out, someone needed to come in and make sense of it all. Summey wanted the job.

Summey was a part of every innovation, every upgrade and every nuance. He took the red clay and molded it into the *new* city of North Charleston—where all things were possible. He built coalitions with other governments. He attracted small industry. He delineated commercial and industrial corridors. He planned the future of transportation patterns.

He stepped up services. He advertised and marketed. He upgraded his police department to fit the challenges. He worked tirelessly to meet the daily tests he would encounter.

And now others have looked at what he did in amazement. The old North Charleston center on East Montague Avenue is now revitalized. Businesses there are a part of the phoenix-like rise. There are law firms, pizza emporiums and banks. North Charleston High School has been revitalized. Madra Rua Irish Pub packs in a lunch crowd daily. It is one of twelve restaurants on that five-block vista. The Intertech Group is only a few paces down from the far corner. Old Attaway-Heinsohn Field is across the street from there.

The navy base complex gave room for another high school—Academic Magnet—that attracted top students from across the community. Other navy complex innovations followed. The U.S. Passport Center and the Federal Law Enforcement Training Center have relocated at the old base. Yet there still remains nearly two hundred acres of prime upside waterfront property. North Charleston is bound to get even better.

Summey reached into government and found solutions. He reached into industry and found partners. He reached even further—to the people he had known for a lifetime to get on board with his vision. Reaching out is what he does best.

Summey has involved the active and ever-available Anita Zucker beyond old East Montague Avenue. Zucker, with her penchant for quality education at every level, has made a dynamic difference across the community. She has been a main character in the storybook revival of North Charleston. She owns the East Coast Hockey League franchise, the South Carolina Stingrays. They are the main tenants of the North Charleston Coliseum. She developed the Carolina Ice Palace, the community's only ice-skating venue. It has been a boon to the area's youth and even hosts high school hockey teams in competition. That's right, there is high school hockey in the Heart of Dixie! The mere location of the Intertech multi-national conglomerate in a newly idyllic and revitalized cityscape is certainly a major coup d'état. Her son, Jonathan Zucker, heads up the Intertech Group, which tentacles to industries in fifty-six other countries. Summey enjoys the association.

Zucker is impressed by what he has done: "I think Keith Summey is an incredible visionary. He has done a tremendous amount to transform the city of North Charleston into the amazing place that it is today, to include improving education, improving the arts, promoting the Coliseum and the Performing Arts Center and all of that Convention Center complex. His support of the businesses in the community has been tremendous as well. I have to give him a ton of credit for his involvement in economic development and making a bright future for a city [of] which we can all be very, very proud."

Old North Charleston is a part of New North Charleston.

"There exists here a better quality of life, a better reputation and a better and more diversified quality of jobs," Summey said with a smile. "We are better in every way that I can count because we all worked to improve."

"Case in point" points to an obvious case. The rate of violent crime in North Charleston in 1994 was nearly 20.0 per 1,000. The 2011–12 rate, at 5.8 violent crimes per 1,000, is well below most cities of North Charleston's size. That's reducing the rate to nearly one-fourth! The previously understaffed North Charleston Police Department was upscaled and repopulated. It grew from 110 policemen and women to 300. North Charleston has gained a new reputation for its safety. Summey was active in upgrading the police reputation and service but also enlisted neighborhood watch programs. He eventually enhanced the salaries of the police officers, as well. There is pride in the entire department where little existed previously.

Though North Charleston has a population of 100,000, there are 250,000 cars that pass through the area each day. To move around metropolitan Charleston, North Charleston will be in your GPS. Again, Summey worked with partners from the federal government (I-26 oversight), along with state and local officials, for partnering in order to benefit all concerns. The road system is much improved.

In even the most difficult times of the recent economic downturn, Summey worked with his council, industry, real estate concerns and small businesses to "keep one business, especially, out of North Charleston: the vacant building business. A vacant building is the sign of a failure. It is what I do not wish to see in the city. So we cut through bureaucratic red tape to attract the best of the best and give them every consideration to compete and grow in our area. We want them here and they know that.

"And you can bet we want Mayor Riley, Mayor Swails, Mayor Collins and all others here to be successful, as well. If something good is happening in Charleston—the Bridge Run, Spoleto, the Wildlife Exposition or just high tourism—we all benefit. Our hotels and motels here get filled. Our service stations pump more gas, and our restaurants have more diners. What's good for one is good for everyone."

The new offices for North Charleston's administration are just to the right from Interstate 26 going west at Mall Drive. The impressive four-story building has very slow elevators. Summey may have ordered them as a conversation piece—literally. There are other important functions within North Charleston's city hall. The Charleston Legislative Delegation has its headquarters there, as well. The once South Carolina State Senate president pro tempore, Glenn McConnell, came in daily. He controversially accepted the constitutional role of lieutenant governor as part of a succession for that vacant seat in March 2012. He and Summey have an agreed interest in North Charleston's optimal development. Slow elevators have made them friends. McConnell is a great teammate to have.

Summey and his city council have developed other initiatives. There are Tax Increment Financing Districts to spur development. Growth has been a catalyst to increased revenues and grants for other services to the citizens of North Charleston.

"I'm basically a salesperson. I'm a project person. We can more effectively incentivize new business and innovation by being proactive in the attraction of the right businesses," Summey explained.

"Hey, I grew up here in the Lowcountry. I played tee ball here. I went to high school here," Summey pointed out. "I care about these people and this community. I was never concerned about what others thought about North Charleston as much as I was concerned about our own self-esteem."

Summey grew up not too far from North Charleston—about thirty-five miles away, in Cottageville. His family moved to North Charleston when he reached his teen years, and he attended Chicora High School with friends like Sheriff Al Cannon and Choppy Morris. Ray Graves was the basketball coach, and Chicora teams were always pretty good. Summey played football at Chicora. Where he led, people moved out of the way.

"Keith was a heck of a football player, and as you would expect as a center offensive lineman, he could open up a hole as wide as he was for the backs to rush through," recalled Sheriff Al Cannon. "Keith has great vision for North Charleston, and there is no question that his passion is making North Charleston a great place for people to live."

Mayor Summey graduated from the Baptist College at Charleston, now Charleston Southern University. Always with a spirit of community, he volunteered assistance to the county election commission, eventually becoming its chair in 1986. He delved into other arenas—as North Charleston city councilman, then Charleston County councilman. He was voted chairman of Charleston County Council and served in that role for three years before running for the position of mayor. The opportunity came about because the prior mayor had resigned. The timing of Summey's transition to take the reins at North Charleston has been propitious. He was exactly what the reeling community needed.

Summey and his wife, Deborah, have two children, Elliott and Annie. They have three grandchildren. Son Elliott Summey has been a member of the Charleston County Council since 2008. His father is quite proud. But he knows the realities.

With a smile, Summey reflected on those early city council meetings, both when he first served on council and then when he became the mayor.

"There were some real turbulent times here. Bobby Kinard had taken over for John Bourne, who was our first mayor and a great man. But Mayor Kinard had some challenges that reminded everyone of a sitcom, not a working city government. There were factions pulling every which way. It was a fearful time. It was also a dysfunctional time," Summey pointed out. "Kinard, frustrated, eventually resigned."

Now in his fifth full term and sixth overall, Summey faced the worst recession in the last seventy years by 2008. There was a dearth of tax revenue to fund the needs of the city.

Summey's initial recession plan called for a hiring freeze without a cut of services. He ordered old equipment repaired instead of expensive replacements. The city needed to catch up on the revenue side in order to operate at peak efficiency. So Summey set out to find other revenue sources himself. It was well within his expertise. He looked for new businesses. He courted industry. In time, he hit the mother lode.

The retail centers spiked. The Tanger Outlet Mall deal was signed. Sam's Club relocated to a bigger store. More hotels opened. And then Boeing flew in out of nowhere. Summey was in on the discussions. With the smiling and confident mayor at the table, Boeing announced its North Charleston factory location. It would build the exciting new Boeing 787 Dreamliner and show it to the world from North Charleston.

"During the recession, we became one of the few municipalities anywhere to grow our revenue," Summey indicated. "That gave us other latitude for other development."

Other positive enhancements ensued. Indeed, the Charleston Aviation Authority granted a contract in March 2012 for an update and expansion of the Charleston International Airport. The older airport had already experienced significant improvements since its opening in 1985. It can only get better from here.

In all of the positives, Summey took time to reflect on a memory that deeply affected him.

"My sister and her husband were killed in a traffic accident. They were victims of a drunk driver," Summey intimated. "It was the saddest episode I ever went through."

Time stopped. The mayor found the time to reflect. His sister and brother-in-law left two children to be raised. It was a very difficult and personal time for the mayor.

Seeing Summey in the sphere of his avocations, one would know that family matters. He and his wife, Deborah, have enjoyed more than forty years of marriage. He is also active in his faith through Cooper River Baptist Church, not far from his home. He sees the emergence of North Charleston in other non-revenue implications. It has become a family-friendly community. Young people have seen the value.

Summey worked with others to enhance family activities in the area from Wannamaker Park to the North Charleston Center for the Performing Arts and the Charleston Area Convention Center. There is also the Seacoast Church Dream Center on North Rhett near Sumner Avenue. It distributes basic supplies like diapers, clothing and food to the needy of the area. The playground system thrives. There remain key enjoyment elements like Frankie's Fun Park, where one can swing at an eighty-mile-per-hour fastball, play putt-putt golf, climb a rock wall or drive miniature race cars. The aforementioned Carolina Ice Palace is booked with weekend birthday parties. There is a butterfly garden at Park Circle. The sleek new Riverfront Park at the old navy base is a gorgeous natural setting for family picnics. One could tour the *H.L. Hunley* archaeological progress while there. The idea of wholesome family life has been an exciting upward spiral that positions North Charleston as a destination—something that was not in the vernacular before the first election of Keith Summey.

He sewed the factions together. He found common synergy with like-minded entrepreneurs and developed an earnest goal of redefining an entire city. He did just that.

"I like what I do but am never sure that there are enough hours in the day to do it," Summey detailed. "I think I gave my cellphone number to too many people."

Summey's availability as a mayor makes him more than unique. He is gregarious, energized and industrious in the ways of building coalitions. He puts people together. Those coalitions have become part of the resurgent story of North Charleston. Ostensibly, it is the story of Mayor Keith Summey.

A Changer in a Changing World

ADMIRAL BILL SCHACHTE

Territorial waters are the provoking proximities that have arguable aqueous borders. One country's definition is another country's dare and vice versa. In the bluster of the Black Sea winter of 1988, the two most powerful nations in the history of mankind nearly reached World War III over this deep and chilling question. A man from Charleston was called upon to resolve it.

Two United States naval ships were commanded to run the nautical heading within the international "right of innocent passage." That right was denied by the Soviets. The firepower of the Stars and Stripes' naval ships far exceeded that of the Soviet frigate. Yet the captain of the frigate decided to run a vector toward the two U.S. ships, the destroyer USS *Caron* and the cruiser USS *Yorktown*.[22] Then, the unexpected happened. The Soviet frigate pulled alongside the *Yorktown*. Many of the crew lined the decks with their furry *ushanka*[23] caps and lifejackets. They were armed with automatic weapons, the hammer-and-sickle flag ominously tethered against the wet, cold wind. The American crews were in response, well armed and ready for battle. Any number of flinches could have started a major confrontation that would have surely escalated. The Soviets used a foolish "exit strategy." Their belligerent captain swung to the right and bumped the *Yorktown* while turning to the left. A pronounced second bump near the aft section of the *Yorktown* nearly capsized the smaller Soviet ship. It was an overt act of aggression with the aggressor leaving abruptly.

The Pentagon and the White House were alerted.

A world expert on territorial waters who served the international community in the proctoring and resolution of maritime claims was called. Rear Admiral William L. "Bill" Schachte Jr. had been serving as "deputy, and then acting, U.S. Department of Defense representative for Ocean Policy Affairs while serving in the Pentagon as the Navy's Deputy Assistant Judge Advocate General (of international law)."[24]

The very decorated admiral had achieved two of the service's highest peacetime awards: the Defense Distinguished Service Medal from the secretary of defense (Dick Cheney at that time) and the cherished Navy Distinguished Service Medal, given by the secretary of the navy.

"The Soviets operated during the Cold War with the sentiment that 'What is mine is mine and what is yours is negotiable,'" Schachte retold. "And if you let them, they'd change that to 'What is mine is mine and what is yours is mine, too!'"

The impulse of instant Soviet scrap iron was scuttled. A retaliatory strike was thus averted. A more prudent course was selected, and the incident—which was not reported by the media until a week later—had already been defused. The episode, along with subsequent negotiations and practicable solution, became the calculated and careful management effort of a Charleston-born naval career lawyer. Schachte met with the commanding general of the U.S. European Command and senior staff at its headquarters in Germany. Schachte and some of his colleagues from the State Department later met with representatives of the Soviets in Washington, D.C., and in Moscow. President Ronald Reagan was in his eighth and final year of office. By positioning the strength of law, the imposing U.S. might and the backing of the international community, Schachte out-negotiated the tough Soviet group. He put a high-level plan in effect that resolved the incident. Those efforts resulted in the "USSR-USA Joint Statement on the Uniform Interpretation of Rules of International Law Governing Innocent Passage," signed by Secretary of State James Baker and Soviet foreign minister Eduard Shevardnadze on September 23, 1989.

There were other untimely diplomatic contortions in this era of decision, barely a year and a half before "the wall came down." Schachte had performed his function admirably and was cited as such by the undersecretary of defense, Walter B. Slocombe, who had strongly advocated the talented Schachte for U.S. tribunal for the Law of the Sea United Nations Conference.

"Admiral Schachte's skills at consensus building are widely known, not only in the U.S. government, but internationally. He has represented the

Admiral Bill Schachte's global experiences have had major effects. His humility keeps him on the quiet end of Broad Street. *Courtesy of the United States Navy.*

department in numerous bilateral and multilateral Law of the Sea discussions and negotiation, always demonstrating an exceptional sense of diplomacy." Slocombe continued, "These have included complex and sensitive issues with Russia, Canada, Greece, Turkey, Japan and several Latin American and South Pacific nations...Admiral Schachte was one of the principal architects of the framework for the administration's Ocean Policy Review."

This was a stirring recommendation for an old Charleston boy.

The second oldest of five children, Schachte grew up on Grove Street within earshot of The Citadel's bugled reveilles. He attended Sacred Heart Parish School and Bishop England High School and earned his undergraduate diploma from Clemson University. His mother and father gave him a pedigree of hard work. His mother attended Anderson College and met the senior Schachte on a blind date when he was a military cadet at Clemson. Clemson had a cadet corps and military bearing from its founding in 1893 until 1955.[25] The Schachte marriage continued the lines of a seminal Charleston family. Schachte's mom later assisted Mayor Joe Riley as a calling coordinator during his first election campaign in 1975 and subsequent campaigns. The younger Bill Schachte, being the mayor's second cousin, spent the next thirty years of his life, from 1963 to 1993, in places that were not Charleston. However, ever sure of an eventual return, Schachte has owned a home on Broad Street since 1973.

Though his dad was one of the early electrical engineers at the Charleston Naval Shipyard, Schachte did not pursue that field of endeavor. The senior Schachte's landmark work on the development of radar became part of the British and American early warning advantage of World War II. His father died seven years after the younger Schachte's 1963 Clemson graduation. Schachte had enrolled in an air force ROTC program at Clemson because there was no naval ROTC training there, and "the army ROTC students had to carry a rifle." Upon graduation and after officer candidate school, he took a commission in the navy. He had no idea that he might be called upon to change the world. He did that a few times.

"When I left Charleston to go into the navy, it was much like Richmond—a dying city. King Street had many vacancies. Buildings were in disrepair. There were only a few restaurants here that were considered decent, one being Perdita's and maybe the Cavallaro Supper Club that was across the bridge. The Colony House was another, but it opened later. There were older hotels like the Francis Marion and the Fort Sumter and nothing with updated conveniences. There may have been a few with window-unit air conditioning. The rest depended on ceiling fans! Market Street had dives and tattoo parlors. It was a place for young enlisted navy guys to get into trouble. There was no real spirit of pride here that I noticed before Joe Riley's regime. The families indeed had pride, but not the community. It was not a place that invited tourists.

In essence, there was no true leadership or vision for Charleston. Now, fifty years later, it's like a miracle happened. In my opinion, that miracle was my cousin, Mayor Joe Riley.

"I remember when he was elected and his father, Joe Riley Sr., was so nervous as the results rolled in, he told me that he had about nineteen drinks to defray the anticipation of the unknown. That jovial exaggeration stuck with me."

Schachte continued: "I happened to be in town for one of Joe's early inauguration speeches at the fountain in front of Charleston Place. I realized that I had come to a changing Charleston. It was so much better. When they built Charleston Place, the other restaurants came. Other hotels came. It was an impressive transition.

"My final return was after I had completed my navy career. I returned to a different Charleston than I left in 1963. I had traveled the world with the navy—meeting with foreign officials in the South Pacific, in Fiji, Indonesia to Papua New Guinea and to Honiara, the capital city of the Solomon Islands on the island of Guadalcanal. I recall seeing cultures that had men in grass skirts with huts and trails that I jogged that ended where no man could go farther. I had been to places so remote that very few will ever visit. I had also been to the countries of Scandinavia, the many European countries and capitals—in Russia, Australia and New Zealand; places like Jakarta and Manila. And then I came back here to move into the house on Broad Street that Carmen and I bought before Joe Riley became the mayor. We're home. Carmen and I are perfectly happy here. It's our last port of call."

Carmen Schachte, the pretty and personable mate whom Schachte met in Puerto Rico, is the other end of the "love at first sight" that many storybook romances evoke. This one really happened. A graduate of the University of Puerto Rico and coming from a highly formal and religious family, she was immediately interested in the suave and handsome Schachte. Schachte invited her to dine in the ship's officers' mess as his guest. Smitten, she did so. In time, Schachte proposed. Carmen's pastor insisted on a letter from Schachte's parish priest in Charleston, Monsignor John Manning of Sacred Heart Church. A letterhead affidavit stating that Schachte was a practicing Catholic—and was not and had never been married—was required. Schachte, understanding the culture and assuring her parents, obtained the letter from his pastor in Charleston. Carmen's parents were assured, and a formal wedding ensued at San Antonia de Padua Church in Ceiba, Puerto Rico. Bill's dad was his best man. The

Schachtes have been married for forty-seven years. They have two sons and two young grandsons.

The Schachte navy career began and ended with his forthright mission to serve. He stayed true to his principles throughout.

Schachte entered the navy's Excess Leave Program to pursue a law degree and transferred to the navy's Judge Advocate General's Corps. He received his jurisprudence degree from the University of South Carolina. After receiving an LLM degree (with highest honors) in international and comparative law from the George Washington University Law School, his discipline focused on international law as it pertains to maritime and U.S. naval activity. The LLM degree, or Latin *legum magister*, signifies an intended pursuit of international law. This new direction followed an astonishing record of service that included meritorious service in combat during the Vietnam War.

A seemingly insignificant incident in those early years made world headlines much later. Schachte defined it as being an innocent bystander who vividly recalled details that turned a presidential election. It was because, as a navy lieutenant, he created a plan to engage the enemy.

It was in Vietnam that Schachte devised a way to entice the Viet Cong into impromptu firefights that were planned traps. It was part of the use of "SWIFT boats" and navy skimmers. A SWIFT boat is an acronym for a "shallow water inshore fast tactical" watercraft.[26] Schachte's plan was well thought out: "Essentially, I would take two volunteers out on a fifteen-foot skimmer towed by a SWIFT boat and then troll alone near a shoreline. I'd have an enlisted man on the motor and another junior officer on one of the two weapons. We also carried an M69 grenade launcher and illuminator flares. I insisted on volunteers due to the danger of the mission. We'd leave the SWIFT boat after midnight with a FAC aircraft on alert. [FAC, or "forward air control," naval planes were used as needed to support such missions.[27]] We were trying to lure fire from the Viet Cong. I'd look for enemy movement or noise of any kind. If we saw something, we'd open up with our weapons—an M-60 machine gun and an M-16 mounted with a starlight (sight scope)—into the area, trying to draw the return fire. If firepower was returned, we'd get out quickly, calling in the positions for both naval artillery and treetop air support, if available."

Schachte explained, "The plan had worked a few times. But I felt like since it was my idea, I needed to be the first volunteer for each mission."

On the night of December 2, 1968, Lieutenant Schachte took a raw volunteer with him on the exercise. That volunteer was Lieutenant John

Kerry. At about 3:00 a.m., Schachte described what he thought was a movement, and he fired a handheld illumination flare. He immediately fired in the direction of the movement, as did Kerry. But Kerry's gun jammed. Kerry then manned the grenade launcher and fired off the first round. A piece of shrapnel from the "blow-back" range of the grenade nicked his upper arm. No return fire was detected. Seeing nothing, Schachte commanded a ceasefire. He then returned to the SWIFT boat that was standing by. Once there, a decision was made to not file the mandatory after-action report since no enemy was encountered. Schachte had admonished Kerry for firing the M69 grenade launcher too closely, as shrapnel could have easily taken out an eye. Schachte went to bed upon returning to Cam Ranh Bay, planning on a late wake-up from his post-sunrise return.

"I was awakened with a message from the skipper, Commander Grant Hibbard. He wanted me in his office immediately," Schachte recounted. "I was startled and wondering what was up. When I got there, John Kerry was already there. He had requested a Purple Heart! Commander Hibbard asked about my report. I had briefed him earlier that there was no enemy fire. When I repeated to him there was no enemy return fire, he became incensed at Kerry. In naval language laced with a few choice words, he told Kerry 'to get out of his office.'

"Kerry was transferred out within about two weeks. I had not heard from him again until he had become a senator. We saw each other under the Capitol, waiting on a Senate subway. He remembered that my call sign that night was 'Batman.' He said we should get together for lunch, but that never happened. I thought I'd heard the last of Kerry and that SWIFT boat incident until he ran for president in 2004. That's when his book came out, titled *Tour of Duty*. In it, it was pointed out to me by someone else that he detailed his Purple Heart awards, including one he did eventually receive somehow from the incident I described in 1968. The doctor that attended him said it was a scratch that he applied a Band-Aid and ointment to. I gave no report because there was no enemy confrontation—one of the conditions necessary for both a written report and an award of a Purple Heart. Commander Grant Hibbard threw Kerry out of his office for requesting a Purple Heart. So, how did he politically arrange this self-inflicted scratch into an actual Purple Heart?"

When the race between Democratic nominee John Kerry and incumbent president George W. Bush heated up, these claims again came to the forefront. A second Vietnam Conflict Purple Heart was characterized as also self-inflicted. It stemmed from Kerry blowing up an absconded container of rice and injuring his buttocks in the process. This was attested to having happened by another SWIFT boat officer. In time, an organization was formed to challenge the Kerry claims. They called themselves the "SWIFT Boat Veterans for Truth." Being somewhat apolitical, Schachte did not join. In 2004, he had already contributed $1,000 to the Bush campaign, likely because he knew Kerry's character. Yet Schachte had previously gone on record as voting for Democrat Bill Clinton in his first election prior to Bush's stint in the White House. The pundits came out of the woodwork. The Dems looked for Schachte's motives. They even made up a few. The Republicans asked for interviews. Schachte wisely stayed the course, not looking for the avalanche of media attention. He declined interviews from popular television network journalist Sean Hannity, along with requests from other networks. He deflected endless criticism from the left.

In time, he agreed to an on-camera interview with NBC's Lisa Meyers. The hour-and-a-half interview took place on August 24, 2004, in plenty of time for the Kerry camp to try and refute the report prior to the November election. In it, Meyers asked in every conceivable way multiple times if Admiral Schachte was calling Senator John Kerry a liar. Schachte fell short of the obvious by referring directly to the chronology and reporting of the incident in question so that the listener could draw his or her own conclusions. Had Schachte, who had stayed on the sidelines, not come forward to tell the facts, many believe John Kerry might have beaten Bush in 2004. To this day, the political left holds Schachte accountable for the loss of the White House. A more prudent view would be that John Kerry brought it on himself.

Schachte had learned valuable lessons from another political fray. He knew the collateral damage that could come from such episodes. After John Kerry lost his bid for the presidency, Admiral Bill Schachte lost an opportunity for a possible judgeship along the way. It was the sacrifice he knew he was making. Author John O'Neill concurs. *Unfit for Command: SWIFT Boat Veterans Speak Out Against John Kerry* details the Schachte incident and others.

In a phone interview, O'Neill noted: "Admiral Bill Schachte was brave to come forward. In the midst of this, he was one of the favorites to be named for a possible judgeship on an International Law Court. I joke with Bill that my book inadvertently made certain that he would not get that judgeship—a position he so richly deserved and was one of the most qualified candidates to be vetted. The Kerry matter made him instantly controversial."

Lawyer and SWIFT boat veteran turned author O'Neill was not the only author with lofty regards for Schachte's integrity. Schachte had also been summoned to review the navy's Las Vegas shenanigans of 1991, otherwise known as the "Tailhook Scandal," and subsequent attempts to cover up. In this episode, some one hundred navy women reported a variety of crimes during an annual navy pilots' convention.

Author William McMichael's book, *The Mother of All Hooks*, characterized Admiral Schachte as part of a three-admiral team that composed the leadership on the navy JAG Corps. The full truth finally came out after an attempted dust-away by a previous navy investigation, and McMichael described Schachte in the most eloquent of terms: "Schachte was a proven and decorated leader who as a young officer had commanded patrol boats in riverine combat operations during the Vietnam War. An unpretentious man, he had risen to become a highly respected attorney in the navy community and had developed a reputation as an expert on international law."

The full Tailhook Scandal was uncovered, and the after-action report included sentencing, military courts-martial and demotions. In another unintended turn, the seat of the judge advocate general of the navy, the highest position in the navy JAG, was lost to Schachte. He had been the "acting" TJAG (the judge advocate general) for more than a year and was thought to be the cinch choice for the permanent appointment. The lost appointment was due to a change in administration and what seems sometimes to be an unwritten rule that once a scandal is resolved, as the Tailhook episode was with Schachte's diligence, all of the principal players become part of the carnage. They are made inaccessible to the press and to future scrutiny. Performing brilliantly in the Tailhook proceedings may well have cost Schachte the judge advocate general's chair.

Columnist and talk show host Robert Novak also detailed Schachte's plight. He reinvestigated the reports, the witnesses and the chronology of the SWIFT boat episode of August 2004 in his book *Prince of Darkness*. The Novak reports clearly edified Schachte's assertions as a true witness. When the story broke, Kerry asserted that he was the only officer in the skimmer. Yet Schachte, who detailed the origin of the mission and manned every one of the operations up to and beyond that time, corrected the senator-candidate. His commanding officer, Grant Hibbard, backed Schachte, as did many other witnesses—except two crewmen who appeared at the Democratic National Convention platform with Kerry. Novak's book detailed the episode from every angle and every possible witness. It's a compelling support case for Schachte.

But all is forgotten, and Kerry is still a Massachusetts senator. Schachte is still active as a counsel to the national law firm Blank Rome LLP. Schachte is happily in the comfort of his Broad Street home, enjoying his grandsons and traveling to places he and his lovely wife, Carmen, like to visit. They are enjoying their semi-retirement years by attending much of what Charleston has to offer. Schachte shares his Monday afternoons with a Bible fellowship that he started in Charleston after he retired from the navy. They meet every Monday at Citadel Square Baptist Church on Marion Square. He corresponds with old friends, mostly by e-mail from his crowded office, filled with photos and other career memorabilia. They include a framed certificate from former South Carolina governor Carroll Campbell naming Schachte as a recipient of the Order of the Palmetto, the state's highest honor. There are many other items that warm his memory of a career honorably spent.

Admiral William L. Schachte Jr. might have helped change the course of the Cold War by way of the Black Sea incident of 1988. He may have rendered full and complete justice to the participants and cover-up operatives of the 1991 Tailhook Scandal, his forthright principle becoming his own fate. He may have changed the course of the 2004 United States presidential election by doing what he has always done: telling the truth. History leaves ample room for abundant conjecture.

What is sure is that Carmen and Bill Schachte are an integral part of what makes Charleston a great place to live. Schachte has earned national and international respect. He has served his country, his family and his conscience. And he is one of us.

A Reach Out to Others

SISTER MARY JOSEPH RITTER

There are devotions. There are prayers. Then there are meals and food distribution, dental assistance, adult language courses and then more prayers. There is prenatal care, high school equivalency classroom participation, recycled clothing, career and budget counseling and more prayers. In every sense, devotion remains.

Sister Mary Joseph Ritter lives where her heart has taken her: to the service of others. The mission of her energy and constancy has been at Our Lady of Mercy (OLM) Community Outreach. It's a miracle place for those who are in need of miracles.

Mayor Joseph P. Riley Jr. has called Sister Mary Joseph the "Mother Teresa of the Sea Islands."[28] Those barrier islands are where she served as the executive director of what tomorrow might bring.

This enclave of hope is near the center of John's Island, South Carolina, the fourth-largest barrier island on the East Coast. Its acclimation to Charleston is due south, and west and east. Well, it is a large island. The complex has been built by the foresight of a board and the insight of its past faithful director, Sister Mary Joseph. It was done with mostly private funding and plentiful public care. Sister Mary Joseph is an avowed fifty-year Catholic sister. The outreach reaches all faiths. There is not an identification narrative at the door. The qualifications are simple: 1) the needy, 2) those in need and 3) others in need, too. No one is turned away.

The OLM Outreach has a historical basis. In December 1829, the first Catholic bishop of Charleston, Bishop John England, brought four women to his young diocese and established them as Sisters of Our Lady of Mercy. Within the year, they had opened a school for girls and, a few years later, an orphanage. By 1838, they had opened a temporary hospital and, by 1841, a free school for "children of color,"[29] a "first" in America. In 1882, they opened St. Francis Xavier Infirmary, the progenitor to Roper St. Francis Hospital. Their industriousness was just beginning! They started parochial schools in Charleston and wherever needed throughout the state. Still devoted to their mission of helping the poor, they opened the Neighborhood House in 1915. During the same year, the Sisters of Charity of Our Lady of Mercy opened Bishop England High School, essentially becoming the school's faculty—along with a few priests of the Diocese of Charleston. By 1933, this same conscientious order staffed St. Mary's School in Greenville and opened Our Lady of Mercy Junior College. They later opened another hospital in York. The Divine Savior Hospital grew, and a nursing facility was added, the first of its kind in South Carolina.[30] The sisters saw another service and education need in Charleston. They started St. Francis Xavier Nursing School and quickly accredited its academic mission. The facility was located on Ashley Avenue at Mill Street—convenient to the hospital. There was no area of interest within the scope of education, indigent care and public service to the needy that this incredible community of women did not impact. The tireless work had ample tireless workers within this amazing kinship of devoted souls.

Our Lady of Mercy Outreach, serving the barrier islands, began in 1989,[31] just ten days prior to Hurricane Hugo's Charleston landfall. The effort was meant to further the Christian service to the poor—a tenet of the Sisters of Charity. The mission was established to serve the 25 percent of John's, James and Wadmalaw Islands residents deemed to be living well under the abject level of poverty. That percentage grew immediately by the displaced and hungry when the massive storm—one of the largest ever to be recorded in American history—came ashore at midnight on September 22, 1989.

The community of enterprising nuns did much out of their normal element in the ensuing weeks and months. Led by Sister Carol Wentworth, the Nun Better Roofing Company was established. All work was free of charge. Another initiative born of the hurricane was NAILS—Neighborly Assistance In Living Safely. The acronym became a popular sign of the times on South Carolina's devastated Sea Islands. Augmented by the outpouring of community largesse and volunteerism, and with Habitat for

Sister Mary Joseph Ritter's calling has led her to assist the needy downtown and on the barrier islands. She exudes energy and hope. *Courtesy of Tommy McQueeney.*

Humanity, the sisters energetically filled the three roles needed: leadership, resourcefulness and prayer. They helped to rebuild the islands. They rebuilt other intangibles like faith in the goodness of others, inspiration for the divinity of God and hope for families that had lost it all in the space of six wind-driven hours.

As one might have imagined, the OLM Outreach had opened in the wrong place at precisely the worst time possible. The result of its opening was the opposite sentiment. It was where it needed to be just in time, as Sister Mary Joseph recalls: "Many didn't have running water or electricity before Hugo occurred. Hugo brought us to them and them to us. Our board of directors had already determined that the community we served had needs beyond emergency. They needed education, budget counseling and healthcare before Hugo was a factor. We brought to them what people brought to us: diapers, clothing and even a truckload of yogurt! They needed dental care and prenatal care. We received grants from the Duke Foundation and MUSC. We have exceeded $1 million in free care and served 3,500 dental patients here through twenty-eight volunteer dentists. We've partnered with the MUSC School of Dentistry and Trident Tech's dental hygienist program. Our language program teaches English as a second language to more students than anyone in the county. We also teach English to those speaking Vietnamese and Portuguese."

Within ten years, by 1999, a Wellness Center was opened for the aforementioned free medical attention—from dentistry to obstetrics. The extended medical services were performed by a wealth of selfless volunteer MDs from the Medical University of South Carolina and Roper St. Francis Hospital—and others as well. There is a miracle-a-day provided to those seeking the kindnesses extended by others. With the expanded educational element, the immigrant Hispanic population, many of them here as vestiges from the days of itinerant tomato crop workers, sought to learn English. The outreach found volunteer teachers for evening classes to allow for daytime jobs. Others seeking a GED, the high school diploma equivalency, found that venue at the outreach. Lives were improved. There were other areas of enhancement to the needy, such as clothing, diapers, nonperishable and perishable foods, counseling and even job opportunities posted.

Sister Mary Joseph tells a heart-warming vignette of one such job opportunity realized by a young minority female teacher. Though beset by economic woes, the young lady donated her very first paycheck back to the outreach to help others. It lifted the spirit of the entire staff. They were doing something so meaningful for so many that the stories of success began stockpiling. Success is the norm.

"Our mission is to help others. With God's blessing and the volunteers who so graciously donate their time and expertise, we can make a difference," Sister Mary Joseph stated.

Sister Mary Joseph remembers her inspiration: "My smile of remembrance came from the happiness of my childhood and the neighborhood I grew up in…where everyone looked after one another. Neighborhoods were safe. You don't really see that as much today. I went to Sacred Heart School. What made me sad was seeing how poor some people were. Sister Anthony was a powerful inspiration to me. I would volunteer to help at the Neighborhood House, where she devoted so much of her time. She would ride out to bring help to families that had very little. It was then that I first saw that not everyone was as blessed as my family. My religious vocation was mentored by this experience through Sister Anthony. Sister Anthony was fearless and committed. She taught me that it was okay to venture out away from the safety of your home to help others. I remember that she would put live chickens in the back of her station wagon to deliver to people. She made a meaningful impression upon me as a young girl."

Sister Mary Joseph Ritter had some characters of future impact in her classroom when she attended Bishop England High School. Her classmates included Joe Riley, Tommy Hartnett, Pat Brennan, Sally Degnan, Billy Runey, Mickey Jones, Patricia Schill, Bill Robinson and Tommy Lavelle. She was born Andrea Marie Ritter, but her classmates fondly referred to her as "Andy."

"Andy was always a top student and was such a good person to be around. She was always cute, outgoing and energetic. When I see her now, I still see the liveliness and spirit of those days we enjoyed as high school students," recalled Tricia Schill Hocutt. "She's simply incredible. And she does all of these things for everyone else as a calling. She's a walking saint.

"We had one of those very positive classes, and several classmates were real leaders, even back then. Tommy Hartnett was always personable. I served on the student council with him. Joe Riley was a hard worker and a perfect gentleman. You could see then that he was going to be someone that would change Charleston. Sally Degnan and I started first grade together. Billy Runey, who passed away, was a fine basketball and football coach at North Charleston High School. Tommy Lavelle coached at Bishop England. Pat Brennan was always a good friend. He's a doctor living in Texas. Our whole class had exceptional people. I think much credit goes to the teachers, many of them were sisters and priests that taught us."

Inspired, the young Miss Ritter joined the convent to become a sister upon her high school graduation in 1960. Her natural choice was the Sisters of Charity of Our Lady of Mercy. She then validated her degree in education by teaching for several years in South Carolina and later in New Jersey. She earned a master's degree at Seton Hall University. It was an appropriate connection since the Patron Saint of the Sisters of Charity is St. Elizabeth Ann Seton, the first American-born saint.

St. Elizabeth Ann Seton (1774–1821) serves as the inspiration for the Sisters of Charity.[32] Sister Mary Joseph explained that the Our Lady of Mercy Outreach Center extends those values that were important in the time of St. Elizabeth Ann. In addition to the poor, there are children, women, the sick and others abandoned or deserted by age or physical or economic circumstances.

"What happens at the Outreach Center is so representative of what the Sisters of Charity in America are all about," Sister Mary Joseph said. "It's a given for all the sisters who continue with [St. Elizabeth Ann's] work." She added that "it is an honor for her whole community because they all walk in the saint's footsteps." [33]

When Sister Mary Joseph returned from New Jersey, she served in administrative and pastoral care at St. Francis Xavier Hospital until the hospital was transferred to the Bon Secours health system. It was partially from the proceeds of the hospital sale that helped to create OLM Outreach.

Through innate humility, Sister Mary Joseph has never been one to draw attention to her monumental works. She credits everyone else. Yet the achievements are compelling. In 2004, the Coastal Community Foundation presented her with the prestigious Malcolm D. Haven Award for community service. The dinner in her honor filled the large ballroom at Charleston Place. The award has a pedigree of community selflessness with past recipients such as Dr. Charlie Darby, Bill Saunders, Henry J. Lee, Henry Tecklenburg, Joe Griffith, Anita Zucker, Edwin Schachte, Dr. Ted Stern, Edwin Pearlstine and Major General Alex Grimsley.[34]

There was a consensus of insight within the banquet hall that Sister Mary Joseph was there to receive an award so that she could further promote the Outreach mission to a roomful of captive donors. It was never about her. Her monthly message through her newsletters to the community of regular donors intimates her perspective: "At the Outreach there are many new faces: fathers who are experiencing cutbacks in their jobs, mothers who are caring for elderly parents and cannot adequately meet monthly rent payments, elderly persons who cut back on food because of medical bills. Financial constraints complicated by health issues, educational limitations and lack of employment challenge many of our neighbors. As the demand for services grows, the need for sustainable support also increases. To address current and future needs and ensure the stability of the Outreach's services, the Board of Directors and Staff are expanding 'The Circle of Blessings,' our annual giving program. Donors commit to give financial support at their level on a yearly basis. Relying on the generosity of our supporters, we encourage your participation in this important effort. May God bless you for your ongoing support as partners in our mission."

In 2009, Sister Mary Joseph was awarded the prestigious Seton Medal, a national designation presented to "people who have contributed in a significant way to social services, education, health care, promoting the awareness of Saint Elizabeth Ann Seton, or spiritual formation in the spirit of the Seton Legacy of Charity."[35]

Thanking people who do thankless jobs, recruiting teaching volunteers, enrolling applicants, sustaining schedules for selfless dentists and doctors and performing the tasks required of a super-fundraiser are all part of Sister Mary Joseph's daily routine. It's her DNA. More so, it's God's plan for her. It's her devotion.

She has learned much from the experience: "I have seen that some tend to categorize different people by some small bias or prejudice. In what we do, there is no race, color or creed. It is just the nature of 'love your neighbor' that matters. At the Outreach, the staff sees everyone as individuals—as families with close relationships, with deep faith and a resolve to do well. There is dignity in every person. There are people that come to the Center from every faith and background. The board and staff guide them to become self-sustaining. They do this with forward thinking and a true spirit of compassion.

"Everyone tries to serve in a holistic manner that looks at a person's entire life and helps each individual address his or her needs with inner strength that either already exists or can be developed. This organization seeks to convey a real sense of respect for people and to see their potential rather than their problems."[36]

She told of a case she knew too well: "A very difficult case was referred to us by the Health Department. The couple had three children, but their baby boy had brain cancer. The father was a farm worker, and they lived in a trailer. It was old and rat-infested. They had rat poison all around the trailer. There was grave concern for a safe place for the baby. We were able to place them temporarily, for two months, in the In Town Suites. We helped get doctors for their care at MUSC. Volunteers took them to the medical appointments. We found the father a job at a plant nursery. He eventually bought a livable trailer. The couple was Hispanic. She learned English at the Outreach. Other volunteers attached to the family. Eventually, they were able to get into a 'Habitat home.' The mother got a job at Kiawah as a housekeeper. But, sadly, the boy died at age twelve. I share the story because of the love that this community and so many volunteers showed for that family. They became part of us. The father learned English. Both parents got permanent jobs, and their other two children are doing well. They are members of Holy Spirit Catholic Church and are working as positive members of the community. Through great tragedy, they have persevered. That family has a higher purpose and a greater sense of dignity."

Somehow, there are higher purposes and greater meanings to life that we should all contemplate. At Our Lady of Mercy Community Outreach, Sister Mary Joseph Ritter should teach that class; that is, if she has the time!

In the summer of 2012, Sister Mary Joseph Ritter was accorded the title of general superior of the Sisters of Charity for Our Lady of Mercy. Her influence will continue to spread and benefit countless others across the wide swath of this most historic order of selfless religious volunteers.

The Bridge that Bobby Clair Built

People seem to aggregate because of Bobby Clair. People from Goose Creek have met people from James Island. People from West Ashley have met people from Awendaw. He's bridged relationships across the community, literally and figuratively. Clair served as the South Carolina Department of Transportation project manager for the Arthur Ravenel Jr. Bridge, completed and opened in 2005.

An older man from North Charleston walked up the new bridge with cane in hand from the Mount Pleasant side to see the view from the top. He took his time, stopping to monitor his energy and take in each heightened vista. Bicyclists and joggers, power walkers and even a Cub Scout troop passed him. A few of the more curious walkers, observing his seniority and assistive cane, stopped to ask if they could help him.

"No, but thanks for askin.' I never thought I'd live to see this. And now I'm just enjoyin' it a few paces at a time," the old man stated. "I'll eventually get there, and then I'll say a little prayer to thank God for keeping me here long enough. This bridge is the eighth wonder of the world!"

That scene observed is not replicated daily, but the sentiment is universal. That bridge is a wonder—for reasons well beyond engineering.

"Yes, it has been a bigger positive than even I would have presumed," Clair said with a smile. "Everyone who lives here has benefited. And the reaction has been more along the lines of community pride and increased physical activity. You see it even on days when it may be too hot or too windy. There's always someone walking or jogging on that bridge."

And they come from everywhere. It has become a phenomenon. They jog from the hotels, the cruise ships, the neighborhoods and even from their offices after work. Everybody sees everybody on the bridge. And that's not even the bridge's primary function.

Clair could never have imagined that so many "locals" would meet at the top just to take photographs or watch the sun go down. It is Kiawah shaking hands with Sullivan's Island, Summerville greeting Mount Pleasant, Seabrook nodding a pleasant hello to Moncks Corner. It's a retired downtown couple meeting Citadel cadets, an established lawyer chatting with an emergency room intern, a Benefit Focus account manager laughing with a Boeing engineer. Nobody could have drawn this up. Well, okay, somebody did draw it up, but that blueprint didn't have this weave of metropolitan Charleston tested for hurricane wind resistance and earthquake tolerance. Clair measured those impacts before the "people effect" was ever calculated. Clair's bridge ended up bigger than what was in those early drawings.

Clair was born in Charleston and, in a bit of later-life irony, lived on the main traffic pattern, at 67 Cannon Street, that led to the John P. Grace Memorial Bridge. Just as Spring Street took vehicular traffic to the West Ashley area, Cannon Street took northbound traffic to the metal monstrosity, the only bridge spanning the Cooper River when Clair was born in 1946. It was the same year that a commercial freighter, the *Nicaragua Victory*, hit the short-side span and sent 220 feet of roadbed and a family of five plunging into Town Creek.[37] The tragedy lurked for decades. That bridge was among the most dangerous in America and underserved the public interests. In fact, many Charlestonians would not hazard a drive into Mount Pleasant out of sheer fear. The bridge had two claustrophobic lanes, one in each direction. As rust started winning the battle over cosmetic layers of battleship-gray paint, the John P. Grace Memorial Bridge became anathema. Following a constant struggle for replacement funding in the state legislature, the Silas M. Pearman Bridge was built—twenty-one years after the freighter tragedy, in 1967. They're both gone now, replaced by Clair's legacy to the city he loves.

Clair has ties to Charleston deeper than the pilings: "My mother moved from her home in Georgetown at age eighteen to Charleston in the early 1940s and took a job as a secretary at a manufacturing plant in North Charleston. She was introduced one day to the late congressman L. Mendel Rivers, who offered her a job as his secretary. She accepted the job and for the next two years worked in both his Charleston and Washington, D.C. offices. By her accounts, the congressman took extreme pleasure in entertaining his

Charleston friends at both of these offices, which she said 'were always well stocked.' Included in that group of close friends was Joseph P. Riley Sr. In 1944, she married my father and for the next twenty-five years dedicated her life to raising her four children.

"My maternal grandfather, William Y. Morris, built concrete forms for the construction of the Grace Bridge in the late 1920s. My mother's brother, Lindsey Morris, worked for PreStress Concrete on the Pearman Bridge in the mid-1960s. I guess you could say that building bridges has been in my blood for a few generations."

Clair's family moved to the West Ashley area during his youth, and he played football, basketball and baseball at St. Andrew's Playground. He remembers that there was not much out that way: "We took the city bus into downtown for a dime. With a quarter, we could see a movie—and that included popcorn and a nickel candy! During the summers, we usually found a way to get to Sullivan's Island for a week with the Condons or the Robinsons, all cousins. The simplicity of that life is something so hard to fathom today, but we stayed busy having wholesome fun every day. Well, there might have been a little mischief here and there, but we were pretty good kids.

"My parents had bought a place on Oak Forest Drive from Arthur Ravenel Jr., for whom the new bridge is named. Oak Forest Drive was a densely wooded dirt road. You could buy dynamite from the icehouse station on Spring Street down by the Ashley Bridge and use it to blow all the overgrowth and trash from the woods. Nobody lived that far out. My parents were pioneers. We took our bicycles to school a few miles away."

Growing up essentially in 1950s Charleston brought back Clair's youthful memories. "We had no air conditioning and no television. I remember the excitement when Channel 5 television went live. Neighborhoods were safe. In a way, everybody's mother was your mother. All the children's rules stayed the same from one household to another. You knew everybody; there were not too many strangers. You kinda miss that now. We walked or rode our bikes to school. What I miss is that simplicity. It'll never be that way again."

Clair's penchant for hard work became a strong foundation for his later focus: "My father was a fine businessman. He owned a couple of service stations and became a fine mentor to me. But I learned that I did not want to work the evening and weekend hours that he did. I liked to build."

Clair's father, Robert F. "Robbie" Clair, passed away in 1991. His mentorship made son Bobby reach a little higher and strive a little harder. He

Bobby Clair stayed on when retirement was an option to oversee Charleston's largest-ever construction project. *Courtesy of the South Carolina Department of Transportation.*

pursued a career of building projects while building a life: "I was in the very first class at Trident Technical College. I took courses in civil engineering, where I had met Mr. W.L. Stevens. He was a veteran student graduate of The Citadel and a very fine teacher and friend. He served on Charleston City Council. He always gave timely advice to me."

Clair returned to assist Trident Tech by serving on its trustee board for ten years, even serving a term as the college's board chairman.

His personal life was proudly described: "I met my wife-to-be, Dena Glenn, when she was a nursing student at the Medical University of South Carolina in fall of 1967. Dena is from Anderson and was one of seven children in her family. We were engaged within a year and were married in 1969. Dena worked as a registered nurse and specialized in patient education until she retired. Her strength and tireless work ethic inspired me and caused me to work more diligently to meet my goals. We were both fortunate to be able to stay in Charleston and raise our two children, Robbie and Kristen. We are also fortunate that both of their families, including our grandchildren, also live and work in Charleston and are able to enjoy the Lowcountry lifestyle."

Clair's post-college view of Charleston was a forecast that came to fruition: "I realized that there was much more opportunity as the community grew and traffic patterns caught up. I went to work for the South Carolina Department of Transportation. It was a great move for me. I stayed thirty-seven years, retiring in 2005."

Clair's innate vibrancy would not allow a sedentary retreat into retirement. He went into private practice to work on other worthwhile projects, most of which he personally selects.

And why not? The Clair reputation was taller than either of the iconic spans that knitted the community together. He had earned a lifetime of respect by planning the Charleston area's largest and most admired success.

"Under budget, under time"—that was Clair's mantra going through the process of building the bridge of the next hundred years. It had to meet every safety criteria presented. The unobvious detail of seismic engineering was intrinsic. So was wind. Charleston owes much of its resiliency to the ever-evident potential of hurricanes. Traffic was to include the potential for future high-speed rail, in addition to the community-friendly bike, jog and walk access overlooking the city's skyline. The accident of the *Nicaragua Victory* from 1946 was studied. Each tower pier would incorporate a defense against ship collision. With the details planned, the design chosen and the engineering models certified, the enormity of the project was still ahead. Clair made heady decisions: "An amazing coalition of funding came together to make the bridge a reality. But what that funding meant was that every day we put on those hard hats was to cost $200,000. Every month of work was $6 million. Time and weather became critical. We could not afford to deviate from our schedule. I insisted upon the timeliness of our progress.

"The chosen contractor, a combination of the Skanska and Flatiron corporations, had plans to finish the project as we all wanted, a year ahead of schedule. This looked impossible at first. But utilizing the capabilities of design-build, where you make the changes as needed without the delays of conventional construction, simplified a lot. It was one of the few projects—and definitely the only mega project ever—that the state allowed to be built in this manner.

"Design-Build as an option saved as much as 50 percent of what it would cost otherwise. There is no better way to take on a project like the bridge construction."

Clair continued the thought process: "We simply broke the immense task that it was down into five manageable projects. We had five independent crews. We looked at the highly potential problems beforehand and decided to incorporate a system of 'checks and balances.' We met constantly at the Sand Dunes Club on Sullivan's Island, away from the project. We tried to anticipate every facet of the project, even focusing on community by having one group that just did community relations. We worked at night to minimize traffic concerns. We gave more than eight hundred presentations on the bridge over four years. We made a concerted effort to keep the public advised and informed. That effect also brought the excitement of each stage as they were completed."

Clair was actually planning to retire before the bridge was built. Looking back, he's glad that he didn't. "The commissioner for the Department of Transportation was Bob Harrell. When it became clear that we were going to get the funds to build the bridge, Harrell contacted me and asked me to manage the project. The DOT followed with their request that I manage it. I thought about it and asked if I could do it on my own terms. I wanted a final say on engineering decisions, financial decisions, and did not want any political mess to hold us up. All was agreed, and I was able to delay my retirement and get busy.

"An example of what it meant was that I was able to handpick engineers. I decided on getting a few younger professionals in lieu of older, more established veterans. I needed people to follow suit and not hold up the project with red tape and too many questions. There were plenty of veteran engineers that I admired, and it was a tough decision, but I had to make a call. I felt that the younger group would be more likely to understand that everything had been thoroughly studied beforehand so that the project could move at a steady pace."

The project started in August 2001. The new icon of Charleston opened on July 16, 2005, to much fanfare. In doing so, it opened taller and wider shipping lanes below, making way for the anticipated "Post-Panamax Class" containerships. The roadbed is two hundred feet above the river. The newer tonnage capacities also reopened the major north–south Highway

17 corridors to commercial truck traffic. The previous bridges had been too rickety to accommodate the increased weight.

Clair did retire from the South Carolina Department of Transportation as he had planned on doing previously. He had traveled great distances. While the bridge was under construction in 2004, Clair was invited to present a paper at the International Bridge Symposium in Shanghai, China. They knew about the bridge. He was asked to come to France in an advisory capacity related to bridge cables. They knew about the bridge. The longest cable-stayed bridge in the Western Hemisphere had made it into the journals, the classrooms and the news programs. It had received twenty-eight national and international awards. *Engineering News Record* magazine recognized Clair as one of the top twenty-five newsmakers in the engineering world for 2005 at its April 2006 awards banquet in New York. He received the Order of the Palmetto from Governor Mark Sanford in 2005, the highest civilian award presented by the State of South Carolina. But most of all, Clair had stayed the course and made the sacrifices. He had proved something to himself. He had served others than himself. The bridge has stapled land across a wide river, but it has done much more than that. It is meant to last many generations past the principal characters—the politicians, the engineers and the people who attended its grand opening.

The unwritten benefit was to better serve other public interests, most notably the growth of the Cooper River Bridge Run. The international 10K (ten thousand meters) race attracts major running professionals, nearly forty thousand runners and walkers and even an occasional celebrity following. The local ambiance complements the event, placing Charleston's notable hospitality at the forefront.

The bridge vaulted the entire community forward. And forward it came—to see the bridge from a pedestrian view. Any fall evening, any Sunday afternoon, any lunchtime jaunts are the timely composites of the secondary uses of the structure. People gather. The breeze freshens. Sailboats circle in the distance. The World War II–era *Yorktown* "Fighting Lady" stands erect as the foreground to the panorama of lighthouses, church steeples, barrier islands and a harbor of aqueous activity. It is the prominence of an unforgettable view.

"That's what I came to see. That's the view. Look at that! Can you believe it?" The old man spoke as he reached the top where the path jutted around to well-placed benches and other awestruck viewers. Digital cameras collected the scenes.

"The walk up was worth every step. I don't know if I'll ever get here again, but I'm here now. I believe I'll stay right here for a while. I'm just enjoyin' being alive," he said. "I made it here."

Somehow, the sentiment was not immediately sensed to be about getting up the bridge but about living long enough to be a part of the excitement. The year 2005—it marked a change in Charleston's "future history."

A project manager might have gotten the new Charleston started and finished in time so that area citizens like the aforementioned elderly man could take a look over the top of old Charleston. Bobby Clair is the man who worked beyond his retirement to make sure we all had a new Charleston to look forward to. He has spanned the ages.

Striking a Chord with Darius Rucker

H e hits high mid-iron shots from strategic positions that make allowances for wind and elevation. Any PGA pro would have found his swing rhythmic and paced. It's effortless—a work incorporating style and purpose. He is more at ease in only one place other than the Bulls Bay Golf Club: the performance stage. He may be the most recognizable American-grown music talent extant. He is Darius Rucker. You know him from one of the world's great bands: Hootie and the Blowfish.

If golf or music were all that motivated his life, he would surely be enraptured by it all. He's excellent at both. His single-digit handicap would be even better if he devoted the time it takes to be repeatedly proficient. His music has something for every fan of virtually every genre. The husk of his singularly identifiable voice is immediately appealing in its rich resonance. But Charleston's own Darius Rucker is a much more comprehensive personality than one could stereotype into either of his favorite endeavors.

"I have always been motivated by 'can't.' That word is a challenge thrown in front of me. I like to think that every 'can't' should become a 'can' when it comes to helping someone," Rucker explained.

Rucker has the heart of a saint and the mindset of a profoundly appreciative child, naming his blessings from the holy hierarchy downward—from God to his two father figures, the actual fathers of friends David Campbell and Richard Johannes. He came from a home devoid of his biological father. He depended on timely direction, long Sundays in church and the encouragement that a caring community fosters.

"Because I needed the guidance of a father, others stepped in. David Campbell and Richard Johannes were my best friends. Their fathers, Mr. Johannes and Mr. Campbell, taught me much growing up. Mr. Johannes taught me how to play golf. They both taught me how to be a man," Rucker cited.

Rucker's road was not easy. At one time, there were fourteen inhabitants, to include his grandmother, two aunts and four first cousins, along with his five siblings, in a three-bedroom apartment. Finding an individual role or even a personal calling would seem precarious. Rucker did just that: "One of my earliest remembrances was singing Al Green songs into salt and pepper shakers to the audience of my household. I was only four. They encouraged me. From those early 'performances,' I felt that I had a compass inside of me that pointed to becoming a singer. It was as if I always knew singing was what I was supposed to do."

Rucker's fortuitous preconceptions were realized. He could always sing. It was while in college at the University of South Carolina that other abilities, especially songwriting, found a nexus with his strong and mellow vocals. College students liked what they saw and heard. And it wasn't just those students in Columbia who noticed. Rucker became an icon before his intention of routine college life had a chance to flourish. Hootie and the Blowfish became the rage. It was 1986. Rucker was twenty. The world was in front of him.

Celebrity beckoned. It is what he and the band had achieved with that celebrity that makes one take notice. They gave back.

Hootie and the Blowfish performed free concerts in the effort to assist several needy causes. They visited hospitals. They hosted golf tournaments. They encouraged young people. Rucker also shared his valuable time by participating on local charitable boards.

The band started the Hootie and the Blowfish Foundation in 2000. In this effort, family learning centers were developed. The range of assistance went from school supplies to dental assistance to backpacks. As if this multimillion-dollar foundation were not enough, Hootie and the Blowfish also had an impact on the South Carolina Chapter of the Junior Golf Foundation. Those efforts infused another $4 million—to date—into various youth golf programs. They host an invitational tournament on the "Monday after the Masters"—again to benefit junior golf. They have made other large donations elsewhere. The school supplies that Hootie and the Blowfish have gathered were used symbolically to fill school buses. They have loaded enough buses to be considered a large fleet. The "Home Grown

Darius Rucker may be Charleston's most recognizable international personality. He loves his golf and plays early. *Courtesy of Tommy McQueeney.*

Tour"—featuring six southeastern cities—has encouraged concertgoers to bring these school supplies. They took the program nationwide over the next three U.S. tours. The enthusiasm from those first events carried over. All supplies are redistributed to selected school districts in need. This continued charitable arm began with a public show in Charleston each fall. The "Round Up" had always been intended for lower-income kids. The simple gesture of a backpack, a haircut, new shoes, free dental exams, other arts and crafts supplies and even a pre-school reading of "story times" has made a difference where differences have mattered.

The band performs prior to the school year at the Family Circle Tennis Center on Daniel Island. The final Saturday "Round Up" event will mean significant supplies for children at a local Charleston school.

"We started here," Rucker recalled. "At shows, we asked people to bring out school supplies. We filled up a couple of buses because everybody here is so great. We decided to keep doing it. We did it all over the country. It's pretty cool."[38]

Hootie and the Blowfish also host a major intercollegiate golf championship every year. The Hootie at Bulls Bay Intercollegiate attracts NCAA teams from across the Southeast. The Darius Rucker Intercollegiate at Long Cove in the spring of each year follows a similar format. It is fast becoming one of the great events of women's NCAA golf.

Closer to home, Rucker busies himself in the assistance of the MUSC effort to build a second regional children's hospital. The growth of the Charleston community to almost 650,000 residents underscores this need. He holds the Medical University of South Carolina in high regard and wants to be there when it calls.

"We ate because of MUSC. My mother worked there for thirty years. I remember waiting to pick her up outside the hospital when her shift was over," Rucker noted. "And we used that hospital a few times. I remember leaping from a height with a cape as if I were Superman only to break my leg and have it set down at MUSC.

"I learned charity from the neighborhood and from military families that lived near us in Charleston. You did not have to go too far away from your home in Charleston to find people who cared about you. That is the one special thing about growing up in Charleston. It made a significant difference in my life as well as my outlook on helping others."

In May 2011, Rucker was honored to be the graduation speaker at MUSC and received an honorary doctor of humanities degree. He was humble in his acceptance.

"Now I know I'm just a bar singer from West Ashley and that there are smart kids like you making it because of a good education. You are the heroes that save lives every day. I am here to honor you," Rucker intoned to the deafening appreciation of the graduates. "We all may not be able to change the world, but in our own world, we can make a big change."

The MD crowd roared with approval. Rucker had found that the width and breadth of his following extended well into the age group of young doctors. Among his closing remarks, he left invitations and instructions.

"Please stay here in Charleston if you can. This is the greatest city in the world." Rucker spoke with earned wisdom. He added, "Don't just find your cause; find causes. Look down the street. Somebody always needs help. You get what you give back, and you make the world a better place because you care."

He intimated three thoughts that the young physicians could appreciate. "Three simple things: 1) Find anything you can laugh at. 2) Always believe in yourself. And 3) Refuse to accept something that makes you cry."

The 2011 graduating class at MUSC received their diplomas and a performance well beyond a concert. They received the true and genuine insights of "Dr. Darius Rucker," accorded this by his timely and sage advice—and by a wide-grinned college president, Dr. Raymond Greenberg. Those young physicians will never forget their graduation speaker.

Rucker had been aptly accorded his rightful prominence in Charleston by his sense of accommodating the community and deep-rooted feeling of responsibility. There was no more evident episode of this dedication than on the CBS *Early Show*, hosted by Harry Smith from Charleston, in the summer of 2008. Hootie and the Blowfish were set to perform from White Point Gardens, "The Battery." Rucker had just experienced what was considered routine knee surgery. An infection made the recovery difficult. It almost took his life. Specialists were called in, and emergency procedures followed. Rucker had two more surgeries in the next six days and was fed powerful antibiotics intravenously. The IV bag and stand went with him to make it on time for this early morning live performance—against his doctor's orders. Perhaps he was Superman with a cape after all.

"I did okay. It wasn't my best performance," Rucker recalled. "That IV got in the way a bit, and I was still feeling very weak. But I'm glad that I got out there and did not disappoint my friends here in Charleston."

Rucker and his knee survived. But it was anything but easy in the recovery process. Not everyone knew what he had been through until Harry Smith exposed his bravado to a national audience up early to see this magnificent band.

One would certainly attach the feeling and emotion in his voice to the range of sincere notions he exhibits in private conversation. Rucker is athletic, truly engaging and warm in his demeanor. He is anyone's and everyone's best friend. And like his fluid drive to the fairway, he is focused and fueled. There is a reserve of energy that indicates there is much more to come. Though he finds himself in the role of Charleston's greatest homegrown celebrity, Rucker would just as easily be a math teacher or a shoe store owner. He expects everything of himself but the loft of an ego and the lack of friendliness others of his posture might evoke. He is down-home Charleston real.

It is that Charleston thing that makes Rucker the Holy City's ambassador. The smile is broader, the walk lighter, the expression happier. He loves everything there is about Charleston and is here, firmly planted in the sandy loam, forever. "Charleston wasn't always this way. I can remember when it was dangerous to walk down King Street, especially upper King. Now it's a thriving part of the world's best city. It has the restaurants, stores and local flavor that says 'Charleston.' I remember when there was not much in Mount Pleasant. Now, it's incredible. Mount Pleasant has something for everybody. The whole community is now an international city that has a magical mixture of people like me that have grown up here and others that came and have done much to better every aspect of the community."

Ironically, Rucker had a lesser opinion about Charleston as a young man growing up. "You know, I always used to make fun of my sisters for all of them ending up back in Charleston. And now, I wouldn't live anywhere else."[39]

The beauty and livability of Charleston becoming recognized across the globe has as much attribute to Darius Rucker as anyone. America's greatest export over the last century has been its music. It's played in Parisian nightclubs, the beach cabanas of Cabo San Lucas and the discotheques of Ibiza. Music videos have edified the phenomena. Rucker's chart-topping "Come Back Song" is featured as a collage of the Holy City—from shrimp boats to bridge views to rooftops and alleyways. The world heard and saw Charleston in melodic four-minute bites.

"That song was written with the thought in mind of a lost love that got away, and she's wanted back. In the way that I left Charleston and went to Columbia only to miss Charleston deeply and then return to the place I love, the 'Come Back Song' has extra meaning to me," Rucker related.

The album, *Charleston, SC, 1966*, went gold (the Recording Industry Association of America's gauge of selling more than 500,000 albums). It was Rucker's second solo country music album. The first, *Learn to Live*, went platinum. The platinum designation is accorded for sales of over 1 million albums. A second single, "This," also topped the charts at number one. In 2009, Rucker attained an astonishing award. He became the Country Music Association's Best New Artist of the Year. It was a natural for Rucker, and he has followed up these successes with even more. The award itself is encased at Bulls Bay Golf Club.

As if the public didn't find more and more about Charleston through travel guides and cruise brochures, Rucker opened the avenue of Charleston in a new perspective—a nostalgic look at his beautiful hometown. Country music embraced it. The mainstream of Hootie and the Blowfish fans could not wait to download the video. There was much more to this album than the bridging of Rucker and country music.

Poignantly, the song "This" contains nostalgic lyrics of the person who meant most to the singer-songwriter. "I cried when my momma passed away, but now I got an angel looking out for me today."

His mother, Carolyn Rucker, died suddenly of a heart attack in November 1992.[40] Her influence on Rucker's disposition, attitude and generosity has been inestimable.

The *Learn to Live* album splashed widely with three number one hits: "Don't Think I Don't Think About It," "Alright" and "It Won't Be This Way for Long."[41] The world wanted more Rucker.

The amazing scale of Rucker's talent is being reexplored in view of his quarter century of production. A look back at those dazzling performances show five top albums, two that went to number one with Hootie and the Blowfish: *Cracked Rear View* (1994) and *Fairweather Johnson* (1996). *Cracked Rear View* sold twenty-five million albums worldwide, or the equivalent of twenty-five platinum awards. Unless you were sequestered during these times in an underground vault, you would have heard "Hold My Hand," "Time," "Let Her Cry" and "Only Wanna Be with You." They are uniquely Rucker signature vocals. Nobody else sounds like that. And that was just from the first album. The hits, like "Old Man and Me," "I Go Blind" (a cover from the Canadian Rock group 54-40), "Tucker's Town," "I Will Wait" and "One Love," solidified Hootie and the Blowfish's place at the center of an entire era of distinctively different sounds. You knew their songs from the first two notes.

The band seemed to gather awards as a seasonal habit. Hootie and the Blowfish won the 1995 MTV Award for Best New Artist. The group garnered two Grammy Awards in 1996 as the Best New Artist, and Best Pop Performance by a Duo or Group with Vocals was given for the song "Let Her Cry." These prestigious acclamations are voted on by the membership of the National Academy of Recording Arts and Sciences. It is considered the very top of all entertainment awards for recording artists. The People's Choice Awards were also distributed along the way. They seemed to have a full house of each and every major music award. So Rucker's walk to the stage to receive the 2009 CMA (Country Music Awards) New Artist of the Year award should not have surprised his enthusiastic country music fans. Why would it? The Stradivarius of new age voices never changed notes, just songs. No other violin can compare.

His 2009 CMA acceptance remarks gave insight: "First of all, to the fans, thank y'all for accepting me," Rucker said. "And I think most importantly, to country radio, you took a chance on a pop singer from Charleston, South Carolina. Thank you so much for that!"[42] Rucker had established himself.

He also sings Sinatra tunes and did so at a special event—Frank Sinatra's eightieth birthday (in 1995). How much more versatile can one singer become? He could certainly perform gospel, soul, jazz or blues. Bluegrass might be next.

Rucker is available solo and as part of Hootie and the Blowfish. The other three accomplished members—Dean Felber, Jim Sonefeld and Mark Bryan—perform with Rucker a few times every year at specific charities that they have held as special. Rucker's foray into country music has him traveling much more but appreciative of home and the good times he's had with his buddies. Coming back home is particularly inspiring. That's when he can enjoy his Mount Pleasant home and time with his wife, Beth, and his children and his early golf rounds at Bulls Bay Golf Club.

"I try to play early. I go off and check back by the clubhouse at the turn," Rucker said. "I like to say hello to the folks here and get a cup of hot chocolate. This clubhouse and this property are special to me. It gives me a chance to relax and enjoy life."

Rucker is one of the founders of the club, started by attorney Joe Rice. The course was designed in a decidedly links fashion by course architect Mike Strantz. Rucker and Rice are good friends. When the club opened in 2002, the first Founders Club Tournament included a foursome with Rice and Rucker in one cart and Mo York and Gordon Lovingood in the other. Joe Rice's cart included a custom stereo that plays a variety of music during his rounds. When Rice turned to the other cart and asked York and Lovingood if they were okay with the music, York's response made even Rucker roll with laughter.

"I suppose that if we're not okay with it we can still get our money back and join another golf club down the road," York retorted. The music played on, and a good time was had by all.

York, who distinguished himself with a magic round that would have rewritten world golf history in 2004, enjoys the camaraderie and prowess of playing with Rucker.

"He hits fairways and is sneaky long. He's a fine golfer who would be many strokes better if his music career didn't get in the way."

York, one of Charleston's best amateurs, hit the cup with a chip at the par-five eighteenth at Yeamans Hall Club in 2005. Had the ball stayed in, he would have been the youngest golfer in the history of the sport to shoot his age (fifty-nine), including every professional from Old Tom Morris to Jack Nicklaus. Instead, he shot a course-record sixty.

"Darius is one of the better golfers here and is a real treat to play with. He is so very likeable, and you'd never know what he has accomplished in the world outside of Bulls Bay Golf Club. And what he has done for others is the stuff of legends. Nobody gives back like Darius does," York confided. "Charleston should be very proud of what he has done for collegiate golf, for school programs and for so many other charities."

For a day or two, Rucker gets in a few rounds, enjoys cooking breakfast for his children, answers correspondence and sets calendar dates with Beth. They enjoy the "vacation" he has back in Charleston, away from the road, the lighting crews and the business of the music business. He loves being home. He loves his family. He loves the outdoors and the waft of the salt marshes. He loves Charleston. He is our most identifiable citizen and, as such, enhances Charleston's worldwide identity. He is from a place in time— with that time bringing him back to the place.

Rucker is from *Charleston, SC, 1966*. There is surely a *Cracked Rear View*, but he has found Charleston to be the most comfortable place on the planet to *Learn to Live*.

The Other Garden of Eden

ANGIE WHALEY LECLERCQ

There are art forms that evoke all of the senses: contemporary cooking, the visual arts, ballet, opera and even poetry. There are few that give the impulse of awe as shown by indulgences of gardening. It is nature resolved. It is God anointing the earth. It is something practiced by those most engaged by the fullness of all senses.

Anne "Angie" Sinkler Whaley LeClercq (pronounced "la-CLAIR") is a lady by every Charleston standard. She is well beyond that heightened measure in her passions. She is an academic, a lawyer, a wife and mother, a lecturer and perhaps Charleston's ultimate authority on the art of floral gardens.

She cannot remember when the beauty of gardens did not enthrall her. "Images of the Garden of Eden before the fall and expulsion of Adam and Eve have descended through the mists of time and linger in the memories of western man. Eden has always served as the superlative metaphor for the beauty we seek in gardens. The serpent of Paradise confronts gardeners today in the protean forms of plant-destroying beetles, insects, rabbits, invasive weeds, drought, excessive heat and high-velocity winds. The creative but Sisyphean aspiration to seek and find beauty through the garden was implanted in me from early childhood, if indeed it did not come to me at birth as an element of DNA."

Her father was one of Charleston's finest lawyers: Ben Scott Whaley. Her mother was among the genteel of society, with family roots still tentacled to the peripheral Charleston plantations. The plantation and homestead at Pinopolis near Moncks Corner still exists.

LeClercq reminisced: "My mother, Emily Fishburne Whaley, loved to say that the women in our family were the gardeners while the men were the farmers. That statement is only partly true. My grandmother, Anne Sinkler Fishburne, and her husband, William Kershaw Fishburne, were both avid gardeners. They had three 'romantic' gardens at their home in Pinopolis, South Carolina. I spent every weekend with them there, as my mother, Emily Whaley, found me to be a belligerent child who needed the kind, loving care of my grandparents, Doc and Nan. Doc had a huge camellia garden, including such varieties as White Queen, Marie Bracey, Pink Perfection and Donklery. He successfully crossed every species and took his spectacular blooms to garden shows all over South Carolina. Nan had her special rose garden with an arbor of yellow Lady Bankshire, a white Lady Bankshire and a white Cherokee rose. She had old climbing roses and all kinds of colorful spring bulbs, a display of lavender and purple irises, a banana shrub tree and a sweet-smelling tea olive tree. The Pond Garden was filled with azaleas of every color, from lavender to magenta, and was a spectacular place for a young girl to hide away and smell the bees, see the rabbits and look for snakes. Nan and Doc were an incredible source of love, support and inspiration for me. Whenever I go into a new garden, be it France, England or Italy, I close my eyes and compare this new exotic wonderland to my memories of my grandparents' garden in Pinopolis. Can I go back? No. It no longer exists. Yet the memory of my childhood days there continues to haunt and inspire my love for the natural beauty of a garden, for the change in seasons, for the changing light of day as the sun passes from dawn to darkness. I can still hear the wind blowing in Nan's 'Harpies,' her tall pine trees. I can still see Doc's beagle and hound dogs treeing a squirrel or pointing a covey of quail in the fields beyond the house. I still remember the many days spent with my best friend, Richard Porcher, as we looked for arrowheads along the dried shores of Lake Moultrie. My memories are poignant, filled with beauty, love and no regrets. I have a saying that I harbor and treasure: Never look back. Tomorrow there is always another Yellow Brick Road."

LeClercq's romantic assessment is vivid. She is dynamic. Her sleek build, long flow of dark hair and deep-set eyes are mindful of the antebellum women in bygone days. She is both brilliant and buoyant. Life has thrown her much, but she appears stronger than the certainty of travail. Her clear pronunciations are "librarious" yet set in the inflection and intonation of the Broad Street brogue. She speaks words that chisel away the distant past to bring everyone to another place and time that only she can describe as her Eden. Her mellifluous voice seems convicted on a chivalry that only Charlestonians would understand. There is nothing overly subtle. She is happy and engaging. She is robust in her retelling and vivacious in her demeanor. Elegance defines her. She and her husband, Fred, also a lawyer, sustain highbrow conversation with a listener's interest, darting from literature to law to languages of another country. Fred is fluent in five. A glass of wine and a tasty hors d'oeuvre camber their interaction. Listen and you will learn: "My very first garden was in the backyard of my mother, Emily Whaley, and my father, Ben Scott Whaley's, house at 58 Church Street in Charleston, South Carolina. Mother gave me a small plot, five by eight feet, in the backyard, where I was free to grow any plant that interested me. Mother was an incredible painter and, in the manner of Miss Gertrude Jekyll, loved to work out the best color combinations possible. She contrasted her colors—like Vincent Van Gogh always said, 'If you paint blue, paint yellow.' Her garden was full of blue and yellow combinations. But she especially loved the pink and blue color combination. She aspired to a spring garden filled with pink tulips, backed by blue pansies and blue larkspur. She would always add a touch of white, such as sweet alyssum and white climbing roses. My mother would say that only in her garden did she find a release from the cares of the world."

Mrs. Emily Whaley passed away in 1998 at the age of eighty-seven. Her oil and acrylic artwork adorns the LeClercq home on Meeting Street. She found color in everything. Her family learned much from her love of flowers.

"My sister Marty Whaley Adams Cornwell, who inherited the garden at 58 Church, is also an amazing painter and continues the tradition of looking for the perfect color combinations. I am partially responsible for Mother's selection of Loutrell Briggs as the landscape architect for the formal features of the 58 Church Street Garden. Mother was pregnant with me when, in August 1941, she was hit in the stomach by a huge wave at our summer home on the Isle of Palms, a house we named 'the Sand Crab.' She was put on bed rest until my birth on January 14, 1942. She was, as you can imagine, distressed; perhaps depressed from the lengthy bed rest 'sentence.' My father asked her what would lift her spirits, and she responded, 'A Loutrell Briggs plan for our garden.' Daddy, like all 'willing' husbands, made sure that his bride, Emily, had her dream come true. Mother and Mr. Briggs were a true gardening team. When Cuffie Robinson Jr. arrived in Mother's life, she had finally found the real thing: a gardener who aspired to make every inch of the 58 Church Street garden beautiful. I often recount the day when I walked down Church Street and saw mother pointing a large stick up into an oak tree on Church Street that was blocking her view of St. Philip's steeple.

Mother said to the chief pruner for the city, 'Cut down that limb.' The chief pruner responded, 'No, Ma'am, I am not going to do that unless Mayor Riley orders me to do it.' Mother called her friend Mayor Joe Riley, who told her, 'You go tell that pruner that he is to do whatever you order.' And so the intruding limb was cut. Another day, I walked down Church Street to find that Mother and Junior had pulled out every Italian cedar in the garden, and they were being picked up by the trash detail."

Loutrell Briggs was a Cornell University–educated landscape expert who came to Charleston and changed many formal yards to something wonderful and comforting.[43] Born in New York in 1897, he died in Charleston in 1977.[44] Briggs wrote a seminal book on his craft and experiences entitled *Charleston Gardens*, published in 1951.[45]

"I said, 'My God! Mother, what in the world are you doing?' and she responded, 'I am tired of those old plants and intend to try something new!' My mother was a garden innovator until the end of her life in June 1998. Do I miss her? Do I wish she could advise me and tell me what the next step might be? Yes, of course. Where do I go to hear her words? To her books: *Mrs. Whaley and Her Charleston Garden* and *Mrs. Whaley Entertains*. You can still purchase both books in hard copy at your local bookstore. She continues to inspire the world of gardeners, including her three daughters, Emily Whaley Whipple, Marty Whaley Adams Cornwell and myself."

The interest that both Angie and Fred LeClercq have shown in gardens has bounded beyond the jetties of Charleston Harbor. They have traveled extensively, mostly in Europe but also to the Middle East. Angie has taken the time to record her travels with both literary impressions and digital photography. She publishes these topical diaries through the *Charleston Mercury*. Her musings and insights are much appreciated by not only her readership but also her many friends who have gained the passion.

Angie LeClercq's book *A Grand Tour of Gardens: Traveling in Beauty through Western Europe and the United States* is in publication (2012) by the University of South Carolina Press. She has also edited an updated version of her aunt's book about her travels to gardens in the Middle East during the 1920s and 1930s. She spent seventeen years doing something else important to a full generation of young men and women: she was the head librarian at The Citadel's Daniel Library until her retirement in June 2011.

Fred LeClercq's career included the practice of law, law instruction and professorial stints as an intern at North Carolina State University, as well

A lawyer and a library science expert, Angie LeClercq is so interesting on a variety of subjects; but the art of gardening is her passion. *Courtesy of Fred LeClercq.*

as a full professorship at the University of Tennessee in Knoxville. He is now law professor emeritus. Though one would assume he has retired, he has not. He has simply transitioned to the collection of historical antiques like clocks, statuary and marble-topped tables. Alkyon Fine Arts and Antiques at 120 Meeting Street was once the law office of Ben Scott Whaley. It is three stories of amazement, astonishment and wonder. It is on the top floor that one would find perhaps Charleston's most unique view. There, on the wide veranda, the comfortable furnishings are spaced with Angie's lovely flower arrangements in large clay pots. Looking left on a vector is the massive sand-brown spire of St. Philip's Church. Panning to the right are several of Charleston's finest architectural offerings standing against time. Next emerges "Old Fire Station No. 1," with its 1887 fire tower—seemingly in their backyard! It was built after the devastating 1886 earthquake and replaced a former fire building and tower at the same spot.[46] Then, to the right, the handsome extension of St. Michael's Episcopal Church pierces the sky. The tintinnabulation is the LeClercqs' evening serenade. A glass of wine enhances the rhythm.

Though the LeClercqs reside in boutique fashion above a most impressive antique and art emporium, and across Meeting Street from the Mills House, there are ample opportunities at gardening beyond. They have several options: "My garden on Lake Summit in Tuxedo, North Carolina, is inspired by all the beauty I have had the good fortune to see and write about from France to Italy to England. My gardening partners are my husband, Fred, and my three sons, Ted, Ben and Kershaw LeClercq. At Summit Gardens, we have two acres with many different garden styles. In our 'formal' garden, there is an 1895 statue of *Dianna and Her Dog* that once graced Nan's garden in Pinopolis. Around that statue, I have pink and yellow bulbs for every season, backed by lavender azaleas. From that spot, I can look down on the Dell garden that is filled with blue and white hydrangeas and pink roses. A white marble mermaid graces the Dell garden. My favorite garden is my perennial garden that overlooks Lake Summit and the mountain vista known as 'the pregnant woman.' There I have every lavender iris that I can find, every pink and white peony that is available and every spring and summer perennial any catalogue has for sale. Across from the perennial garden is my butterfly garden that is a maze of lavender and white butterfly bushes with orange and black butterflies by the thousands. And, oh yes, of course, I have a bird feeder where titmouse, wrens, mockingbirds and towhees abound, making the air lively with their songs. How I wish I could be a bird and fly and sing!"

The world that presents itself to Angie LeClercq is stunning. She takes it all in. She has a heightened sense of appreciation: "Finding happiness for me? Watching the sunrise over Lake Summit; watching the stars come out, especially Orion's Belt; having my three sons near."

The three grown boys are all in their forties now. They are a constant source of pride for the LeClercqs. There are plenty of photos on the third floor espousing their stages of growth from youth. And now there are six grandchildren. "I enjoy having Ted, Ben and Kershaw, and their precious children—Douglas, Price and Susan Anne LeClercq (Ted and Courtney LeClercq's children) and Peter and Will (Kershaw and Dr. Anne Hawk LeClercq's children) and Benjamin Edward McCrady (Allston and Ben LeClercq's son)—at our home. The sound of laughter, the smell of good food, the waft of roasted marshmallows is always around when the house is filled with family and grandchildren."

It's a good bet that they love the view from the porch!

There is a sense or supposition that the LeClercqs' next generation and the one after that will be well versed in all of cultural Charleston. And they will know about gardens.

Catching Up with Matt Wieters

B eing an all-star is not limited to sports. Matt Wieters is Major League Baseball's cyborg—with personality. He unfolds from a crouch to six feet, five inches and 230 pounds. He bats right and throws right and, oh yeah, bats left, too! He could probably throw left if the Baltimore Orioles' front office asked him to do so. He is considered by many as all-of-baseball's best young talent. He was the American League's Golden Glove catcher in 2011, as well as an All-Star Team selection. He is bright, brawny and boundlessly energetic. He practices when nobody else is watching. He is Charleston's own, the kid from Goose Creek.

Matt Wieters was trained for twenty years by the very best instructor in the game: his father. The instructions went well beyond baseball. His father, also six-foot-five, pitched and played third and first base at The Citadel. The 1977 Bulldog graduate went on to a fine minor-league pitching career with the Atlanta Braves and Chicago White Sox before an injury forced retirement. There are those who still maintain that Richard Wieters was the best player to ever don a Citadel baseball uniform. They would be both statistically and factually correct. Richard Wieters was a gangly athlete who was also a fine high school football and basketball player. His teammates at The Citadel included current Bulldog head coach Fred Jordan and Marty Crosby, a football quarterback who graduated with the college's all-time passing record. Richard Wieters was one of the few Citadel baseball players ever to gain All-American status.

Matt Wieters's father would know much about statistics. Richard is a well-respected CPA. His tutelage accounts for much of what has been the sum total of Matthew Richard Wieters. Young Matt remembers the lessons: "My dad was my biggest fan. He was there for everything. We'd play catch, he'd pitch to me and he'd give me a kick in the butt if I became a little lazy, and he was always such a competitor. Even today, if we play golf, he's mentally into every shot, and my only chance is to not let him have the scorer's pencil!"

Wieters and his wife, Maria, have been married three years, and they now reside in the Tampa Bay area, mostly by design. They do not live far from the Orioles' spring training facility spread over fifty-three acres in Sarasota. It's where Wieters can get in extra work. Each January, he begins to get pumped up about baseball. Each February, he reports early to camp. He wants the extra work. It's all about getting better.

The Orioles' camp surrounds Ed Smith Stadium,[47] where the club hosts its spring training schedule and can prepare for Major League Baseball's grueling 162 games. The national pastime requires durability that is especially demanding for a catcher. In addition, the O's face teams from the best division in all of baseball. They play more games (18 each) against the Yankees, Red Sox, Rays and Blue Jays than any of the other twenty-five major-league teams. Those four teams were an astounding 70 games over .500 during the 2011 season, none with a losing record! The Orioles have made great steps but must lengthen their stride to compete. That's where they have a "leg up," with a young, aggressive, multitalented catcher. Matt Wieters brought out the lumber in 2011. His average came up, and his strikeouts went down. He bombed twenty-two home runs and drove in sixty-eight runners.[48] He's getting better every year, every month, every at-bat. Why? Because of what dad Richard Wieters taught him over his youthful summers on local playgrounds: work ethic.

Wieters played at every level of Dixie Youth Baseball before entering Stratford High School. There, he teamed with fellow major-leaguer Justin Smoak to beef up a "Murderers' Row" for a high school. Smoak is now the first baseman for the Seattle Mariners. Both Wieters and Smoak went on to sterling careers at Georgia Tech and the University of South Carolina, respectively. Wieters distinguished himself at Georgia Tech as a first-team All-American twice. In his three years, he amassed a batting average of .359, with 35 homers and 198 runs batted in. He accumulated 418 total bases. He also recorded sixteen saves and eighty-

three strikeouts in his eighty-seven innings of pitching for the Ramblin'
Wreck. The Orioles took him as their number one draft pick in 2007.[49]

"I still keep in touch with Justin [Smoak] and so many of my teammates
from Stratford and Georgia Tech. They can keep me humble," Wieters
reflected. "Coach [John] Chalus from Stratford High School was a positive
influence to me and helped me to understand so many of the little things—
the situations that come in baseball."

And there were others who afforded the inclinations that make a fine
athlete into a meaningful person: "My grandfather, Marion Wieters,
affected my life by just being himself. He loved to bowl, go crabbing and
even shrimping. What better place in America could you enjoy time with
your grandfather than in Charleston? Crabbing is fun, and when the
shrimp season starts, it's just great." Grandfather Marion passed away a
few years ago.

Wieters did not follow his father to The Citadel, the military college whose
flagship sport has been baseball. It was difficult to not go there, given his

The man they have built their team around—Matt Wieters's handling of the Orioles' young
pitching staff in 2012 got them to the playoffs. *Courtesy of the Baltimore Orioles.*

dad's relationship with the college and its very successful coach, Fred Jordan. The Citadel's baseball program has, historically, been well recognized across America. They played in the 1990 College World Series and have won eight Southern Conference championships. But Wieters wanted to play in the vaunted ACC, a perennial powerhouse for college baseball. Though he opted to play close to the Atlanta Braves, his favorite MLB team growing up, he did gain quite an appreciation for The Citadel's successful baseball coaches, Chal Port and Fred Jordan.

"Coach Freddie Jordan is the best. He's 100 percent baseball, and he can teach. His fundamentals apply at any level, and just being around him because of my father, growing up, helped me to better understand game situations," Wieters recalled. "And my dad was really good at situations as well. He could predict pitches and locations when we watched the Braves play, and he'd be right so often that you just knew he had to be good at it as a player.

"My father has a simple saying about sports that I keep at the forefront. He says, 'Work hard, but have fun.' I am so fortunate to be playing baseball because it's what I love to do. Yet baseball can be a humbling experience.

"My sister, Rebecca, is not only a better athlete than I am, but she excelled at more sports. She played softball, volleyball and basketball. Rebecca worked harder than anyone. I was always just baseball. She did it all. Being two years older, she became a model to me with her work ethic and determination. You know, she was a terrific fast-pitch softball player."

The striking six-foot-two Rebecca Wieters became the Southern Conference Female Athlete of the Year in 2005 while playing volleyball at the College of Charleston. Rebecca Wieters married Matthew Moake in 2010 and is working toward her PhD in history at the University of Maryland–College Park.[50] Rebecca was a graduate of the College of Charleston's Honors College. She was also an Academic All-American at the college.

The gene pool is rich. Wieters's mother, Pamela, is "gritty and mentally tough, but accident prone. She fell through a glass table once and through the attic another time. She always says, 'There is never an excuse to not do anything.' And she will try anything. She is especially susceptible to accidents when we are on vacations," Wieters noted.

His uncle Billy Wieters (Richard's brother) also pitched at The Citadel. Billy Wieters was a more-than-formidable competitor. The Wieters family knew baseball. Indeed, the name "Wieters" in Charleston would almost automatically conjure a playground, a batting cage and the smell of Neatsfoot oil on leather mitts. "I miss Charleston enough, but I try to come home every chance I get. There is no place quite like Charleston in terms of real southern hospitality. That friendliness is special. You're not likely to find anyplace quite like it traveling the Major Leagues, though there are some nice cities."

How does Baltimore suit his personality? "Baltimore, fortunately, has so much to offer. It has that small-town feel like Charleston. The people are polite and outgoing. It seems that everybody knows everybody, and there are so many fun things to do there. Being a port, like Charleston, makes all the water activities important. When you think about it, Baltimore is the major-league city that is closest to being like Charleston.

"But you know, Charleston is by itself in every good category I know. When people find out that I grew up there, they are likely to tell me how much they love Charleston. That makes me proud."

Father Richard Wieters graduated from St. Andrews High School in the West Ashley area before his career at The Citadel. Matt and Rebecca grew up in Goose Creek, where the Wieters family cultivated one of Charleston's greatest athletic families. The academics were off the charts as well.

The adjustment to the very top level of baseball has been steady. There have been many expectations into which Wieters has had to grow, but the Baltimore fans have been patient and supportive. Each year, Wieters's offensive production numbers have increased. The 2011 season brought other accolades. The Gold Glove distinction proclaims Wieters's arrival into the elite. He is considered the best defensive catcher in the American League. Or, as one source termed it, Wieters is "Mauer with power."[51] Joe Mauer, the franchise player of the Minnesota Twins, has been the foremost catcher in baseball over the last six seasons. But Mauer cannot bomb the ball out of any field at any park. Wieters can do that. And he is just coming into his own.

Being named to the American League All-Star team for the first time in 2011 was not only an attestation to his hitting and defensive abilities but also to the reputation he is gaining for his clubhouse skills. He leads by example, by timely and helpful advice and, importantly, by being one of the most likeable players in all of baseball. Oh yeah, and there's that other intangible: he works hard.

Wieters has seen every great player in today's big leagues and is more than impressed by the talent level. Each league has an All-Star team each year for the midsummer All-Star Game. It has gotten more and more competitive with the winner gaining the home field advantage for the World Series. Wieters took the time to cross both leagues with his own version of a major-league All-Star Team—based on what he has seen up close. It's the view from his catcher's crouch: "Excluding catcher, a position I would like to earn on the team I'd pick, my infield would have Miguel Cabrera of the Tigers at first base. He can hit better than anybody in baseball. I'd have trouble at second base between Robinson Cano of the Yankees and Dustin Pedroia of the Red Sox. Either would be fantastic. The guy I emulated growing up as a solid middle-of-the-lineup switch hitter, Chipper Jones, has got to play third base on my team. J.J. Hardy of the Orioles, with his consistency, has earned the role of my shortstop. He can also hit the ball out of the park. In left field, I'd go with Matt Holliday. He's a strong right-handed hitter. Ichiro Suzuki would man right field because he hits, fields and runs the bases. My center fielder would be Jacoby Ellsbury of the Red Sox. His speed changes games.

"My left-handed starter would be C.C. Sabathia because he logs a lot of innings every year. He's a horse. My right-hander would be Felix Hernandez. He's got electric stuff. The reliever would be Mariano Rivera, simply because he's been the best for a long time. And I'd have our manager, Buck Showalter, manage that team. He's got a great baseball mind. It never shuts off."

The players on that team would be hard to beat. It would be fitting that their catcher is a bright young star who handles his position with the best and has scary power in any ballpark.

Wieters refers back to his sandlot days when he describes the kind of everyday play he respects. He likes the guys who go all out. "Ty Wiggington and Derek Jeter are good examples. Those guys are classic baseball players. They finish every game with dirt and grass stains all over their uniforms. They scratch for every advantage. I like those kind of players. And I like the intangibles that some players bring to a clubhouse. There are players who are natural leaders. A great example is Derek Lee. The entire team benefits by having Derek Lee in the locker room."

Matt Wieters is living his dream. The year 2012 framed his fourth full major-league season. He began it at the remarkable age of twenty-five. The impressive physical and mental tools he has commanded combined with his family-tradition strong suit—hard work—continued to elevate his career. He performed the little things that, added together, equated to team success. The Baltimore Orioles were the surprise team of the entire American

League in 2012—in no small part because of Wieters's handling of a largely inexperienced pitching staff.

In time, Wieters will walk away from baseball and perhaps come back to his roots in Charleston. In time, he will still be humbled by it all yet remain an exemplary model of devotion for so many others. In any event, his wife and children, his parents and his city (Charleston) will be proud. Hyping the axiom of being an All-Star is a baseball denominator that defines career accomplishment. But for Matt Wieters, the journey to success has never been limited to baseball.

Literary Charleston

Pat Conroy

Was it Oden or Thor, Apollo or Zeus, Midas, Prometheus or the Sun God, Ra? We find them laced across eternity by the simple act of looking up. And eternity will select even more.

It was the gods that gave us the planets and the stars and even time. A half century seems like fifty years to some, but it's only one-twentieth of a millennium to others. In time, the postmodern phase of American literature will be defined by several entertaining novelists of the last five decades. Write them down. John Grisham, perhaps. Add in Stephen King, Michael Crichton, Danielle Steel, Nicholas Sparks—we recognize them all. There are others. But none will likely raise our minds to the place and time of our destiny. Only gods do this. Perhaps, there you will see Donald Patrick Conroy, the literary god of elegant description, the "transitioner" of humanity into humans and the conductor of page excerpts into the dramatic repartee. His stage is Charleston, where the buildings are low enough to see sunrises and the steeples high enough to spirit wonder. Pat Conroy rebuilt the long-troubled city in his unique rapture of eloquence. It is now alive within the literary consciousness of America and beyond. Gods can do that.

Conroy came to Charleston from the disjointed itinerancy of military family displacement. Add in the emancipation of a woeful upbringing. It was 1963. He had signed a grant-in-aid to play basketball for The Citadel. He would play baseball, as well: "I was a lousy baseball player, but I loved Chal Port more than any coach I ever had in any sport. My one great memory as a baseball player was hitting a double off the wall at West Virginia and driving in Brian Irvine with the tying score. An observant West Virginia coach suggested that Irvine had not touched third base, and in a study of his tracks, Brian had missed it on both sides by two feet. In the dugout, Chal Port said, 'I can't blame Irvine. I, too, went into a state of shock when Conroy got a hit.'"

Conroy's exploits as a point guard on Coach Mel Thompson's 1966–67 Citadel basketball squad are sadly—yet humorously—recounted in *My Losing Season*. The book gained highly favorable reviews and again revealed Conroy's affinity for wide contrasts—reality versus sport, conformity versus individuality and inspiration versus terror. The book takes him back to reacquaint the insights of his teammates years after the horrific guidance of a lamentable and failing coach. This narrative experience of writing the book also brought Conroy back to his own father.

The Citadel experience was a source of plentiful creativity. He found the college to be a wealth of balanced scenery, questionable tradition and robust personality. He arrived more ready for the experience as a military "brat" than most incoming freshmen. He even plied his early mastery of language against its stringent backdrop: "I pulled off one prank in my life. It happened during my third week at The Citadel, and I've written about it before—I thought I could get some laughs from the cadre and other upperclassmen, so I composed a four-line poem:

> *The dreams of youth are pleasant dreams*
> *Of women, vintage, and the sea.*
> *Last night I dreamt I was a dog*
> *Who found an upperclassman tree.*

"That was the first and last prank of my life. I had the cadre from four battalions walking down to Romeo Company to make my life nightmarish. They were lining up to beat my chest, and I got called 'gauldy knob' more than anyone in history. I still don't quite know what 'gauldy' means, but I'm positive it is something that upperclassmen loathed. It led to a prank-less life."

He recalled the exalted books, the enduring quotes and the meaningful writers. He loved what books did for him. They took him to the constancy of place and the nourishment of normalcy.

It was the author Thomas Wolfe who wrote, "The whole conviction of my life now rests upon the belief that loneliness, far from being a rare and curious phenomenon, is the central and inevitable fact of human existence."[52] Conroy quilted life in the brilliant novels of his own introspective loneliness. "When I came to The Citadel in 1963, I had already fallen in love with the books of Thomas Wolfe, a southern writer from Asheville, North Carolina. My love affair continued through my four years at The Citadel, including the time I invited Thomas Wolfe's brother, Luke, to address the Calliopean Literary Society. Since The Citadel could not provide Luke Wolfe with a hamburger or a tank of gas, he could not justify the trip. But just talking to the great writer's brother on the phone provided me with my first cheap literary thrill."

He continued: "There is one story of Thomas Wolfe that held a great power over me. It was called 'Only the Dead Know Brooklyn,' and it tells of Wolfe's long walks through the borough of Brooklyn, where he tries to let the essence of the city enter the pores of his skin and press the images of a great city asleep into his heart. I tried to do that with Charleston. I found myself on weekends in Charleston with no money, but with a dazzling, upraised city to wander in at my leisure. I developed a crush on a girl who lived off Bedon's Alley and watched her family have a late-afternoon brunch on Sundays for four years. By chance, I saw her sweep out of her house in a bridal veil on the day she got married in St. Michael's, and it was a glorious accident that this splendid coda rewarded all those years of Charleston watching. The city has lived inside me for all these years, but only when I got to South of Broad did I find the venue to make the city a character in my book."

Charleston came alive in Conroy, and the beat of the city's heart reached the world beyond. He experienced the genteel and centered people who stayed in the comfort of a most perilous place, where epidemics and cannons, wind-blown water and the shake of the ground converged. They persevered for the solace of the placid periods between. They were much unlike the vagabonding commensurate with the military family plight. These "pluff mud" families had been here by the extension of bloodlines since 1670. They were not leaving anytime soon. Conroy had found the permanent home of his novels and the grounded yearn of his life at the same time.

"I lived in Charleston several times that are not widely known. For several summers, I 'housesat' for Joe and Charlotte Riley while they summered at the Isle of Palms. I wrote several chapters of *The Great Santini* on their dining room table. Joe Riley was the lawyer representing Lieutenant Colonel Courvoisie and me for our book, *The Boo*, the worst book ever to be written by an American.

"For six months I rented a home on Sullivan's Island from Captain Woody Holbein when I was writing *The Lords of Discipline*. He and I had become friendly when I was at The Citadel, though I regret he never taught me. Each morning, I would go over to The Citadel library to claim the chair I had come to every night as a cadet in a cut-off, unseen row of desks that sat up against the library's east side, which looked off to Hampton Park. I wrote major parts of *The Boo*, *The Water Is Wide*, *The Great Santini* and *The Lords of Discipline* while sitting in a place that centered and defined me."

The Daniel Library (1960) on The Citadel's campus was scarcely completed upon Conroy's arrival. The three-story Spanish Moorish design balanced the campus along the Avenue of Remembrance, buttressing the Summerall Chapel on one side and the wrought delivery of Lesesne Gate on the other. The world happened out there, beyond Charleston's most famous park. Conroy took it all in.

Conroy came back often, sometimes crowned in laurel, other times wound in quarrels. He found controversy when he was looking for truth. Tripping along, life can be difficult. Great writers enunciate great truths: "The truth is the only subject that makes any difference to a writer like me. It comes from a great and honored tradition among writers over the ages. I grew up in an era dominated by Faulkner, Hemingway and Fitzgerald, with Eudora Welty, James Dickey and Walker Percy bringing up the rear as beribboned kite tails. Has it been painful? I've found it agonizing. I tell people if you want to live a life of solitude, write a novel that will get you banned from your own college for thirty years. But I've been engaged in these drone attacks for my entire life. I put a Predator missile through an entire school board and then blew my family out of the water with *The Great Santini*. Without some shivering alliance with truth, art is meaningless, simpering and inert."

In time, truth finds shelter from the exigencies of other lesser perceptions. Conroy was never afraid of confrontation. His true-life association with the father was factually described as a son protecting his mother from a tyrant. Conroy eventually reconciled with his contrite father and developed a loving bond until his father's passing in 1998.[53] It is but one of the contrasts Conroy lived. He brought Hollywood to The Citadel as a favorite son but was cast away and demonized in his honestly earnest attempt to benefit his college. The stipend to film *The Lords of Discipline* at The Citadel was estimated at $225,000. The Citadel's board of visitors thought the well-written novel would be mistaken for reality and applications for the vaunted military college would rapidly decline. It might have sensed the obvious, as no other American military college or academy took on the project. Instead, *The Lords of Discipline* was filmed at Wellington College in England in 1983.[54]

Conroy's discernments to the class of 2001 as their graduation speaker touched on that conflict and others. It was his emotional return as a favorite son. "Because of various aspects of my character and fates, I did not get to address the Corps of Cadets in the last century. There were many years when I thought that Saddam Hussein or Jane Fonda had a better chance of addressing this class than I did.

"I tried to think of a line or words that would sum up better than anything how I felt and how other people feel about this college. I wanted it to be something ringing and affirmative, something true and something to be true for every person who has ever gone through the long gray line. I came up with this line, 'I wear the ring.' I think it is the best line I have ever written and the best English sentence I am capable of writing. I love that phrase. I love that sentence. Thirty-four years ago, I sat in this field house. My mother and father, my six brothers and sisters, sitting in the audience as your parents are sitting now. My parents—it was their proudest day. My mother wept when I came off [the stage] that day. She wept so hard, and I said, 'Mom, what's wrong?' And she said, 'Son, you are the first person in my family who has ever graduated from college, and you did it at The Citadel.' And she said, 'The best college in America.'"[55]

Conroy was back. The controversies dissipated. Previously, he had sent words of encouragement to the females trying to break with 150 years of male traditions at The Citadel in 1995. He did so on a promise kept. The promise came from a discussion with female cadets enrolled at the United States Coast Guard Academy during the previous year. While deep inside the broil of the public banter, Conroy had anonymously written a large check to support The Citadel basketball team's trip to South America to compete in spirited rivalries with national teams from Argentina, Cuba and Chile.[56] He had stayed in touch with those who mattered to his career as well, many from The Citadel. He remained true to his convictions throughout all scrutiny.

There were mentors, professors and deep-rooted friendships. Impressive people had taught him, inspired him and some might have even changed him a bit. He reached back to recall the influences: "The Citadel English faculty when I was there was superb, and I loved my time among them. Though I didn't know it then, I became famous among them my second week when Colonel John Robert Doyle would pass around the forty novels I had read to his colleagues until I was hissed down by my classmates. Nor did I know that Colonel Doyle was passing my essays

The southern traditions seem to center on Charleston in author Pat Conroy's world. *Courtesy of Steve Leimberg.*

around the teacher's lounge of the English department—including my first one, an analysis of *Bells for John Whiteside's Daughter*, by John Crowe Ransom. Colonel Doyle became my faculty advisor, and he personally selected every course I took at The Citadel, and the major criterion he looked for was great teaching.

"Then, I entered the world of the History Department, where I found stupendous teachers like the astounding Captain Addington, Colonel Anger and a man I portrayed in *The Lords of Discipline*, Colonel Charles Martin, who was known as 'Fat Jack.' Being taught the History of England by 'Fat Jack' was like being taught the same subject by Henry VIII. Periodically, he would stand me up in class and tell the cadets that I descended from the sewer pipes of Europe, and as an Irishman, I was a fitting example of all the scum of Ireland. When prodded to respond, I would say, 'With all due respect, Colonel, it seems like you Englishmen are descended from a very fat and snotty nation.' He would thunder at me to hush my rapscallion Irish mouth, but we enjoyed each other, and he stands tall as one of the greatest teachers I ever had. As does the dashing Dr. Oliver Bowman, who introduced me to the mysteries and wonders of psychology, which would remain a fascination through my whole life. His teaching was charismatic and captivating at the same time, and he was the one that would first tell me my world would be tempestuous. Yes, that was great teaching."

The Citadel's well-respected English Department had a healthy overflow of characters in the mid-1960s. Every "knob" who had ever spliced commas or split infinitives feared the department. The *Writer's Harbrace Handbook* was the Bible therein. For business majors, the preferred grade was "C minus." But a "D" would also suffice.

"In the English Department, my career began and ended with Colonel John Robert Doyle. He taught me six courses during my career and assigned and passed judgment on my senior essay. He and his wife, Claire, seemed to like fussing over me, and they invited me over to their house for tea and crumpets (literally). After my graduation, my classmate Jeff Benton and I gave a retirement party for Colonel John Doyle and Colonel Charles Martin. I called him at his Virginia plantation every year for the rest of his life.

"Colonel James Carpenter taught me Milton, and Colonel Achurch taught me literary criticism—my William Hazlitt years—and Colonel James Harrison taught me American literature, and I would run to get into their classes each day. They were bright, kindly gentleman, and I was lucky they found me in my young manhood.

"Here's what I've told all the Ivy Leaguers I've met in publishing, and they are a million-headed legion of soft souls. I can tell they think my attendance at The Citadel has crippled me as a writer, as though I had contracted some spiritual form of polio. 'Au contraire,' I say. 'The Citadel is the best college in the world for a writer to attend. Anyone who survives that nasty crucible we call the plebe system knows everything there is to know about the cruelties and contradictions in man. You get that at The Citadel—not at Harvard, Yale or Princeton.' While they were having philosophical discussion in their rooms with the greatest young minds of their day, I was sitting at The Citadel library lost in the greatest books ever written for three straight years during every study period. My boast to them is that I plan to be a better writer in my generation than anyone who ever went to an Ivy League college gets me [targeted] with derision and anger. I keep up with the field. The kid ain't doing that bad."

Well, that assessment is a matter of destiny. There will be English Departments at Harvard and Yale and Princeton that will study this noble and timeless author. They will recognize characters like Bull Meecham, Tom Wingo and Leo King. They are each exquisitely developed and contemptuously flawed.

The Lowcountry of South Carolina is bathed in Conroy's creativity. He longs for the breeze of the marshlands and the swaying moss of the live oaks. It inspires him daily.

Conroy even looked at Charleston as a permanent home. He explained: "My wife, Cassandra King, and I looked seriously to buy a Charleston house when we got married. It was my lifelong and pretentious ambition to one day own a mansion South of Broad, and we looked at fifty of them or more. But both of us came to believe that we would be caretaking a museum instead of living in a house. My friend Anne Rivers Siddons and her husband, Heyward, bought a gorgeous house on Church Street, and we could use this guesthouse at any time. Beaufort was the first town that called out my name, and we decided to remain in the area until we die. But *South of Broad* was my genuflection to my time in the city of Charleston, and I can only hope that time was well spent."

Conroy had come back, like a team at the buzzer, winning in overtime. The thrill of living the life of America's most endearing—and perhaps most enduring—writer returned as well. He had become both Thomas Wolfe and William Faulkner with a dash of the unbounded version of Prometheus. He modeled characters from his reality-sprinkled experiences as the gods had modeled man from clay. And yet, there were the other things Conroy did when he was not sensing the scintillations of life beyond movie script hacks and loud-voiced producers. He looked up. He realized there is more. He wrote about those insights along with other stories of audacity and bravado.

More is to be known of Conroy. But we are in the wrong century. Not enough was ever known of Hyperion. He remains a god yet unembellished.

From Toddlers to Builders

Mikey Bennett and Hank Hofford

They were not born alphabetically; they just ended up that way. In fact, Hank Hofford was Mikey Bennett's neighbor, Hofford being two years older, as preschool toddlers in Northbridge Terrace. That was over fifty years ago.

"We both came from larger families. My mother, Virginia Bennett, had an awesome influence on our home—where there was six kids—as well as the kids that played in the neighborhood. Hank and I were playing together almost every day," Bennett recalled.

"We were young and driven. I always said that Mikey would load the wagon, and I'll pull it. Mikey always had determination and a winning attitude. He was undefeatable," Hofford added. "So how could you not make something positive happen?"

In that sense, Bennett told the serendipitous story of the biggest leap in their careers.

Bennett and Hofford started in business together renting mopeds in the downtown Charleston area. It was a seasonal business, but it was orchestrated well enough to make an adequate income. From the experience, they looked to find some off-season work. A bid was put out for a renovation of an old building that interested them. They obtained a contractor's license and priced the materials. They won the bid. They paid close attention to the detail of the restoration and performed the work meticulously. Their future reputation for other jobs would rest on the performance of their first completed building. It went well. They decided that there was more of a future in the restoration work than in the moped rentals. The Bennett Hofford Company was established—in alphabetical order. It was just as well because of the order of their process. Mikey Bennett sought the bids, did the pricing and submitted the proposals. He also looked for all avenues for financing the hopeful projects. Once the job was secured, Hank Hofford did what he performed best. He ordered the materials, organized the work crews and managed the project to completion. He was pulling Bennett's loaded wagon. The team concept had them each relying on the other from project to bigger project for what each did best.

And build they did. They did a small strip center in the West Ashley area on the Savannah Highway, rented the spaces and sold it to another investor. Others followed. In the coming years, they found a chance to do something significant. The old Chicco Apartments were two large brick structures covered in dank and aging stucco on Meeting Street, a block uptown from Marion Square. The building dated to 1880 as an old Reconstruction-era bagging manufacturer. It was in 1938[57] that Vincent Chicco saw the opportunity to convert the buildings into a needed apartment complex for the influx of navy yard workers to the area in anticipation of World War II. Chicco added retail and office space. But in time, the building proved to be too dated to be effective as apartment rentals. Vacancies occurred and, in time, vagrancy.

"We approached the family of Vincent Chicco, one of the great old Charleston families," Hofford detailed. "They were willing to sell it because the times had changed, and there was really no upside to an apartment restoration. It was much too costly for the expected return. It was also becoming an eyesore, and they didn't want that to happen. So Mikey and I approached the Hampton Inn corporate folks. We talked to the key planners with the city. In essence, our idea worked, but we had no money."

"I remember paying an enormous sum—$400—to buy a giant Rolodex of well-researched commercial-lending institutions when Hank and I first started trying to negotiate the Chicco Apartments into a Hampton Inn," Bennett remembered. "It was 1990. It seems like I called every card on that Rolodex to get the financing. I called thirty contacts a day for almost a full year. I'd get answers like, 'You seem like a nice guy, but...' and 'No way, pal' and more than my share of hang-ups. I had nearly exhausted the Rolodex when I was able to put financing through a Japanese bank and Credit Lyonnais, the largest bank in France."

Meanwhile, Hofford was approaching the best way to salvage and then renovate the buildings.

"I first went there to look at the building to see if we could save anything," Hofford laughed. "There was not much inside to be saved. As I went through it, I ran off a wino sleeping in the alley. The windows were mostly broken out, and there were pigeons and who knows what else living in those old rafters."

With financing secured and approvals in hand, they began the demolition and reconstruction. That forgotten part of Charleston was still in decline. This Hampton Inn project would be the first step in bringing it back. It set the momentum for the redevelopment of the entire corridor of Meeting and King Streets north of Calhoun Street. Propitiously, as they neared completion of the Hampton Inn, another opportunity presented itself. Bennett recalled: "The county put out an RFP [request for proposal] to do something with the old county offices located in the Old Citadel. We had just finished doing the Hampton Inn in 1992. Both Hank and I liked the property, and it being historical, it only had a few possibilities that would work as a restoration. We had met the president of the Hampton Inn group, named 'Promus Hotels.' They had done a few other things outside of Hampton Inns like Embassy Suites and Harrah's Casino. Some of their top people were outdoorsmen. They had invited us to visit their lodge, Five Oaks Lodge, in Arkansas. Hank and I decided to go just to see if we could speak to the top guy."

"This was a posh lodge, as good as any in America," Hofford added. "They had arranged some hunting. During the evening, we had a nice meal, some drinks and some cigars. These were some corporate big shots. Mikey and I had the feeling that we were a few hundred million short of the average net worth there. But we knew we were where there were some avenues for money for the project. We had one shot at it."

"The timing was right," Bennett noted. "We were out on the porch, and the president of Embassy Suites, Promus Hotels, Clyde Culp, came out to enjoy his cigar. I remember thinking, 'It's now or never.' Besides, the worst he could do was to turn me down. I told him about our idea, to turn the Old Citadel into an Embassy Suites because of the structural footprint and the room sizes.

"'That old building wants to be an Embassy Suites but just doesn't know it yet,' I said. I expected to be laughed at or embarrassed, I guess. I had figured this important corporate CEO knew everything there was to know about hotels and would blow the idea away, possibly. But instead, he

As one who has invested much into the community, Hank Hofford is most proud of his Charleston roots. *Courtesy of Susan Ford.*

smiled, looked at Hank and I and said, 'I need to tell you that I have very little knowledge of the hotel business. They hired me away from being the CEO at Wendy's a year ago. So I could tell you a whole lot about hamburgers, but not much about hotels. I'll have our guy that does that call you at the beginning of the week, and he'll decide if we should look it over. If it works, great!'"

"Mikey and I were stunned," Hofford recalled. "The guy was awesome! He put us at ease. The fear of approaching the issue was over, and we had the president of the corporation telling us he would have his top people look at it. We now had an avenue for financing the project. The door was open."

Bennett added: "They called us on Monday. We had their top investment guy on the phone by the instruction given to him by the president of the company. He came to Charleston in short order. He looked at the property and our proposal and, over the next few weeks, decided to back the project. That singular conversation in Arkansas, looking back, was our vault from being a single hotel owner to launching the hotel development side of our business. The Embassy Suites restoration project at Marion Square became one of the finest hotel restoration ventures in America."

It got better. The Embassy Suites Historic District gained several significant accolades, including an article in the *Wall Street Journal*. The Bennett-Hofford reputation soared. The residential side of the business grew with the economy. They built other commercial projects, including another signature restoration, the Rice Mill Building at 17 Lockwood Drive, within the city marina, in 1993. They were able to find several high-end tenants and eventually placed the Bennett-Hofford corporate offices on the top floor.

The team concept was in full swing. They found unique projects. They assessed them, carried them to the city planners, looked for financing, found likely tenants and then performed the work at a level of craftsmanship that exuded the pride of their specialization. Bennett-Hofford buildings gave the expected ambiance of Charleston's revival.

Hofford carried the concept to Kiawah Island, with its mid-1990s emergence in the upper-scale housing market. In time, the island gained its well-earned celebrity as a premier golfing community and later was named both number one tennis resort in America and the number one beach resort in America. Kiawah became the biggest and brightest ornament on Charleston's tree.

In time, the two childhood friends became the celebrated builders of 500 new homes in the Charleston area, 350 of them on Kiawah alone. Economic impact? Immeasurable! That was only part of the story. They built other hotels and commercial applications across the tri-county area. They have restored seventy buildings in downtown Charleston.

But they did other things outside of their careers. Bennett smiles at the story of his kindhearted partner going to see the tall ship *Spirit of South Carolina* being built from the ground up. He had an inclination to donate $5,000 to help. By the time the conversation was complete, Hofford found out that they were about to give up the project. He bristled at the thought. After a lengthy conversation with the volunteer builders, Hofford was the new "on-the-spot elected" chairman of the $5 million project. That cost Hofford much more than the donation intended, in addition to his valuable time. Hofford helped raised well over $6 million. The ship was completed, and another great Charleston story was made into legend.

"He went to go and give them $100, and it cost him $5 million in his time, energy and out of his own pocket! That ship took out nine thousand

An athlete, an outdoorsman and a man of deep family values, Mike Bennett has found "hospitality" to extend to other interests. *Courtesy of the Bennett family archives.*

kids and taught them many more lessons than how to tie knots," Bennett said of Hofford while Hofford smiled and nodded.

Bennett's lifelong love of sport manifested when his children began playing baseball. He began to coach his two children, Jack and Brennan. The complications of practice times kept his busy schedule in such disarray that he finally decided to no longer be subjected to other people's whims. He built his own baseball practice facility. It was not just any practice facility. He found an excellent amount of acreage to create the field, with parking, a full-size field and batting cages. Think *Field of Dreams*. Bennett's facility was better than anything Hollywood could muster. It was on the breezy banks of the Intracoastal Waterway near that other Hollywood in South Carolina. It is routinely viewed from the water by boaters. Bennett gets calls frequently offering to buy it with some unique pricing overtures. His answer is always the same: "It's Bennett Hofford Field of Dreams. I'm the GM, the coach, the owner, the ground crew and the maintenance supervisor. I'm the modern-day Connie Mack for little leaguers. It's like an old school sandlot. I built it so that kids could play baseball. The field has kids there all the time, and they can hone their young skills. I suspect that when I'm gone, kids will still be playing baseball on that field."

Bennett has coached youth baseball for more than a dozen years. The time he spends is what he refers to as his "fun time": "If I had paid Bobby Cox what the Braves paid him and used that time to work on hotel deals, I would have made more than enough to cover his salary—and the kids would have had a better coach. But I would have missed the experience. That experience to me has been priceless."

Bennett's dedication to community has shown up in other areas of generosity. He became a major donor of Our Lady of Mercy Community Outreach's Wellness Center. He also made the lead gift to the City of Charleston to begin an Irish Memorial (completion 2013) at the foot of Charlotte Street. Bennett is proud of his Irish heritage. Also, he gave a major gift to the SPCA. As Bennett says: nuns, Irish and dogs.

Bennett knows the dedication it takes to make it as an athlete. He was a high school standout who played football and wrestled. But neither was his best sport. Bennett learned the art of boxing and progressed through the Golden Gloves and into the college level of boxing at his alma mater, the University of South Carolina. His record over his amateur career was 98-1. He won the collegiate East Coast Championship in 1975.

"Mikey has always had a winning attitude, and I appreciated that most when we went into business together," Hofford offered. "He's undefeatable because, as I say, he's determined, tenacious and he never gives up."

Bennett had plenty of inspiration. He spoke about his parents. His father, Red Bennett, "was a real hustler. He was a true Irishman with a seventh-grade education but an entrepreneurial approach to everything."

Mother Virginia kept up traditional family values of chores, church, schoolwork and regular family meals. She was, and is, tireless. Father "Red" tried every way possible to make money, from shining shoes to restoring sunk boats: "A number of years ago, knowing the stories my dad had told me about shining shoes in front of Convertino's Cleaners on King Street, I had the opportunity to buy that building. I did so. I brought Dad to the closing just to make him happy and so he could see that his life had come full circle. It was a meaningful day for him and me. Dad had this great idea to pull up sunken boats and restore them. He was a fine craftsman. He'd buy them from the insurers and make them look brand-new. He'd sell them for a healthy profit. He made some good money when Hurricane Hugo came through.

"I had others that mentored me, and I never forgot them. The late Nick Theos, the fine principal at Bishop England, was a hero to me. Father Robert Kelly was an unforgettable legend. And Coach Jack Cantey was the best. He's a great man."

Hofford has had the same sentiments for some of the same people: "You could certainly add in my father-in-law, Joe Ford. I emulated him, and he was a fine man to copy. My own father died young. So in a way, [wife] Susan's father became a father figure to me. Mikey's dad was someone I also admired. Red Bennett...there will never be another like him."

There are some stark differences between these two partners. Hank Hofford graduated from Clemson University. The rivalry exists! Hofford acclimates himself to the nuances of technology; Bennett remains unfazed by what is new in cyberspace.

Bennett has no computer and no e-mail. He has a staff of people with both, including an in-house attorney, Tracy Masters Ray. His youngest sister, Kim Bennett Brown, is his office manager. Her husband is former U.S. congressman Henry Brown's son. She is largely responsible for the necessary correspondence that frees Bennett to do what he does best: deal with corporations, financial institutions and even governments. His lifelong friend and partner, Hofford, is always there, in a room down the hall, to make anything coming from that distinctively Charleston entity as a hardened bond of masterful performance going forward. Not having the modern convenience that computers allow in Bennett's office could be, in the pace of his world, an asset for Mikey Bennett.

Hofford loves to sail and has participated in the Charleston to Bermuda Race five times. He and his lovely wife, Susan, have moved to the "country." They live in a remodeled and updated plantation house on the back river side of Edisto Island. There is a dreamlike peacefulness there. The James Hoban–style architecture of the three-story plantation house is austere but elegant. It's called Prospect Hill, an old cotton plantation that dates from 1792. The house was built in 1800 and is surrounded by woods and marsh.[58] Hoban, from Charleston, also designed the White House in Washington, D.C.[59] The Hofford home overlooks a pond on one side and the river on the other, adorned by countless centuries-old live oaks.

Bennett and his wife, Amy, are inseparable as well. They even hunt and fish together. Bennett enjoys visiting a few hotel projects in Montana, where he has rolled up saddle blankets and ridden along fences to repair breaks. He loves the cowboy way. He also loves the waters off

Charleston, but for different reasons. He and Amy go deep-sea fishing to enjoy special time together. Bennett's home is also a revitalized old land tract, Quinby. It is a two-thousand-acre former rice plantation near Huger, South Carolina. Bennett has been a proponent of preserving the greenbelt tracts surrounding Charleston to preserve livability, wildlife and the pristine forests.

"Watching all that has happened here makes me have a deeper appreciation for our mayor, Joe Riley. He has been a personal friend but, even more importantly, a steward for the city we all enjoy," Hofford stated. "Where would we be today without his vision?"

"I can't tell you how many times he has guided me personally. He always challenged me to do the very best. We're lucky," Bennett added. "Joe Riley built the base of the best city in America. We can never thank him enough. Now, the big boys like Boeing have come. There will be others. We're no longer a secret. There will be more jobs, more diversity and more opportunities. In the economic climate we've all struggled through, what a breath of fresh air it has been to be a part of something as magical as Charleston during the time of Joe Riley."

Bennett and Hofford are beyond an institution. Their pre-retirement advice from those who opine avenues to preserve their accomplishments for the coming generations has had them "reshuffle the deck" in recent years. Hofford has taken on most of the new construction, and Bennett has continued his mastery of hotels. In fact, Bennett Hospitality has now developed hotels in Montana, Florida and Georgia, in addition to the hotels in the Charleston area. Each has promoted congenial epicurean establishments—39 Rue de Jean, a decidedly French bistro; Coast, a seafood restaurant; and Virginia's, a traditional Lowcountry restaurant—in honor of Bennett's mother. One other major effort, the proposed Marion Square Hilton, which is destined to become a landmark property for Charleston's brilliant future, has been fraught with delays and revisions for ten years.

"It is on a timeline of its own," Bennett suggested. "We would just like to build this as a legacy to the city we love. The luxury hotel will add more ambiance to the upper King Street area while bringing another top-end hotelier within walking distance of the abundant attractions and vistas downtown Charleston has to offer. But we have had to modify it at every stage to please one group or another. Meanwhile, the mayor has been most supportive, and we are thankful. But really, we proposed this Hilton on land we owned ten years ago."

"I told you he never quits," Hofford attested. "He was 98-1. What's that tell you?"

It says that Charleston will have a stunning Hilton on Marion Square, and Mikey Bennett will be there to cut the ribbon and welcome the first guests. Hank Hofford will nod his head approvingly and pull the wagon again.

Meditations and Mediations

BISHOP DAVID B. THOMPSON

The pope sent him to heaven. Well, almost.

"Becoming the bishop of Charleston was like going to heaven without the inconvenience of dying," Thompson intoned upon assuming that important liturgical role in 1989. It was in the spring of that year that the Holy Father, Pope John Paul II, appointed Monsignor David B. Thompson as coadjutor bishop of the Diocese of Charleston. He was ordained in the Cathedral of St. John the Baptist, the see of the diocese, on May 24. With the retirement of the former bishop, he became the eleventh bishop of Charleston, a succession that started with the Irish immigrant Bishop John England in 1820. Bishop Thompson's influence from his residence on Broad Street changed Charleston.

A native of the Keystone State of Pennsylvania, Bishop Thompson had been to Charleston before and was enthralled with the appointment.

"I stayed at the Mills House a few years earlier to attend a conference on canon law. I fell in love with Charleston but never dreamed I would have the opportunity to come back here. And now I'm here permanently," Thompson confided. "I have so many wonderful friends here, and the climate is just perfect."

That first year did not exactly deliver the weather he was hoping. On the evening of September 21, 1989, Hurricane Hugo became the most powerful recorded storm in U.S. history. The path was a direct hit on Charleston. It arrived at midnight. Bishop Thompson had been in Charleston for only four months. He witnessed the power.

"I had been at a funeral in Pennsylvania traveling back to Charleston when I noticed the plane had many journalists and photographers going to Charleston," Thompson recalled. "I thought, well, 'This could be an adventure.' I landed and headed to Broad Street, not knowing what people do in the way of preparing for hurricanes."

The bishop's office and chancery in Charleston are located at 119 Broad Street, diagonally across from the Cathedral of St. John the Baptist.

"Mayor Riley had put out a warning that those living on the first floor should leave because of the potential of flooding. I was living on the first floor behind the building on Broad Street. So I checked into the Omni [now Charleston Place Hotel]. It was new and quite solid, so I felt I would be safe on an upper floor. I was up on the fourth floor," Thompson recounted. "Monsignor John Simonin and Deacon Joe Kemper invited me to St. Mary's Rectory for a nice spaghetti meal as the winds began to become deafening. We called it the 'Last Supper of Charleston.'"

St. Mary's Rectory is situated next to Charleston Place. It was a short walk back to the new and expansive hotel. "By 9:30 p.m., the wind was wreaking havoc upon the windows, and the hotel manager brought all residents and employees back down to the second-floor ballroom. It had no windows. They issued flashlights for everyone and had set up food for not only the guests but also the hundred or so employees they brought in for safety. They really did a great job."

As the morning daylight approached, the winds had subsided enough for the new bishop to return to his Broad Street residence. For many areas of Charleston, it took weeks to get electrical services back to the homes and businesses. The sounds of the ensuing weeks were echoes across the peninsula from gas generators and chainsaws.

"I remember that I could not hear anything the night before because of the sound of the wind. I went back to find an oak tree across the front door of my house and the surrounding brick wall blown over. I could get into the back door. I still had hot water but not much food. The Griffiths, Joe and Bette, lived next door. They had plenty of food but no hot water. We worked out a good swap over the next few days.

"It occurred to me that in a major storm, it's good to be Catholic. I had an abundance of candles!

"My first major task as coadjutor bishop was to assess and resolve hurricane-related crises in every parish, every church and school across the diocese. That was a comprehensive assignment. We had some churches with severe damage. There were the insurance matters, the adjustors, the inspections, the financial concerns, the school's academic schedules and the damage to the residences of the pastors, even in the upstate. I remember going over to the Our Lady of Mercy Convent on James Island and seeing three nuns on the roof trying to remove a tree!

"There was a 7:00 p.m. curfew here, enforced by the National Guard. Things were in much disarray then. I remember going to Nativity that first Sunday after the storm and the warm reception those parishioners gave. They were happy to see me. Perhaps they thought I brought a claims adjustor. Divine Redeemer Church in Hanahan was a total loss. Other churches here, in Florence and in Sumter, were not safe to hold Mass. It was then that the goodness of others so impressed me."

He remembered the support from so many contributors for the parishes: "One point two million dollars came in from those that wanted to assist from parish collections and other means. There was a tremendous amount of physical repair work ahead, so much so that it seemed impossible. More than $300,000 was made available to Stella Maris alone [on Sullivan's Island], where the South Carolina National Guard took up residency for a while. Later on, Bishop Donald Wuerl, serving then as the bishop of Pittsburgh, personally gave me a check for $50,000 to assist our emergency. Later on, Bishop Wuerl, acting on behalf of the Southwestern Pennsylvania Ministerial Association, sent a check for $176,000 to be channeled through the South Carolina Christian Action Council. This was meant to aid the six churches, not Catholic, which had been burned down here in the Southeast. What a great gesture of kindness that was! No wonder he is now a cardinal!

"In ways that God provided, Hurricane Hugo had many happy circumstances," the bishop summarized.

By Christmas 1989, the cleanup process still dominated Charleston. In another oddity of weather, an ice storm arrived on that Christmas Eve— very rare for the Holy City. "I remember saying the midnight Mass that very first Christmas in Charleston. I began my homily with the words: 'I never intended to take Charleston by storm, but Charleston has taken me by its charm,' and I have been here ever since with no plans ever to leave. In time, all was done, and I could turn much of my attention to other areas."

That was when Charleston and the state of South Carolina received his full focus and the wide benefit of his ability.

Bishop Thompson's influence on the spirituality of the community, especially in his landmark interfaith relationships, has lasted well beyond his decade as the head of the diocese. It was in 1992 that Bishop

Thompson published his pastoral letter, "Our Heritage—Our Hope." He had been laying the groundwork for a diocesan synod (pronounced *sin-id*)—a planned look at the church from within the organization and from the eyes of others by reaching out to other faiths. The letter outlined the plans for the first such meeting of the faithful in Charleston since 1956. Subsequently, Bishop Thompson published "Enthusiasm for the Faith: A Design for Implementing the Vision of the Synod of Charleston" in 1996.

"I was inspired by the Vatican Council of 1962–65. I felt the Church of Charleston needed an in-depth look. Canon law was revised in 1983. I told my people that we needed to take a good look at our church in a synodal process. It was a four-year study of our deanerys, our parishes, our priests, our seniors and our youth. A particular subject addresses our 'Women in the Church.' I sat with them and asked for frank answers. This was a process that needed participation. We met with other church leaders to widen our knowledge and deepen our mutual respect.

"A diocesan synod is primarily an 'in house' look at the local church. It was my decision to make it more than in house—to reach out to those of other faiths. We involved both Christian churches and other religious groups to ask their help in our look at our church, how they saw us, how they thought we could be renewed and improved. They didn't disappoint. They were constructive, positive and magnanimous in reaching out to us as brothers and sisters in the Lord. They all became closer friends.

"The celebratory conclusion at the cathedral in 1995 was conducted in the presence of His Eminence Joseph Cardinal Bernardin and in the presence of the synod officers and delegates, including those of other faiths." Some twenty-six bishops attended the closing Mass.

Bishop Thompson's second pastoral letter, "Souvenirs and Promise," officially closed the synod, with his "Enthusiasm for the Faith: A Design for Implementing the Vision of the Synod in Charleston" forthcoming in 1996.

The impact of the synod has been enjoyed for almost a generation of parish and church leaders and the faithful. Charleston was again elevated and bettered by the vision and the scope of spiritual leadership and the enthused renewal of religious community interchange. Among Bishop Thompson's residual citations for this masterful synergy throughout the various faiths was the Jewish National Fund's highest honor, the Tree of Life Award. It remains a testimony to his commitment of respect and understanding. It validated his chosen vocation in ways that will impact future generations of Charlestonians.

When stepping outside of his vocation, Bishop Thompson took refuge in a most confounding avocation: he loves to play golf.

"I tried to play when the weather permitted on a Friday. I told others that it was my holy day of obligation!" Thompson winked.

When asked about the extent of his progress in the sport or even his latest score, Thompson merely reflects on the exercise, the weather and the good company he hosts: "I play. Let's enjoy that for what it is and not what it could be! I play golf. I am not a golfer. There's a difference."

He lives very close to the driving range and resides in a small but sturdy town house near the Dunes West Golf Club. "It's nice having the driving range there, but I don't see the need to use it and waste any of the very few good shots I have left."

Bishop David Thompson arrived shortly before Hurricane Hugo and brought all religions together. *Courtesy of the Diocese of Charleston.*

He's both a pragmatist and a wonderful playing companion. He usually plans his Friday round when his very active schedule allows—over the years with good friends like retired Charleston Credit Bureau founder Bobby Molony, real estate entrepreneur Joe Griffith, U.S. Airlines pilot Carey Budds, ten-time Charleston mayor Joseph P. Riley Jr., Colonel Larry McKay, Rick Cooper and Dennis Atwood, his former chief financial officer with the diocese. There are many others who have received his blessing prior to a critical putt or a tough carry across a water hazard. He often offers partners and opponents the Last Rites.

"He's a fine man and has a great sense of humor. You cannot play a round of golf with Bishop Thompson without leaving the golf course glowing with a wide smile," Molony attests. "We would all give him a putt here and there, but he just won't take it. He's a marvelous gentleman with an incredible mind."

He has used his pastoral warmth and depth of canon law training to benefit others across the diocese.

"The Diocese of Charleston" is an interchangeable geographic term for the state of South Carolina, with a Catholic population approaching 200,000. Unlike secular government, which is normally map centralized, a Catholic diocese is faith centralized relative to mostly historic beginnings. Thus, Charleston is the center. It's where the ships traveled the currents and trade winds from Europe to deliver mostly Irish and then French (Haitian revolution) Catholics to the Holy City. The establishment of St. Mary's Church on Hasell Street (1789) was the first house of Catholic worship in the original three lower colonies (the Carolinas and Georgia). The peninsula of Charleston grew in Catholicism over the next two centuries to include other parish churches: St. Joseph's, Sacred Heart, St. Patrick's, Immaculate Conception and St. Finbar's, which later became the Cathedral of St. John the Baptist. Most incorporated parochial grammar schools and a high school were started in 1915, the high school named for the aforementioned Bishop John England.

Bishop Thompson's early commitment was to get out and meet the people, from Beaufort to Spartanburg, Aiken to Myrtle Beach. He did so. He visited every parish in the state, traveling thousands of miles in a matter of months. He reinvigorated the churches and established his gregarious charm that has been thematic throughout his life. He simply loves people— all people. His reputation was well founded. His personality could reach outside of Catholicism, and it did.

When the world was watching Charleston for a much happier occasion, the 1991 Ryder Cup at the Ocean Course on Kiawah Island, Bishop Thompson was summoned for an invocation at the players' dinner the night before the first match. The "War by the Shore," as it was called, ended in a thrilling American victory on the last putt on the last hole. It would seem that the invocation set the stage.

Bishop Thompson famously invoked the spirituality of the moment with his prayer:

> *Bless the knights in search of golf's Holy Grail, the Ryder Cup. Reward those who have planned their course with a setting so wondrously reflective of your boundless beauty. As we gather this evening to honor our golf teams, eager for action, desirous of victory, may we remember, Lord, golf is your game: holy, straight, honest, with fairways, warnings against traps and roughs, even with an Amen Corner!*

The Ryder Cup had the perfect admirer of the sport. He had come a long way from his roots along the Atlantic seaboard.

In 1999, Governor Jim Hodges awarded Bishop Thompson the State of South Carolina's highest award available to a citizen: the Order of the Palmetto.[60]

"There could not be a more deserving recipient," the mayor commented before the presentation of the award. "Bishop Thompson was a healer and a builder. The Catholic Church has grown in South Carolina in both numbers of faithful and churches as well. He brought the people together in the diocesan synod, which was a blueprint for the future." Riley continued by saying that the bishop was a leader in the state in both spiritual guidance and civic guidance: "I'm proud of the way he has distinguished himself and the Catholic people in South Carolina." Then, in alluding to some of the golf outings the Riley family has had with the retired prelate, he said, "You measure great people and leaders by their sense of humor, the way they make those around them feel at ease. Bishop Thompson has an inner spirit of light and optimism that a sense of humor brings. He is a man of God, grace and a powerful leader."[61]

The Most Reverend David B. Thompson's childhood and young adulthood were spent in Philadelphia. His undergraduate work at St. Charles Borromeo Seminary earned him a master's degree in history. He was ordained into the priesthood in 1950 and earned other postgraduate certifications and diplomas relative to his legendary appetite for learning, including a licentiate in canon law.

There are so many personal highlights to Bishop Thompson's extraordinary career that but a few are addressed herein. In addition to being an avid golfer, a voracious reader and an accomplished literary contributor, he is a sought-after public speaker—even on subjects well outside of religion. His celebrated homilies at his current parish, Christ Our King Catholic Church, include his extemporaneous humor, his passion for the sanctity of life and his incredible abilities of recall. He knows almost every member of the choir, every altar server, every reader and Eucharistic minister by first name, though these personages are apt to rotate from service to service. His mind is deft and his spirit humble.

The Sunday morning service following South Carolina's Republican presidential primary of January 28, 2012, impelled him to pastoral oratory that revisited Jesus' appearance at the Synagogue of Capernaum. It is recorded in the Book of Matthew. Bishop Thompson made comparisons to the public life of Christ and to differences he brought to the mindset of the rabbis, as well as the people. The homily was cogent and thought provoking. It was well received by the early morning congregation at Christ Our King Church, many of whom were quite relieved to see the end of television campaign advertisements that had run their course the day before. Bishop Thompson closed his homily with his point that Jesus was the most qualified of all before him to become the Savior of Man. He then turned to step toward his seat at the altar, suddenly stopping halfway and then turning to add, "My name is Bishop David Thompson, and I approve this message."

The entire congregation broke out in laughter, followed by clapping in unified approval. In the solemnity of a Catholic Mass, the instinct of applause for a moment is generally not practiced. Special occasions can overcome great traditions. The unbridled enthusiasm won out. The appreciation of the kindness, understanding and inherent self-deprecating humor of this universally appreciated man made clapping a most appropriate response. If one listened intently, the whistle from the back might have come from Jesus. Who is to say it did not?

The tireless man has not retired. He is the bishop emeritus but not even remotely the retired bishop. He is likely as active as he has ever been. His daily work begins early, with a Mass in his chapel, reading, preparation of a homily and devotions. He visits friends—well and sick. He has a few favorite weekly visits, including a Friday breakfast with friends across the community and across many faiths as well. He drives himself to his "rounds," always ready to assist another family or another cause. He reports in as the most esteemed chaplain of a downtown society monthly, with prepared blessings of grace and benediction. He corresponds with family and loved ones, especially his twin brother, Monsignor Edward J. Thompson, who lives in Florida.

His lifetime would seem always ahead of him with his penchant for organization and planning. It was those particular qualities that had him pursue an early idea that earned him the distinguished moniker of "Father Bandstand."

Then Father Thompson was the founding principal of Notre Dame High School of Easton, Pennsylvania, in 1957. It grew from 413 students to over 2,000 students. Responding to students requesting a social outlet similar to the success of *American Bandstand* in Philadelphia in November of that year, Father Thompson hired a disc jockey from a Bethlehem radio station as host and put together perhaps the greatest repeating show in the annals of U.S. high schools. Easton is about halfway between New York City and Philadelphia on the regular bus and train routes. The hit television show *American Bandstand* was in its infancy, hosted by the ageless Dick Clark. This Philadelphia classic lured the great performers of the era, by way of the Big Apple. On the way back to New York, the rock-and-roll celebrities could pick up extra money by playing a "gig" at Notre Dame High School. The gate receipts more than covered the expense. The teen idols who appeared at gym dances hosted by this creatively postured priest and principal included Paul Anka, Chubby Checker, Fabian, Connie Francis, Herman's Hermits, Bobby Rydell and Brenda Lee. Lucky parents served as chaperones each Saturday night. They wanted to see the stars, too! Father Thompson became "Father Bandstand" to an entire generation of Notre Dame High School students. Easton, Pennsylvania, would never be the same.

"My motto has been that I want to have big ears, to listen to my people and all others. Sometimes the church comes off as being too imperious, too powerful. It's best to be more open and more receptive. We saw this work well in the synod. The process is just as important as the product. We strengthened both the ecumenical and the interfaith communities. In our own Catholic experience, you look around and see that people have taken more ownership of parishes. There is such a powerful resurgence in our laity. There are fourteen non-priest managers of parishes in the diocese. That's progress by the process, and it makes us better.

"I learned so much as a teenager and young adult from the radio broadcasts of Archbishop Fulton Sheen. *The National Catholic Hour* on radio was a compelling program that brought so many to Christ."

Archbishop Fulton J. Sheen hosted *The National Catholic Hour* radio program from 1930 to 1950, before a seven-year television program of the same syndication titled *Life Is Worth Living*.[62] He is considered the world's first televangelist.[63] Sheen wrote seventy-three books related to theology, instruction and Catholicism and was eventually appointed by Pope Paul VI as archbishop of Rochester, New York.[64] His cause for canonization to sainthood was opened in 2002.[65]

"Archbishop Sheen elevated my life in numerous ways. He was such a learned, yet humble, man. It was his influence that helped compel me to the priesthood," Bishop Thompson recalled.

"Then there was my great advisor, Bishop Joseph McShea, whom I had served with for over thirty-eight years. Any time I needed advice, there he was. He was the very first bishop of the Allentown Diocese. He remained there until his passing in 1991. He was such a giving man. He taught me how to be a bishop.

"Another influence, my twin brother, has been part of who I am from the cradle on. We were 'womb mates!' He is like me, still serving as an assistant pastor in a Florida parish. He's a monsignor. He is someone I have always looked up to because of his sincerity and wealth of knowledge. He puts fire in my belly.

"There were so many welcoming families here from the very first day. I have been blessed by their friendships over the years. Three or four families stand out—Joe and Bette Griffith, Henry and Esther Tecklenburg, Joseph and Helen Riley (parents of Charleston's mayor) and, later, Bobby and Sadie Molony. So many others came to my assistance as well. Other abiding influences were and are Dennis Atwood, Monsignor James Carter and Sister Bridget."

As he approaches his ninetieth year, the bishop astonishes those he encounters with his amazing memory and impressive acumen. He is both brilliant and humble. He still offers a Sunday Mass at Christ Our King Church in Mount Pleasant, as well as saying his own daily Mass in his private chapel. His depth and breadth of reading are well beyond what one would ascribe to most PhDs, and his devotion to others equals his prayer. To the greater glory of God, he reserves much appreciation for other joyous avocations, like pleasant conversation, a legendary sense of humor and, of course, a penchant for golf.

His best avocation, however, is being your friend.

A Reservoir Reserved

Lonnie Carter

M r. Carter was born into a small southern farming community. They grew peanuts. He exhibited a keen intellect and a cheerful disposition. He left his small high school for a prestigious military college. His life emerged as his abilities widened. He gained influence. Power is central to his life. People equate him with energy. He saw opportunities in the road ahead and became the president.

Wait…it's not that small farming community or that military college. It's not that kind of energy and power. It's not that Carter. This is that other Carter: Lonnie. He's the president and CEO of Santee Cooper, one of the great utility success stories in America.

It's true that Carter came from quite humble beginnings, the third in his family of six children from the quaint rural setting of Ehrhardt, South Carolina. The Carters, including several uncles, have been farming the land there for several generations. They still do.

Lonnie Carter is much like the guy who opens the door for you at the IHOP even though he got there first. He is bright, personable and gentlemanly. He owns the smile of a county fair duck call defending champion. He likes to connect the dots of the people he knows in common with you. He presents a down-to-earth quality in the upper echelon of corporate altitude. He is unpretentious.

Carter comes from reality.

The town of Ehrhardt celebrates the German heritage of its founder of the same name by means of its annual Schützenfest. The population of 600 crowns a new king marksman, the "Schützenkönig." Ehrhardt's identity is somewhat inseparable from the next farming community over, Bamberg. Six times the size of Ehrhardt, at about 3,600 residents, Bamberg is the hometown of current South Carolina governor Nikki Haley. The joint communities represent Old World values and a wholesome work ethic, despite more than 20 percent of their population living well under the lowly watermark of poverty. Carter recalled that abrupt statistic: "When people talk about those that are unemployed and cannot find work, some people have deep misconceptions that they do not try to find work. I have a completely different perspective. In Ehrhardt, there are times when unemployment might reach 25 percent or more. And they're all trying to find jobs."

He saw it all around him growing up: "We didn't have anything, but we never thought about it. Nobody else had anything. My family only knew farming, and that was what I had in front of me growing up. It was a good life with hard work but decent people with healthy outlooks on everything. Heck, I never really got outside of Bamberg County until I went to college."

Carter was the first member of his family to attend The Citadel. He received ample support from the high school guidance counselor, Eugenia Hiers. Carter was the student body president and had the abilities needed for college. But college was not a certainty for Carter until Mrs. Hiers got involved.

"She was relentless, all business and tough—but cared deeply for her students," Carter recalled.

When he decided to go, two other members of the class joined him. He went to study business, especially accounting and economics. He graduated in 1982 as a business major and went right to work in Moncks Corner at Santee Cooper.

"When I came to Charleston in 1978, I was the naïve boy from the small town. Other cadets had to explain to me punch lines from jokes and tell me when I had been insulted. I was straight from the farm. My roommate was Steve Cannon, a great guy from Atlanta who was always the first one to recognize the best ethical solution to anything. He impressed me as a fine human being in every way. Charleston was starting to mature and come of age. As cadets, we didn't venture north of Calhoun Street after dark back then. Now it's as vibrant as any other area of Charleston. The downtown area will host people from all over the world on any given weekend. Charleston has earned prominence and notoriety. The community is often thought of as the tri-county area, but I really think it has grown even beyond that. The growth has been positive, and the fact that it will continue to grow is a positive. We must all accept it and plan on it. Certainly we have to plan on it in the power business. If we grow with appropriateness, it works best for all. The traffic has not been crazy like other places. There is so much here that is a blessing."

The post-college years seemed to indicate a return to Ehrhardt for Carter. Carter's family farm business in Ehrhardt was calling. But graduation pointed him to another career. "I was released from many responsibilities at home to go to college. My parents expected much from me. So going to college was quite a privilege. Going to The Citadel was the best decision ever. I was undisciplined in high school. The Citadel would change that. Working twelve-hour days on the farm was not unusual, so having me away at school was difficult for my parents. But my mother and father were the only ones in their own families not to go to college. They wanted me to have every opportunity. Working on a farm relates to the perception that farming was to be in my future. My respect for farming and those that I saw growing up that put everything into it could not be more sincere and deep. But I had no desire to farm."

Carter had gotten involved with the Ehrhardt community in the anticipation that he would return. He was invited to men's suppers by his boss. There he learned about local politics by listening to the men gather from around the farming community. Other adults he admired included Ray Rentz and Harvard Henry. As a young adult, Carter made friends easily. One night, he even drove the county sheriff home after a meeting. The host felt that the sheriff had had too much to drink, so Carter delivered him home safely.

"I came from a good Christian home. My parents were not socialites. There were six children, but one, Jakie, died young from a farming accident. One brother, Andrew, later inherited the farm. I have two other brothers and one sister. We were eighth-generation farmers and worked the four hundred acres in corn, soybeans, peanuts and cotton. But we couldn't all work the farm. In fact, I worked for cash at another farm while I was in high school. That made sense to my parents. But farming was not the perfect world. I was like most kids. I got in trouble for doing things I wasn't supposed to do, but I found out one true thing while

Lonnie Carter has made his life about providing energy for two million South Carolina residents. *Courtesy of Torrey Monroe.*

growing up: you can get away with a lot by telling the truth. I always told the truth.

"I had some college experience working for an electric utility company, and Santee Cooper liked that. I had been dating the general manager's daughter at the Edisto Electric Coop and got a summer job there. I worked with the line crews, and I even collected past-due bills. That was an experience I'll never forget. A third of those that didn't pay were simply deadbeats, another third were just sloppy paying their bills, but that bottom third was the most difficult. They had no money and no way of paying. It was a hard lesson for me. It was good experience but a difficult job."

Santee Cooper happened to be looking for someone to train in the accounting department to write computer programs. Carter had learned the technology of computer punch cards at The Citadel. That one course came into play. Carter was selected: "I was the brand-new computer guy that transitioned Santee Cooper to electronic records. They thought I could be an analyst. After nine months, I was moved to planning. I saw that my talents would best be suited in areas where Santee Cooper was poised for growth. I moved sideways to another department that dealt with the exciting world of potential and strategies. It suited my personality."

It defined his career.

Santee Cooper is simply amazing. The New Deal project made American and world history. When twelve thousand workers cleared over 177,000 acres of land for one singular project in the 1930s, two lakes were created: Lakes Marion and Moultrie. The clearing activity was the largest in U.S. history. The resulting dams and locks also featured new statistical achievements, one lock lift becoming the largest the world had ever seen. In the process, the striped bass, South Carolina's most sought-after freshwater prize, had to be reintroduced to other ecological environments. The South Carolina Department of Natural Resources exported these fish to other areas. Striped bass are now found in thirty-four states.

The largest employer in Moncks Corner, the county seat of Berkeley County, Santee Cooper is a state-owned public utility that supplies electricity and water to much of the lower part of the state. It also exports power. Directly and indirectly, over two million South Carolinians benefit from the power source that is Santee Cooper.

Carter saw the growth analytics. He knew the population trends. He was able to calculate the nexus of his training and experience to benefit his passion for the ongoing projects of this massive utility. In time, he also gained important trust from the higher levels of management. He became their president and CEO in January 2004.[66]

"I read the future. Debt ratios, rates, financing options, investments and relationships with others in the industry were all components of what Santee Cooper was all about. I learned from people like Mark Glenn, my supervisor, and John Bishop, our comptroller. Graham Edwards was a mentor and was the president. He was so very dedicated. Mrs. Emily Brown was the veteran chief financial officer. Ironically, I competed with her for the CFO position. She had such great experience. She opened herself to me and really became a great person for advice. She read people well and managed those important business relationships. She took the time to teach me. I had great professors at The Citadel, like Jim Whitney who taught me a love of accounting. Professor Chris Spivey taught finance and the mechanics of financial models and calculations. What does the time value of money really mean? Professor Bruce Strauch taught economics. He analyzed all of the strategies. He made me an analyst, as well as teaching me the tenets of business law. Within time, all of these lessons and the influence of so many selfless and brilliant people propelled me to advancement in the business I came to love."

In his thirty years at the utility, Carter has drawn from much departmental experience, along with his training in more analytical disciplines. He sees the idea of energy as a balance of many viable sources. "We need 'all of the above' solutions. There is no one resource answer to energy needs. Energy for the future will include nuclear power, coal, natural gas, hydroelectric renewables and the balance of conservation. Energy conservation is essential. The other experimental and technological additions are helpful, like solar and wind, but they have not been developed to support the volume the world requires. In addition, the cost to build must be balanced against the future energy gained. We have the complete record on solar and wind, so we're not dealing with rhetoric but reality. In South Carolina, wind turbines may be years away from cost-effective clean energy."

Carter has studied all forms of modern energy venues: "Clean energy has been done. We're all getting better at protecting the environment. Even in our industry, the particulate matter in air has been so greatly reduced. My problem now with the subject of green energy is that people tell you the theory of how to do it and then want to spend your money to get it done without any guarantee that it will even work. There is a future in green energy, but we need to be smart and effective. We've got to stay balanced. The research needs to advance. But we still have to supply homes and businesses with current energy resources, as well as large industry, going forward."

Santee Cooper is the state leader in the field of green energy production, research and advancement.[67] Carter looks at the entire spectrum of energy and water use as part of Santee Cooper's due diligence. "The growth of South Carolina is intimately integrated with Santee Cooper and other providers. There is a strong correlation of economic growth and energy consumption. Most of the growth of South Carolina trends along the coast and east of Interstate 95. South Carolina grew by nearly one million people in the last ten years. The demand for potable water will grow. This is good news economically. We are all bettered by the influx of business and the demand for services. And we plan at Santee Cooper with that growth as our focus. We have to be ahead of the grid.

"I applaud the combined efforts of everyone with a stake in the future. Clemson University has a grid simulator and a drivetrain facility. The simulator is the biggest in the world, and there is only one other that exists. This was the idea of a PhD student at Clemson and it's being done right here in South Carolina. The idea of taking something simple and making it effective for energy use is exciting. And to think that a college student had the idea! The excitement of new technologies will provide other potential solutions to our needs going forward."

Carter and his wife, Laurie, live in the Moncks Corner area. Their oldest daughter, Emily Lauren, graduated from the University of South Carolina. Their younger daughter, Sarah Elizabeth, was the valedictorian at Berkeley High School and attends Wofford College. Son Jacob, named after Carter's father, is still in high school.

Everybody seems to revel in Carter's expert oversight of Santee Cooper. It is as if the utility and Carter were one and the same. The sentiment came to the forefront in 2011, when Carter was unanimously reappointed by the Santee Cooper Board.

Bill Finn, the utility's human resources chairman, noted that the board "was uncomfortable with the possibility that the CEO could retire or resign at any time."[68]

"The board felt that in the interest of financial stability that Santee Cooper required some continuity of leadership at this time," he said. "We are in the midst of some of the largest projects we have ever undertaken, and he has done an excellent job."[69]

Glen Brown, who serves as executive vice-president of human resources, reflected on the Carter career from a different perspective: "I was part of the team that recruited Lonnie here. It was obvious from the start that he was intelligent and focused. It was not as obvious that he would develop into a very dynamic community leader. He has passion, and when he believes in a cause, he puts his heart and soul into the task at hand. He generously gives his time, talent and treasures to make our community a better place."

When the lights go out at Carter's office, a full day's work has been accomplished. The parade of energy experts, politicos, suppliers and financial wizards has expanded Carter's periphery. Employees and vice-presidents, supervisors and janitors have all made their way through the wide steel reinforced boulevard of a hallway. The energy efficiencies are measured. The security is again entrusted to protect this major Lowcountry asset. Carter drives home to his loving wife of thirty years.

Lonnie Carter enlightens his constituencies. He illuminates his responsibility to nearly two thousand employees. Carter lights up the world around him. Through his vision and ability to analyze, a wealth of available energy will be available to South Carolina's future.

Acting Up

Bill Murray

He could have still done what he has done without doing all that he had done. Bill Murray could have won the amateur golf championship at the Pebble Beach Pro-Am if he were the CEO of an airline or a race car driver. He could have been a baseball team owner if he were a stockbroker. He could have been a *Saturday Night Live* comedian without the Catholic school conformity found in his Chicago-area upbringing. He could have been an Oscar-nominated actor without his entrée into the entertainment business as a comedian. He could have been your best friend from college or the best bowler in your Tuesday night league. Somehow, he could be all of this and more.

He is a father, a friend and a businessman. He is his own agent. That means he lives life on his own schedule within his own time and syncopated to his own pace of living. That's a commendable trait that is otherwise inconvenient in an instantaneous world. There is no situation that hints at *his* people calling *your* people to agree on an arranged meeting. He has no executive assistant, no driver, no secretary and no promoter or publicist. He has himself.

"It's just practical for me. When the phone started ringing too many times, I had to take it back to what I can handle. I take my chances on a job or a person as opposed to a situation. I don't like to have a situation placed over my head," Murray explained in an interview with *Esquire* magazine.[70] "To the degree that I can get the things that want to control me out of the way, then there's less stuff in my field of vision. Then I can work."[71]

The affable Murray came to Charleston because he liked it. He liked his friends here—the Lord of the Charleston RiverDogs, Mike Veeck; the late Ashton Phillips and his son, Al Phillips.

"If you get to know Al well enough, you can call him 'Gator,'" Murray winked.

Murray's four youngest children—all boys—are in school in Charleston. He also has two older sons. Veeck is a fellow Chicagoan who pioneered the Midwest–Charleston migration. Murray and Veeck have other commonalities. They are both from Catholic families of nine. They both love baseball (Murray the Cubs, Veeck the White Sox). They are both soulful heroes of the common man—unpretentious and well adjusted. They both have an uncanny sense of humor. Laughter is their mortar. There is an abundance of mortar. And they are bound by an unassuming and tight friendship.

Murray is there for Veeck and vice versa. Veeck introduced Murray "as the man who still embodied a magical child." Indeed, the sixty-one-year-old Murray was seen in a rare Sunday afternoon rainout display of youth at Joseph P. Riley Jr. Park. He dashed onto the tarp-covered diamond, splishing and splashing. The cameras had captured the robust moments of his slide to home plate. The video made ESPN and the world via YouTube.

At the 2012 South Atlantic League All-Star Game luncheon, held in Charleston, Murray was inducted into the league's Hall of Fame. He appeared to sheepishly accept and then left a message for the aspiring young baseball talent in attendance. He wore the non-matching ensemble of a Goodwill recipient, and his complementary clownish personality flourished. The room of hopeful Major Leaguers found him both insightful and hilarious.

In private, Murray talked about his friendship with Veeck and especially what components make a friendship last.

"Friends should always be special. We should endorse them, support them and promote them in every way possible. I am lucky to be friends with people I admire like Mike Veeck," Murray stated privately. "We should cherish our good friends."

Veeck, being rooted in Charleston for two happy decades, found it a natural occurrence that Murray would find Charleston a welcome home. It was as if he knew the Murray thought process.

"Bill has been a great friend. I think it's because we have a common background, both from large Catholic families—nine children—from the old neighborhoods," noted Veeck. "He never bought into the stardom and celebrity bit. He stayed grounded and within himself. That says a lot knowing all that he has accomplished."

But Murray did not find Charleston within his pace at first.

"When I first got here, I thought that nobody here knew how to drive," Murray recalled. "But after a while, I found this pace much easier on my system. That adjustment has been good for me."

Murray enunciated other life views to the All-Stars after the acknowledgement of the Hall of Fame award.

"Well, I never thought I'd be elected to a Hall of Fame for anything. I really don't deserve it. But I'm not giving it back!" Murray stated flatly. "This is probably the biggest honor I've ever [had]. I did win a Golden Globe once, and I was nominated for an Oscar, and I've won some other kind of things like that. But they cannot explain this to me, and that's why this one is at the very top."[72]

He continued, "Living the game of life can be a lot more interesting if you live it as a game, not taking anything too seriously except for really, really serious things like oil changes and tire rotation. But, then again, you decide."

There are realities that begin early in life and appear again late. What is lived in between may not always be as real for many. For the actor Bill Murray, navigating between the two realities has been among his most commendable achievements. Mind you, there have been other feats.

Murray is the middle issue of a nine-child family from Wilmette, Illinois, that had harsh realities to face—especially when Murray was a young man. His father died in 1967, when Murray was barely seventeen. His father was a lumber salesman. Young Murray worked his paper route and caddied, along with his brothers, at a local golf club. They needed to pay their tuition at Loyola Academy, a strict Jesuit high school. Murray sang with a local band and spent two years in college, his personality and antics vaulting him forward while concurrently impeding his formal education. The vault was impressive. Sure of himself, the satirical Murray began working with his older brother, Brian Doyle Murray, in the unpredictable venue of stand-up comedy. They both progressed to the Second City, a famous Chicago comedy venue. His personal warmth and natural timing won over his audience. That audience grew to millions upon millions.

The sheer breadth of his comedy defined a generation from *Saturday Night Live* to *Caddyshack* to *Tootsie*. His roles defined characters—all different and yet all believably real. He's Carl Spackler, Frank Cross, Phil Connors, Ernie McCrackin and Dr. Peter Venkman. There are fires of humanity that burn within. Murray could just as easily be your neighbor or your barber. He is all too real.

Sighting the affable Bill Murray in Charleston has become part of a new tradition. Murray is humbly based within his simple values. *Courtesy of Mike Veeck.*

Murray is a throwback. He's tall and athletic, a fine golfer and so comfortable with his celebrity that he uses it to help others. At Veeck's Hot Stove baseball banquet in 2012, Murray took a seat out in the crowd of six hundred fans, his back to the head table. The crowd was there to hear an address by former Atlanta Braves pitching ace John Smoltz. Prior to the banquet's beginning, an auctioneer raffled off the head table seat next to Smoltz. The crowd saw only the bid paddle going up time and again, first outbidding a handful of others and then actually outbidding his own last bid. There was a roar when the crowd saw the winning bidder, a smiling Bill Murray. He donated the proceeds to the Storm Eye Institute of the Medical University of South Carolina. Veeck's own daughter, Rebecca, has retinitis pigmentosa, a rare eye disorder that has caused her blindness. Murray has been there for father Mike and especially for Rebecca. Murray believes that friendship transcends all else.

Murray related, "I think if you can take care of yourself and then maybe try to take care of someone else, that's sort of how you're supposed to live. There's only so many people that can [do that], and the rest of the people, they're useful in terms of compost for the whole planet."[73]

His friendliness and reputation for mingling in any public situation with comic effect have made him all the more popular. He melds. He merges. He fits. And people admire that quality in him.

To be sure, Murray has exhibited a larger repertoire than the sidesplitting roles he's played in comedy. He's a leading man. Make that an Oscar-nominated leading man. He is not dashing like Cary Grant or heroic like John Wayne. But then again, these two past movie legends were Archibald Leach and Marion Morrison. Murray is Murray. He never wanted the Hollywood hype. Instead, he prefers Charleston.

"It's really nice here. The people are so mannerly and helpful," Murray pointed out. "The kindness of people is not a given outside of Charleston. It is what is expected here. You just don't see that community of goodwill anywhere else quite to the degree you see it here."

Charlestonians may see Murray at his favorite two venues—a golf course or a baseball game. With the Goldklang group, he revels in the fun of ownership of the Charleston RiverDogs. Mike Veeck is the ownership partner who promotes perhaps the best show in the minor leagues.

To say that Murray is a casual golfer would be like saying those in the Holy City occasionally sip sweet tea and eat red rice. Murray studies the game and challenges himself to perform at an optimum level. The cameras never bothered him, so to record a landmark championship win at the AT&T Pro-Am at Pebble Beach in 2011 seemed natural. His professional golfing partner, D.A. Points, rode the momentum with Murray to his first-ever PGA tour victory. True to form, Murray announced the win as a "Cinderella story," from a line he spoke as the dreamy greenskeeper Carl Spackler in the movie *Caddyshack*.

Murray lives vicariously through himself. He does not try to be anyone else. He finds that the art of acting always seems to return him to the center of his own personality.

"One of the things I like about acting is that, in a funny way, I come back to myself," Murray noted in an interview.[74] It's refreshing that, in being himself, he is the same person the public acknowledges as the down-to-earth Charleston icon we might see walking down Meeting Street or in the ten-items-or-less line at the Piggly Wiggly. Make sure you count his.

Murray's brush with the Oscar for best actor came from a sterling performance as an aging actor alone with his thoughts in Japan to film a whiskey commercial. The 2003 film *Lost in Translation* became one of several serious acting roles that have redefined the depth of Murray's abilities. The winner was Sean Penn for his role in *Mystic River*. The Oscar was not the goal for Murray, though he was certainly deserving of the acclamation.

"If you want the Oscar really badly, it becomes a naked desire and ambition. It becomes very unattractive. I've seen it," Murray stated following the event.[75] The deadpan humor is sometimes difficult to distinguish from reality—and it is Murray's reality to discern.

There has to be another category for Oscar-types who are able to enhance a performance from script to persona using the edginess Murray employs. Nobody does that like Murray. There has been nobody quite like him. He can be dorky and sarcastic and yet romantic and witty. He has played the famous Franklin Roosevelt and a symbolic Ebenezer Scrooge. He's even been the voice of the feline Garfield.

Murray is perhaps the best-known diehard Chicago Cubs fan around. He has contractual provisions in each production to see the Cubs if they were ever to reach the World Series. It hasn't happened since 1908. He sings "Take Me Out to the Ballgame" during the seventh-inning stretch when he attends games at Wrigley Field. Baseball's Opening Day 2012 found the affable Murray throwing out the first pitch to the roaring approval of the Chicago crowd. The Cubs played well but lost in the later innings, to start their 104th season streak non-world-championships ominously.

"The Cubs are always in the game, except either early or late, when they seem to find a way to get out of the game," Murray said. "They're my Cubbies, win or lose or lose again."

The youngest four of Murray's six boys are being educated in Charleston. Murray enjoys the personal time to watch them in playground leagues and at Charleston's First Baptist School activities. The simple lifestyle afforded in the Holy City—even given his lofty celebrity—allows Murray to relax and remain in perspective: "Being here is important for them. They're not in a plastic world, and they can grow up with good friends and wholesome experiences."

Murray's considerable list of performances beyond his legendary *Saturday Night Live* beginnings is indicative of his energy and resolve. Though selective of artistic projects, he never feared the rigors of hard work. With deference to his comedic hits like *Ghostbusters, Caddyshack, What About Bob* and *Groundhog Day*, another career developed that placed him among the best of the best in serious and dramatic comedy roles. As a wide-range character actor, he has performed in an amazing array of movies featuring believable, ribald and earthy eccentrics. In doing so, he has made sense of a remarkably productive career.

The list of more than two dozen important film contributions includes *The Limits of Control, The City of Ember, Coffee and Cigarettes, Kingpin, Get Low* and *Get Smart*. Add in *Wild Things*, the highly acclaimed *Lost in Translation, Broken Flowers, Nothing Lasts Forever* and *The Man Who Knew Too Little*. He was a hit in *Stripes* and *Meatballs, Tootsie* and *Scout's Honor*. There were so many others: *All You Need Is Cash* and *Quick Change, Friends Like These* and *Loose Shoes*. He carried the action in *The Lost City, Larger Than Life, Passion Play* and *The Moonrise Kingdom*. Murray could act. He could also hang in there. He did *The Life Aquatic, The Wedding Contract* and *Hyde Park on Hudson*. *Scrooged* brought back the Charles Dickens Christmas tale. *Rushmore, Little Shop of Horrors,*

Osmosis Jones and *The Royal Tenenbaums* may have stretched other actors. Not Murray. He even did *Hamlet*.

These are not all of his life's work.

Murray has musical inclinations and can sing or even mesh within a live local band. He has done this. He can cook. He will even cook for charities. He has read poetry and caught the first pitch of a baseball game—when he has not thrown it out. He leads Cub fans from the booth in the seventh inning as if they just won it all last year. He has been seen entering Mayor Riley's office as if he were checking the electrical power box or emptying the trash. He has been celebrated, yes, but never calibrated to his celebrity. That makes him one of us.

The tireless actor has been sought for special roles owing to his relationship to the common man and for his devotion to reality. That's why he could have still done what he has done without doing all that he had done. He's adaptable to all of life. Those adaptable actors are very rare in Hollywood.

In a sense, that's why Murray is here in Charleston.

Winning

JOHN MCKISSICK

No coach of organized football has ever compiled a record of more wins than John McKissick of Summerville High School. The numbers are beyond reasonable imagination. Over his first sixty years, he had amassed 594 victories. That's nearly 10 per year. There were years when his team only played 10 games. Along with the yearly caché of wins are 10 state championships. Yet the wins are not what necessarily drive this legendary coach each fall. They are simply a part of his purpose.

"I'm not sure how others have accepted a calling in life, but I know I have long accepted that coaching is what fulfills me. It's why I get up in the morning," McKissick intimated.

McKissick is still stoically imposing. His wispy white hair is thick enough to avoid Hair Club membership. He has a resonant country get-it-done demeanor, much as you'd expect from a high-impact, high-expectation leader of young men. He is warm and direct at the same time. He exhibits a sincere down-home smile and a glaze in his steely auburn eyes. He wears a broad-brimmed hat when outdoors and moves around decisively with energy. There are fifty-year-olds who may not approach his impressive physical zeal.

"I suppose I have been lucky. God has given me the gift of health, and I have been able to avoid so much that others have suffered by the time of my age," he noted. "I take everything a year at a time, and every year, so far, I have been able to participate in the sport I love."

McKissick has no outside hobbies that inspire within him the same passion as coaching football. He plays golf about four times a year. It's not enough to wear out the little cart pencil. He likes to spend a little time at home in the yard and might do a bit of gardening here and there, but not to the point that the earth needs him to oversee its sustenance to all varieties of flora. His wife, Joan, is always at his side, except for her Tuesday evening church choir practice.

"I walk on the beach some from time to time at the little place we have in DeBordieu. It's a nice way to get a little exercise and enjoy the weather," McKissick noted. "But other than a few simple things, my hobby is coaching. It's what I want to do every morning when I get out of bed. They're nice enough to let me stay here and coach as long as I want, and that's what I was hired to do.

"I coach and serve as the athletic director here. The coaching is 'Job One' during football, and the AD job fills the rest of my time. The high school has never interfered with my mission to coach, as I think they see great value in the full development that young men—and women—can benefit from sports. At some schools, that latitude is not given because someone decides that athletics have no importance in education. I'm here to tell you that they most certainly do."

Being a head coach in a state that has elevated itself nationally for its love of high school football has been rewarding. McKissick is the name synonymous with the state's football fortunes. He has certainly defined his community, as well. Along with recently retired Summerville mayor Berlin G. Myers, age ninety-five when he stepped down, the town announces itself. Summerville is famous.

Myers has a bust at city hall. He served as mayor for forty-five years. He led by individual persistence, careful delegation and perceptive instinct. The same could be said of McKissick. A decade younger, McKissick was coaching at Summerville High School fifteen years before Myers ran for his first term.

"Our mayor has done so many fine things to make Summerville a better community. I hate to see him step down, but I'm sure he has deserved some time to himself," McKissick lamented. "He's also been a great supporter of Summerville football."

The cycle a mayor repeats is the rhythm of all things community, from traffic to crime to livability to finance. But football is different. There is but one focus for the legendary McKissick—to compete every year with the top priority of winning a state championship. In that effort, he has appeared fourteen times, winning ten and losing four. Every practice, skull session, conditioning program and coaching clinic is aimed at that one difficult achievement. Anything less is below the goal. Yet McKissick has many stories of teams that did not win yet made him beam with pride. One such team played in the 2005 championship.

"Though I have a deep respect and appreciation for what officiating crews have to do, especially in championship games, the film shows that we would have had another championship in 2005 when A.J. Green made an end zone catch that would have won it on the last play. The official ruled it out of bounds. We lost 33–32 to Gaffney High School. That comeback to set up that last play would have been among the greatest in the history of South Carolina high school football. The official simply missed the call. What can you say? They usually get those calls right. They just missed it this time. My point in even bringing it up was that I was so deeply proud of that 2005 team and the way that they conducted themselves on and off the field. I'll never forget how proud I was."

McKissick went on to name other great teams that persevered but did not necessarily win "state" and individual players who have passed through his legendary program.

Grandson Joe Call under the tutelage of the winningest coach in football history, the legendary John McKissick. *Courtesy of Tommy McQueeney.*

"So many of them went on and did great things. Stanford and Keith Jennings, Kevin Long, Jamar Nesbit, A.J. Green, Ian Rafferty, Fred Worthy and Mark Slawson went on to play in the NFL," McKissick pointed out.

McKissick has coached nearly 3,200 young men over those sixty years going into the 2012 season.[76] Over 100 have appeared in the North-South All-Star game and the state's Shrine Bowl game.[77] College scholarships number into the hundreds. McKissick has had an impact on young lives well beyond the gridiron. He has helped to mold characters: "I've coached young men who made a lifetime doing important things, and that has made me smile. Converse Chellis played for me and at The Citadel. He became a state representative and, later, our state treasurer. Harry Blake went to West Virginia on a football and track scholarship and now runs a fine insurance business here in Summerville. Tommy Ervin was a linebacker for me. Good teams have to have good linebackers. He played at The Citadel and then went into the financial industry and has done very well. Billy Long is a fine businessman here in Summerville. There are so many that went into coaching and others that have had great success in other walks of life. I'm proud of every one.

"I had the great fortune in my life of learning from others. My high school coach, Jimmy Welch of Kingstree High School, was a steady influence who taught me plenty. Lonnie McMillan at Presbyterian College motivated me to become better—as did Coach Cally Gault, who coached at North Augusta High School and at Presbyterian."

Coach Calhoun "Cally" Gault became one of the most respected small college coaches in the nation, often leading his Presbyterian Blue Hose as a preeminent power. During his tenure at North Augusta High School, he won forty-two straight games. His stint as head football coach at Presbyterian College in Clinton, South Carolina, lasted twenty-two years and is considered the heyday of Presbyterian football.

McKissick is quick to compliment opposing coaches, as well: "Some of the football coaches I've met and enjoyed over the years would have to include Gerald Moody at Berkeley High School. Coach Moody could compete with anyone. He was always a great guy. Pinky Babb at Greenwood High School always had fine teams, and he sure could coach."

McKissick taught nearly fifty assistant coaches over the years at Summerville. Many went on to other high schools and colleges in the coaching profession.

One of his former players, Billy Baker, took the time to write a book about McKissick in 1993 titled *Called to Coach*. Nearly twenty years later, that calling has many more chapters.

All three of his grandsons played for him at Summerville. Richard and Joe Call were both quarterbacks. The third, Donny McElveen, also played quarterback. The younger Joe Call is currently the Green Wave's offensive coordinator. Call, a college quarterback from The Citadel, takes great pride in the lineage and his grandfather's amazing record: "He's got that banner of four hundred [wins] hanging over there and wears a ring for five hundreed," Call said with a smile. "I think it means more than he lets on."[78]

McKissick's oversight of Team Summerville, along with his added duties as the school's athletic director, has not vaulted his self-worth beyond his next football game planning session. He possesses erudition for the task at hand, rarely taking the time to gaze at the long trophy cases and preponderance of felt-lined banners. He has received three national high school coach-of-the-year awards. They only give one of those per year, and there were 14,445 high school football teams in the United States as of 2008.[79]

McKissick encounters interruptions like a band of excited players carrying him from the field, a plethora of Hall of Fame induction ceremonies and even an appearance in 2012 at the Super Bowl. He's been awarded the Order of the Palmetto, the State of South Carolina's highest civilian achievement awarded by the governor. His presentation was several governors ago. The aforementioned Don Shula Award as NFL High School Coach of the Year was presented in Indianapolis during ceremonies surrounding the 2012 Super Bowl.

"It's the latest, so it has to be the best one," McKissick was quoted as saying shortly after winning the award.[80] "Like I've said before, awards and honors are a result of having good people around you working for a common cause. I have been blessed to work with some great people, and I have been blessed to work for Summerville High School."[81]

In a twist of irony, celebrated NFL coach Don Shula personally presented the award to McKissick. Shula, at age eighty-three, with the most victories in the history of the National Football League (347), handed the trophy to McKissick, at age eighty-five, who at that moment in time had amassed 594 victories—247 more than Shula or any other NFL coach had ever experienced. With the advantage of 247 more victories over his career, one would think McKissick would also have many more losses than Shula. Not so. Shula's teams have lost 173 games. Going into the 2012 season, McKissick's Summerville juggernaut has lost only 143.[82] Shula had 6 ties. McKissick had 13. That's a full season, including playoff rounds, of just games that ended in ties.

McKissick has had only two losing seasons. Two! Fifty-eight winning seasons were left in their wake. He has missed only one game in his career, though he was there in the stands to make sure that a win was in order. It seems that his hat was blown from his head at the precise instant that a referee made a controversial call in favor of the other team. A lesser competitor might have used an older hat. The official noticed McKissick's shiny new hat, and the South Carolina High School League hesitantly enforced a suspension. No one was more apologetic about the incident than McKissick. And that football referee has a story he can tell his grandchildren.

"It really looks different from the stands. I like it better on the sidelines," he stated. "That's where I think better."

His wife, Joan, has never missed a home game. There were quite a few times when attending was difficult, including hip surgery in 2010. But she made it to the opener. Their marriage has been a complement of direction that has sustained both of them for nearly six decades.

No Fear of Failure, a book published in 2012 by author Gary Burnison, revisits success through the lives of the successful. The chapters include articles about Michael Bloomberg, New York's mayor, and Carlos Slim, the current richest man in the world. There are twelve chapters that relate the stages of success to the reader. Chapter Six is "Building Teams." The interviewee is coach John McKissick.

Burnison records an exchange with a student that occurred while he was there: "At one point in our interview, McKissick stepped out of his office for a moment and into the hallway of the high school where the students were passing classes. 'Hey, Coach!' a young man called out. 'Next year I'm playing for you!' The student turned and walked backward a few steps as he continued down the hall. 'I'm ready, and I'm playing for you.'

"Reflecting those words, I couldn't help but wonder: what business leader wouldn't want to hear the same thing from his team? As a team builder, McKissick has exhibited an uncanny ability to mold, motivate and lead others. His first priority is to engage his team. 'I don't coach football,' McKissick said, 'I coach kids.' He knows that one of the biggest motivations for any individual is a sense of belonging to something bigger than one's self. For the players on Summerville's Green Wave that means being a part of a winning legacy."[83]

That kid has a better chance of getting a state championship ring than every kid at every other program in the state. It may be more a matter of whether Coach McKissick has a place for the exuberance of youth, resplendent with a new direction.

McKissick was once that kind of young man himself.

A native of Greenwood, South Carolina, McKissick's family moved to Kingstree. There, the young McKissick starred on his high school team, earning a spot on the Presbyterian College squad. Military service intervened, and McKissick spent two years as an army paratrooper. He returned to Presbyterian, earning a degree in economics. After a brief stint working with his father, he took the coaching job at Summerville High School, then with fewer than three hundred students, in 1952.

Though McKissick set a winning pattern early, his biggest victory of the 1950s was gaining the hand of his wife, Joan. John and Joan McKissick were married in 1955. He won his first state championship in 1956. The successes kept coming—the birth of two daughters and a nice sturdy home followed. The American life, simple as it was, sustained every moment of their combined interest.

Summerville High School, like the rest of the Charleston area, began to grow. Neighborhoods sprang up. Industry came. The wide berth of an interstate veered through. Shopping centers opened. A few hotels and food stops followed the interstate. Another inn, the highly regarded Woodlands Hotel and Spa, is a converted mansion that dates to 1906. It has long been the only five-star resort in the state.

The engaging Summerville Flowertown Festival grew, as well. It is considered the state's largest arts and crafts festival and boasts an attendance of 100,000 for its ten days. The explosion of color is attributed to the thousands of blooming azaleas and dogwoods. If the Masters is on television, the Flowertown Festival is in its stride. It has been named by the Southeast Tourist Society as one of the top twenty events in the South.[84] It raises money for the Summerville Family YMCA and was founded in 1972, during McKissick's twentieth year as coach.

Summerville itself is an old town that grew out of coastal health concerns. In Charleston County, they are called mosquitoes. They were thought to cause several illnesses on the peninsula, and some brave Charlestonians headed up the Ashley River soon after Charleston's founding in 1670. A few hundred years later (1899), the International Congress of Physicians proclaimed Summerville—aptly named for the time that the mosquitoes are at their worst in Charleston—one of the two best places in the world for people suffering from lung disorders. The turpentine scent was thought to be a cure for many respiratory ailments and a fragrant defense against the mosquitoes.[85] Now there is Deep Woods Off. It's the lotion that has saved many golfers and the McKissick summer practice sessions.

Nobody prepares better than John McKissick. He studies players for their speed and strength. He positions them accordingly. He finds heart in others. They will play for him as well. His schemes include a preference to find great athletes to play key positions. They start with quarterback. He has had the best of them from Perry Cuda, who played at Alabama, to Matt Vaughn, an All-ACC baseball player at Clemson. They include Ricky Bustle, now the head offensive coordinator for Virginia Tech, and Bennett Swygert, the quarterback's coach at Newberry College. His other athletic priority is to find linebackers with strength and speed but, importantly, with instincts. As he intimates to others, "Great teams have great linebackers."

He studies film. It didn't always happen that film was available. In the early coaching days, it was better to study coaches and personnel. The technologies have changed. Now, the game is worked in the film room.

In spite of all that McKissick continues to accomplish, the pundits insist on predicting his last year in coaching. It was in 1999, 2002, 2006, 2009, 2010, 2011 and is now predicted for 2012. One can find these end dates within the endless affirmatives accompanying the explosion of digital media: the Internet. These pundits have to be right at some point. Yet they have not fully vetted the unpredictable.

When will John McKissick not want to get up in the morning and coach football? That will be the year he retires.

Overlooking the Obvious

JOE RICE

Those kids have no one else."

Well, actually, they do. They have Joe Rice and his partner, Ron Motley. The Dee Norton Lowcountry Children's Center has gotten their attention.

The "Center" is for the victims of substance and sexual abuse; it also offers counseling for their families. It is a nonprofit organization founded in 1991. The center is supported by donations from individuals and several local businesses. The Dee Norton Lowcountry Children's Center is located on upper King Street in Charleston.[86] Importantly, it is the favorite charity of Joe Rice: "Ron and I are not into as much bricks and mortar as we are about getting assistance directly to those in the greatest need. This is an entire community need that, I think, gets overlooked too often."

It could be said that partners Rice and Motley have made a career of helping millions of others who had been heretofore overlooked.

Attorneys Joe Rice and Ron Motley formed Motley Rice, LLC. Look up and you can easily find them. Their building at the mouth of the Cooper River overlooks Charleston Harbor much like a sentinel from its Mount Pleasant prominence. Rice's office is a window vista of all that is Charleston—from the *Yorktown* to the downtown church steeples, from the Sullivan's Island Lighthouse to the Arthur Ravenel Jr. Bridge. It may be the best view in America.

"I watched the entire *Hunley* episode as they moved the submarine from the harbor on up the river," Rice noted. "All of their brave crew were still inside some century and a half after the incident. They were back in our consciousness and could finally be honored. That was a day I will never forget."

The *H.L. Hunley* submarine made world history by sinking the USS *Housatonic* in Charleston Harbor during the Civil War. Its subsequent loss had puzzled historians and other scholars for well more than a century. The sub is being archaeologically restored at the Warren Lasch Laboratory in North Charleston. Rice noted: "This is one of the most inspiring vantage points in Charleston, and I feel fortunate that I get to experience how beautiful Charleston is every day. To the left I see those historic churches, and to the right is that amazing bridge. So, in a way, I look at the past and the history of Charleston in one direction and the future, being the bridge, in the other. That bridge symbolically and physically takes Charleston to the world. It is a new and modern dimension for the community. I watched it going up in stages and tracked the changes and could see it was being completed well ahead of schedule. Even the *Hunley* episode speaks volumes about the latest technology. They are discovering new information by new methods almost daily. So Charleston is now a blend of the best of the old with the excitement of the new."

Technologies have also played a role in the creative and celebrated genius of the Motley Rice law firm. It is not a Broad Street tradition. Neither Joe Rice nor Ron Motley is often seen in a light blue seersucker suit approaching the bench in any of the courthouses near Charleston. Their cases are usually docketed elsewhere—places like Washington, Houston or New Orleans. They specialize in cases that impact citizens of every country.

It was Joe Rice and Ron Motley who took the tobacco industry to court over what was determined to be its intentional negligence in attracting millions across the world market to begin smoking and deflect the sense to break the habit by what was considered an addictive conspiracy. That "cause" was rewarded in 1998, when Rice led the negotiation of the Tobacco Master Settlement Agreement, which was joined by every state and remains the largest financial or public health settlement in the United States. It was again Motley and Rice who sued on behalf of the victims of the terrorist attacks of September 11, 2001.

"Congress established a victims' relief fund right after the event. We represented victims who did not find the fund to be fair for them. We continue to represent victims against those alleged to have helped finance and support terrorist groups," Rice clarified.

The firm has become engaged in much other litigation of public interest, most notably the 2010 BP oil spill (also called the *Deepwater Horizon* spill) into the Gulf of Mexico. That three-month ordeal dumped crude oil in amounts estimated between 205 million gallons[87] and 540 million gallons[88] into the Gulf of Mexico. It was the largest ocean oil spill in history.

On March 2, 2012, Rice agreed to a financial settlement for the Gulf businesses and individuals he represented that is estimated to exceed $7 billion. Rice was one of the lead negotiators for the PSC (Plaintiff's Steering Committee), which reached this settlement. His statement to the press explained the process and settlement: "I am excited about the ability to have Motley Rice clients participate in a settlement process that was designed to be victim friendly. We wholeheartedly support the court-supervised claims process and think our clients will receive the full and fair compensation they deserve."

It was an amazing agreement from two standpoints. First, there was no cap on the amount to be paid by BP. Second, BP would fund the court-supervised settlements—irrespective of the previous $20 billion it had set aside for settlements.

The Motley Rice statement further explained the dynamic: "BP agreed to two separate class action settlement agreements, the first of which compensates individuals and businesses that suffered private economic loss as a result of the spill, including lost profits and property damage. The second compensates people having medical claims in connection to the spill and also provides them with 21 years of regular medical consultation. Eligible claimants can participate in one or both settlement programs under the settlement in principle."[89]

These mind-boggling awards and settlements could not be possible without the astonishing teamwork Rice and Motley receive from associate legal teams and partners they have in other key cities. Though Charleston will forever remain its headquarters, Motley Rice law firm has legal offices in New York as well as Los Angeles. There are additional offices in Hartford, Connecticut; Morgantown, West Virginia; Washington, D.C.; and Providence, Rhode Island.[90]

The Motley Rice firm litigates cases in numerous other national and international areas, including a few prescription drug atrocities where victims received lamentable and even fatal results. Notably, they have also taken on several defective medical devices, including pelvic mesh, a surgically implanted design supplied by nine manufacturers that had seriously adverse impacts to nearly thirty thousand patients between 2008 and 2010.[91]

The team aspect has worked well for these two super lawyers. They each bring astonishing assets. Rice recognizes the synergy: "Ron and I make a great team. I know of no one who can effectively litigate a case better than he does. He is such a force in the courtroom that it makes my job as a negotiator much easier. We become dynamic together in that regard. He does what he's best at, and I do what I enjoy to best benefit our clients. His intellect in understanding law is not surpassed in the United States by anyone. He is dedicated. His mother died of emphysema. It was from the effects of smoking cigarettes, so he is quite engaged in the tobacco case and has been for his life."

Rice earned his undergraduate and law degrees at the University of South Carolina. He met his future wife, Lisa, at a fraternity party. He was in Alpha Tau Omega; Lisa was a member of Alpha Delta Pi.[92] Lisa and Joe Rice have one child, Ann E. Rice Ervin. Ann E. married Tanner Ervin in May 2010.

Ron Motley, the senior of the tandem Motley Rice, remembers the early days and the notice served on the legal profession by Rice's obvious talents. "I hired Joe Rice right out of law school. He at first tried jury cases with me and then tried them on his own. Soon it became apparent to all in the firm that Joe's prowess as a negotiator was unparalleled. His talents have not abated over time. He is widely respected by some of the better-known defense attorneys and especially in New York City. We have a great team!"

Indeed, Ron Motley and Joe Rice command a wealth of respect among the local law professionals in Charleston. Perhaps they're happy that Motley Rice, LLC, works cases in so many other communities that the Charleston market gives all other lawyers ample opportunity.

Local defense attorney Joe Griffith Jr. knows them both and appreciates their mission: "With its national reputation, the Motley Rice law firm has been quite an asset to the legal profession here in South Carolina. Founders Joe Rice and Ron Motley have always raised the bar as victim advocates, and their leadership role in major cases of national importance is undeniable, particularly in the mass tort area. These two gentlemen are also a great resource for the law community, as they are always willing to help their fellow attorneys in analyzing the merits of potential cases

Most people love to meet Joe Rice. Defendants may disagree! *Courtesy of Motley Rice, LLC.*

and providing co-counsel assistance. Their commitment to charitable and civic causes is also highly commendable. They stay involved with, and give back to, the community. All of Charleston benefits from their generosity."

Rice's expansive office sports a decidedly western décor. It fits Rice's adventurous spirit. His photos include a few of his favorite horses, including a beautiful Paint quarter horse named Thunder. He enjoys equine pursuits. There are also photos of his dogs and a few remnants of cows (rugs) and deer (antlers)—evidently acquired within his various hobbies. He loves wildlife and the great outdoors. His desk usually features a glass of his favorite Lowcountry potion: sweet iced tea. Rice is effervescent and upbeat yet contemplative and pensive. You would not want to engage him in rhetoric. It is what he does. He has a quality of ego-less invitation. He can easily be your friend. The tuft of thick gray and charcoal hair spills over his opened collar. He is relaxed and confident. His tanned face and cheerful countenance hint that his friends may be waiting for him at the driving range. It would seem that he has even more friends than stock certificates and bank deposit vouchers.

Indeed, there is a golf course. There, Rice enjoys the recreation moments and a healthy number of friends. His development of the private Bulls Bay Golf Club has elevated Charleston's already impressive list of golfing venues to an international level. The course has Scottish and Irish seaside features. The elegant clubhouse sits atop a hill. That's already a departure from Charleston's noticeably flat topography. The Mike Strantz design has inspired those who see it for the first time as a layout that should welcome bagpipers and leprechauns. Strantz, a good friend of Rice's, succumbed to cancer in 2005. They enjoyed riding horses together, and Strantz, Rice noted, "made the course look like it had always been there."

Strantz had designed nine courses after serving as a protégé to Tom Fazio. Strantz not only designed courses, but he was also an artist, his portfolio including Civil War and Citadel pen-and-ink renderings. He also had a reputation for operating all equipment associated with the building and maintenance of a golf course. A native of Ohio, Strantz had made his home in Mount Pleasant. He had few better friends than Joe Rice.

"Mike's loss was tragic for everyone, especially his wife, Heidi, and his two daughters, Dana and Andrea," Rice lamented. "You can see he was special."

Rice's friends at Bulls Bay have expanded to include another famous Charlestonian, musician Darius Rucker. They play golf together and enjoy each other's camaraderie. Rucker and Rice enjoy the quiet charm of the uniquely challenging course and their mutual love of the game of golf.

Rucker's friendship with Rice became quite evident at the Rices' 2010 wedding festivities of daughter Ann E. to Tanner Ervin. Rucker filmed a personalized video for the wedding couple because he was out of town on tour and could not attend the ceremony and reception. On it, he invited Ann E. and her new husband to be in one of his music videos, "History in the Making." They did so.

That wedding has Charleston abuzz.

Rucker's good friend and celebrated musician in his own right Edwin McCain wrote and performed a song especially for the event. "Walk with You" became a top hit recording. It has fast become a wedding standard.

"It was the song we did our first father-daughter dance to—I could not use it to walk the aisle. I would never have made it," Rice intimated.

Left: An evening view of the Intracoastal Waterway near Awendaw, just north of Charleston Harbor. *Oil on canvas, by W. Thomas McQueeney*.

Below: Bird's-eye view of Morris Island Lighthouse, currently under restoration. *Acrylic on canvas, by W. Thomas McQueeney*.

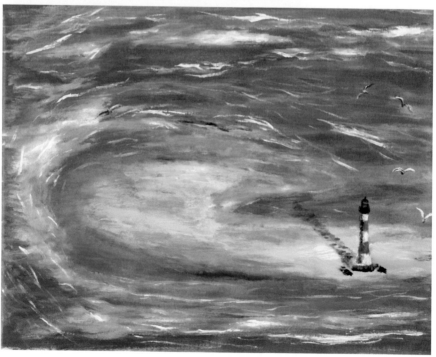

The evening sky appears afire as the sunset lights the southern end of the Isle of Palms. *Photo by Tommy Ford.*

The Arthur Ravenel Jr. Bridge at sunset, seen from Mount Pleasant. *Photo by W. Thomas McQueeney.*

The descending sun in Charleston Harbor silhouettes the daily return of a shrimping boat. *Photo by Tommy Ford.*

High Battery seems in peril from the raging surge of a Charleston hurricane. *Photo by Tommy Ford.*

Silhouette of Charleston at sunset from the Old Village in Mount Pleasant. *Photo by W. Thomas McQueeney.*

St. Michael's Church spire is the focal point against a backdrop of another of the Holy City's surreal sunsets. *Photo by W. Thomas McQueeney.*

A lone recreational sailor prepares the rigging after an evening beach landing. *Photo by Tommy Ford.*

A soft rain shower at the foot of Broad Street introduces the majesty of nightfall in Charleston. *Photo by Tommy Ford.*

Pelicans parade across the dunes at Sullivan's Island. *Photo by Tommy Ford.*

From the waterfront homes at Mount Pleasant's Old Village looking to Fort Sumter, reflections emerge. *Photo by Tommy Ford.*

Lightning in a purple sky over the Ashley River. *Photo by Tommy Ford.*

A view to the low brow of the city from Mount Pleasant. *Photo by Tommy Ford.*

Placid reflections of the homes bordering Rutledge Avenue on Colonial Lake. *Photo by Tommy Ford.*

Rice's wide circle of friends and longtime neighbors may have witnessed one of the greatest weddings ever. There were special moments there to be enjoyed by the lucky list of invitees.

Mentioning neighbors in particularly distinctive ways celebrates the uniqueness of Rice's home. Rice's neighborhood is an exceptional place. The neighbors are mostly friends whom he has known from other previous neighborhoods. They had made multiple moves together. Many lived in proximity in two other Mount Pleasant neighborhoods. A neighbor to one side, Joe Griffith (whose son is the lawyer previously cited), developed Olde Park, Rice being his partner in the enterprise. On the other side, banker Forrest Edwards has been his friend since 1973.

"Forrest knows more about mortgage banking than anybody. It seems he has booked half the loans around here, and I'd bet if you've been around Charleston long enough, you're friends with Forrest Edwards," Rice indicated.

Across the street is Rod Moseley, to whom Rice refers as "Mr. Citadel." "He's all about supporting the standards of The Citadel. That's Hot Rod! He's intent on having Citadel values as focal to Charleston in his own low-key fashion. You have to admire that," Rice added.

Living in Mount Pleasant has its advantages, but Rice is not too cozy with some of the recent changes. "You have something special here that has to be preserved. Look at the canopy of trees over Mathis Ferry Road. Will progress become the force that takes those beautiful oaks away? The widening of Highway 17 can help the traffic, but I'd hate to see Mount Pleasant look like any other place. Putting what amounts to a freeway through the center can diminish much of the residential appeal. Not all change is good change. It would be good to preserve the integrity of the community by preserving its uniqueness."

Mount Pleasant has a charm not realized elsewhere. There is the working fishing village atmosphere of Shem Creek, where the shrimp boats still make their evening return. The seabirds dip the still waters for the abundant fish there. The Old Village, a vestige of Charleston's past, surrounds the creek. Coleman Boulevard and Rifle Range Road have a quaint southern feel. There are marsh vistas and bird sanctuaries. Alhambra Hall recalls old Labor Day picnics and the annual Blessing of the Fleet. Boone Hall Plantation and the site of the Charles Pinckney home serve as historical markers. Pinckney hosted first president George Washington there in 1791.[93] The pier at the Arthur Ravenel Jr. Bridge brings walkers, fishermen and children to enjoy an evening ice cream.

The *Yorktown* will host military service veterans, Boy Scouts and tourists, peering into its massive decks or waiting for a harbor ride to Fort Sumter. There is a public golf course there that may be in danger of other development. Money drives the algorithm. Patriots Point Links has been the subject of a potential sale to a town house developer. It benefits those who seek to make a fortune but will not advance the ambiance of a community. Rice understands this dynamic and feels that these community issues deserve a greater degree of foresight.

"The town will get more tax revenue and the community will have even more traffic. But what will that do in the bigger picture but make Mount Pleasant just like anyplace else?" Rice explains. "Where do you draw the line?"

It would make one realize that the fleeting times need to be coddled. There are perfect days of idyllic settings. Rice can conceive what his ideal day would entail: "I'd have played eighteen holes in the morning with good friends. Of course, I would win the bet. I would have a nice lunch and then ride my horse for two hours in the forest. Then I'd go out on the boat, do a little fishing and greet sunset with a cocktail. Now that would be a nice day here in Charleston."

Rice has extended his largesse to another beneficiary. The University of South Carolina benefited by Rice's friendship with its past athletic director, Eric Hyman, and its football coach, Steve Spurrier. It needed a facility to upgrade the dated coaching center. Rice visited the site, looked at plans and has committed to the Rice Building, one that will provide the benefits of modern technologies and proximity to the student-athletic facilities to promote assistance and oversight. It is being built next to the student enrichment center. It is the newest privately funded facility at the university.

It will only be part of Rice's life's legacy. He has a tight-worded philosophy that he espouses.

"What are the right things to do?" Rice postulates. "In all things that should be the control mechanism."

Rice explained: "We should always set our sights on what should be done, not what is expedient or what best benefits profit. Wouldn't it make sense that some law would not have to be in place for a manufacturer to install shatterproof glass? Shouldn't factories want to have the highest safety standards possible? Instead of paying money out in courts for the penalties, shouldn't people who care about the right thing to do invest in a better workplace? The right thing to do should always prevail over profit or the inconvenience of schedule."

It is a striking anomaly that Joe Rice's perfect world would likely never need lawyers. There is a collective of plaintiffs, most of whom have never met one another, that is profoundly appreciative that since the world is far from perfect, there is a place for Joe Rice. They number in the millions.

Assistance from the Bench

Judge Arthur McFarland

When Arthur McFarland was twelve, he knew much about who he wanted to be. He had aspirations. To some, that comes early. With McFarland, it came early and stayed late.

McFarland, the seventh of nine children, showed brilliance in the classroom and a deep spiritual disposition. "I grew up on the East Side in the Wraggsborough area. I went to an all-black Catholic elementary school, Immaculate Conception, until I reached the tenth grade [1964]. With only eight other black students, I transferred to Bishop England on Calhoun Street. That severed relationships and began a drastically different life. Unlike my older sisters, I did not finish ICS. But in many ways it was a positive experience. I graduated with honors and was accepted at the University of Notre Dame.

"I was put on a new mental path by experiencing the changes of culture relative to integration. I had mentoring help from Holy Ghost Fathers, Father William Joyce and, later, Father Egbert J. Figaro. Father Figaro, the first African American parish priest in Charleston, has a legacy that still remains strong today."

Father Figaro was the long-serving pastor of St. Patrick's Church at the corner of Radcliffe and St. Philip Streets. He was born in New Jersey, ordained a priest in Ridgefield, Connecticut, and became a monsignor in Charleston. He passed away in 1999. A diminutive gentleman with a strong rasp of a voice, Figaro endeared himself to the entire community.[94]

"The societal changes were difficult for all, but it helped that you had a mindset to adapt. That wasn't always the case. In the summer of 1963, I was only about fifteen, and I participated in a 'sit-in' at Felder's Drugstore at the corner of King and Calhoun. I was arrested. This was the year before I entered Bishop England," McFarland stated in measured words that told of the troubling times. "This was the long hot summer of civil rights. It was the slow and awkward merger of two worlds."

McFarland's father, Joe, was a Charleston Trident Chamber of Commerce employee, serving the organization as the custodian. "He rode a bicycle to work daily for forty-two years, never once missing a day. He worked at the corner of Broad and Church Streets before the Chamber moved to Lockwood Boulevard. The only day he ever missed was the day he died. He had a massive stroke," McFarland lamented. "He was a true breadwinner and a model father.

"I sometimes think about my father. He always said, 'Be kind to people on your way up because you'll see them again on your way down.'

"My mother, Thomasina Jenkins McFarland, supported me in more ways than you can imagine. Our family was immersed in another church—the historic Emanuel AME Church on Calhoun Street. When I was in the sixth grade, I decided to become a Catholic. She asked me about it, saw how sincere I was and supported that decision from that day forward. She wanted me to follow my faith, uphold solid values and always be motivated. She had the skills of an educated economist, though her opportunities for education were lacking. She finished the ninth grade, and at that time, that was all she could expect. She always told me that there was something magic about a seventh child, as if she expected me to do something great in life. My mother became my biggest supporter. When Mayor Riley swore me in as a municipal judge in 1976, my mother held the Bible."

Going to a previously all-white high school challenged McFarland, but his mother was there to allay his trepidation. She encouraged him to accept the opportunity and make the best impression for others who would follow.

James Owens, the Bishop England High School basketball captain, remembered the travails of the times as McFarland joined the team.

"I never saw anybody deal with the things Arthur did," stated Owens. "He was the first minority player to ever play basketball in the South Carolina High School League. At first, he even caught it from the students at our school, but after a while, they saw his goodness and his dedication. People were insensitive about race, especially in the late 1960s. Arthur handled it all with a great deal of personal fortitude. I had gained a deep respect for him early on.

Judge Arthur McFarland has been an advocate, a volunteer and a major component of Charleston's cultural growth. *Courtesy of Dr. Elise Davis-McFarland.*

"We had a good team. Arthur was a forward and one of our first six players. He was a fine athlete—very quick and smart. He could defend as well as anybody we had. There are a number of games that Arthur's play made a difference and helped us to win. But when we went to other teams' gyms, they were merciless. He caught hell from everybody. I remember him getting stitches over his eye. He was targeted everywhere he went. They tried to distract Arthur by the racial slurs and insults. As we got into our schedule, our team rallied around Arthur. In time, the school student body came to appreciate him. But he had a rougher time of it than anyone could imagine."

His high school basketball coach, Charlie Gallagher, was also an English teacher in the Honor Group classes. He remembered McFarland's challenges: "He was as fine an English student as I ever had. He earned straight As in just about every subject. He was always getting the class work done at a high level. I had the opportunity to coach him. We were already the team everyone wanted to beat because of our tradition of success. Now, with Arthur as the first black player in what was an all-white league, those opposing gyms were especially hostile to us. But we would just go out and win. Arthur was a key player, and I would usually match him against the other team's best scorer. I saw that team get better, and a big part was accepting Arthur."

Gallagher detailed a story that made his point: "We went to another conference team's gym. It was hectic, and the game was close. They had ridden Arthur the entire game. He heard every insult in the book. In the last minute, we made a few good plays and put the game away. One of the opposing players ran at Arthur to take a swing as the buzzer went off. One of our bench players, Timmy Griffith, intercepted the guy and nailed him right in front of Arthur. A small riot started. We got our guys together and got out. But it showed me that our players were going to protect Arthur no matter what."

"Arthur McFarland had a lot more going than basketball," Owens added. "He's a first-class human being. He was always one of the neatest dressers I ever saw. He was meticulous. We became like brothers. I had such a high respect for him back then, and I still do. When he became a judge, I had not seen him in a few years. I saw him at the courthouse one day, and we hugged. It was just like going back and living those few years over again."

Success was not an easily attainable commodity in the mid-1960s. There were certainly obstacles.

McFarland recalled those early days: "It definitely was not easy. Our coach, Charlie Gallagher, was a hard disciplinarian and demanded players in great athletic shape. We ran more than anyone, and though I didn't see myself as a skilled player, he gave me opportunities, I believe, as a reward for my hustle and attitude. But you could bet he put a team on the floor to win. Losing was not an option."

McFarland's contributions to the classroom were duly recorded. He was an outstanding student and had earned several post–high school scholarship opportunities. One of the most prestigious academic universities in the land showed interest.

Indeed, McFarland gained acceptance to the University of Notre Dame. He had vaulted to the doorstep of even greater opportunity. Though this path would take him to a wide array of postgraduate choices, his sights remained set on making a name for himself. McFarland finished in South Bend and then entered the University of Virginia Law School. He continued to perform impressively. Someone noticed. That's where he met his future wife. Dr. Elise Davis-McFarland is the vice-president of student affairs at Trident Technical College. Their two children, Kira and William, were raised in a highly academic environment.

They were raised in a new city and a new time but still within the old qualities that hinted of McFarland's memories. He explained: "I never really left the peninsula. The overall quality of life is still strong in Charleston, especially downtown. I have a comfort level there. I sometimes get stuck behind tourists going too slow, but it's worth the experience. It's part of the price. I learned to appreciate Charleston by leaving it. The people seem to relate to folks of all racial and socioeconomic levels. And that downtown area keeps me grounded. The physical changes of the city have been very accommodating. The idea of intra-racial as well as interracial separations still has a ways to go. But it has come a long way from where it was.

"I reflect back about my daughter Kira writing a paper when she was in the seventh grade at Buist Academy. She won a navy award with it. It was about getting a good education and using it, building a strong family and making contributions back to the community. It spoke of her admiration of my role as a father.

"I can remember trying to make it in the field of law by the same determination it took to play basketball in high school. I sometimes needed to go home, read Kira a bedtime story and then return to my office to finish my work. I worked for ten full years on one school desegregation case, from 1982 to 1991. I also worked closely with the Diocese of Charleston on the Charleston Catholic School, a really important innovation in the advancement of education, race relations and the diocese simultaneously."

What was once a burgeoning network of downtown Charleston Catholic parishes diminished as the city spread away from the central peninsula. There were distinct provinces of competing churches. Cathedral School was on Broad Street, St. Patrick's at Radcliffe. Old St. Joseph's was near the auditorium and was sold. The church still stands. St. Mary's, the oldest Catholic church in the Carolinas, is on Hasell Street. Sacred Heart Church is at Huger and King. St. Peter's Church is on Wentworth Street, and Immaculate Conception Chapel is on Shepherd Street, both serving the African American Catholic community. Retired bishop David Thompson conceived the idea of an excellent central school, the Charleston Catholic School, to be housed in the previously named Sacred Heart School. It made perfect sense for economics, centralization and maximizing resources. McFarland helped to put it all together. The highly regarded school opened at the corner of Huger and King Streets in 1991.[95]

The new Charleston Catholic School incorporates the four remaining vibrant parishes of the downtown area: St. Patrick's, Sacred Heart, St. Mary's and the Cathedral. It starts at K4 and continues through the eighth grade.[96] The ample funding and ability to attract top teaching professionals have made the school a landmark success and a study for other urban parochial schools. Along with like-minded others, McFarland made himself available to see it come to fruition.

Perhaps by his reputation of assisting others in volunteer matters, McFarland was approached to serve as a municipal judge. This gave him an opportunity to expand his knowledge and experience in civil law. He performed these municipal duties for thirty-five years. His court would have every walk of life but mostly traffic violators. Yet he did have his share of odd cases: "One day, this lady walked up when her case was called. She calmly told me, 'I am the mother of God.' Things went downhill from there! She had been brought in for disorderly conduct. This went on for a while. In the entire exchange, we never were able to get her correct name. I suppose that, given a high number of cases, this was my crazy case. She was more than crazy." McFarland smiled at the silliness of that experience. "The police officer there was undercover, and it was all he could do to keep a straight face."

McFarland stayed involved in other areas. He serves on St. Patrick's Parish Finance Council and other church committees. He is a central player in the yearlong 175th anniversary of St. Patrick's Parish. He loved that old church. His spiritual life revolves around it.

McFarland held the highest office in one of the great American Catholic organizations, the Knights of Peter Claver. St. Peter Claver was a Spaniard who eventually became the patron saint of African Americans. Though born in Spain, he lived his entire adult life in the early 1600s in South America and took exceptional care of those enslaved or imprisoned. In his lifetime, he is credited with over 300,000 baptisms.[97]

McFarland was elected supreme knight at the Knights of Peter Claver Annual Meeting in 2000. He held that position for the maximum tenure of six years. "That almost happened by accident. I had been their national lawyer for six years. It was all about timing. I had run as national advocate. The previous supreme knight was retiring. There were a few gentlemen there that expressed interest. I ran, never expecting to win. Somehow, I got the most votes and have enjoyed that relationship since. We see friends from all over every year at the convention.

"It has helped me to become more engaged with my Catholic faith. I was able to travel to Rome, to Austria and even to Australia. The experience grew me in the church. My values are grounded in Catholicism. During my tenure, we established the first international council on San Andres Island, Colombia, South America. This is symbolically important as our patron saint, Peter Claver, spent his priesthood serving African slaves, arriving in the port of Cartagena in Colombia."

There is even a sense that the travels have made McFarland better realize his appreciation of the beauty of Charleston. There are parallels.

Historically, Charleston was the entry point for more African slaves than any city in North America. Charleston was once a walled city, presumably for protection from the Spanish and the chance of Native American uprisings. But seeing other walled cities in other parts of the world seems to give an opportunity for comparison. "Where St. Peter Claver spent much of his time was in Cartagena, another walled city. It's like Charleston, very historic. Like Charleston, there is an emphasis on preservation. You marvel at some of the buildings and walls dating back centuries. I have been to Rome on several occasions, where preservation and archaeology are commonplace. In addition to religious pilgrimages, so many academicians travel to Rome to study the ruins. Coming back here, you have to really appreciate what Mayor Joe Riley has done, along with others who saw the benefit of aggressive preservation. Charleston is a living museum.

"Downtown has so much of what I knew growing up, and yet it has so much more that has been restored or even added in good taste. The peninsula in some ways is better, but I am concerned about the displacement of native Charlestonians. That's why I still live there."

McFarland has come a long way from the Wraggsborough housing project but is geographically close to that beginning. He has seen the strife, the racial tension and the melding of cultures. He could be considered one of a few true pioneers of the time of integration within what were the brittle dry twigs of a potential community firestorm. Mostly, he is considered by everything he represents—faith, justice, family and the solid values that his mother advocated years earlier. He is that magic seventh child, after all.

Media Moments

NANCY MACE

S cientist Alfred Nobel invented dynamite in the mid-nineteenth century. Hedy Lamarr was one of Hollywood's great actresses of the 1930s and 1940s. Babe Ruth pitched the Boston Red Sox to the 1918 World Series title. In each case, these celebrities were known for something much greater than their early and seemingly defining notoriety.

Is a lifetime demarcated by the flash of a luminous moment? Inside the parenthetical brackets belong the insights but not the completed journey of the traveler. The myopic look at the moment has mitigated and marginalized many greater lives.

Alfred Nobel left his fortune to the furtherance of his passion: world peace. Hedy Lamarr, demure and sexy, found the right algorithms to discover the patterns of radio wave frequency hopping. That premise became the basis for today's Wi-Fi and Bluetooth technologies. The Sultan of Swat, George Herman Ruth, changed an entire sport with his prodigious ability at hitting the home run.

Enter Nancy Mace.

Those not familiar with this energetic and creative dynamo would point to an early career event—perhaps a trivia answer—to define her. She became the very first female graduate of The Citadel, thwarting nearly 150 years of tradition closeted in its former existence as an all-male military college. No woman could have done it better. But to Mace, it's a line on her résumé that she does not view as anything more than what it is: a statistic. She is more than that. Much more.

A striking and shrewd green-eyed brunette, she is the personable progeny of two incredible parents, each endowed with a deep well of originality. Her husband, Curtis Jackson, is a success in his own right, in the precarious technology world that has freckled the face of nearly two decades. Her children, Miles and Elli (Ellison), are nurtured from one of the most unique and creative child cultivation processes imaginable. They are the Mace and Jacksons' properly mannered and favorably fortunate offspring.

Mace is one of four siblings, the third daughter who was anything but conventional. "I was the rogue child. I raged against authority. I was anti-everything. So my expected course of adherence and discipline at The Citadel was not a given at all. But I found out a lot about myself. Curtis says that I am still undisciplined, but I find that I can be very disciplined when motivated. I have an intense inner drive when I want to get something done."

Her dad, Emory Mace, a retired army brigadier general and a part of The Citadel's long gray line (class of 1963), is the college's most decorated living alumnus. His two tours of duty in Vietnam were highlighted by his uncommon bravery in the face of close enemy fire. He saved the lives of three soldiers in two separate instances and risked his own life in the performance of other maneuvers to save his battle-riddled company. Yet among his most amazing escapades, there is no merit badge applicable. That's because there was no mission other than to retrieve his Citadel ring under the cloak of darkness in the middle of the previous day's harsh firefight—in the bog of a rice paddy, no less! The ring was in a foot of water. The enemy had taken the ground and was in the immediate proximity. He found the ring and returned to his troops. Nancy states: "Who else but my dad would take that kind of risk? In fact, who would poach alligators to pay their college tuition? Crazy, huh? He did that, too. He always operated on a 'risk-reward' basis, but the risks were wild. Dad always had that side of him, the wild streak. In a way, I have a little bit of that from him.

"Dad always exhibited a veritable work ethic. I feel I have that going—especially when I have my mind made up on something."

Meeting Anne Mace, the diminutive and enthusiastic mother of the Mace clan, one would easily see the connection to daughter Nancy. She has a strong presence and a glare of expected clairvoyance. She is a step ahead of the thought you left behind: "From Mom, I seem to have gotten her debating skill. She is so very well versed in many subjects. She's a conversationalist, while Dad is more of a storyteller. Mom is also driven and independent. So I have a touch of that, too. In the business I'm in, that's a must."

She has a Sam's Club lifetime supply of drive and independence. It was a forklift delivery on multiple pallets loaded at birth. Her demeanor is the soft side of femininity. Yet therein emanates a casual sequence of underlying intensity. It builds. She is ready to go and aching to achieve. Her confidence exudes.

"I was rebellious and undisciplined. So, coming to The Citadel in 1996 was good for me. I needed The Citadel," Mace intimated. "Technically, I was a high school dropout. Halfway through my junior year at Stratford High School, I went to my parents and told them I was quitting school. There were a number of reasons. They, at first, resisted. But I persisted by explaining that the process for me was not effective. I could do well enough, but I was not at all focused. Some of the work was so redundant to me, and in addition, I was having other student-related issues. There was one kid there that stalked and threatened me. It was scary. So, I home-schooled the remainder of my junior year. I then took a few courses at Trident Technical College, which my school district credited toward the two credits I needed to finish school. I took my ACT and did well enough to get accepted into college."

The path into The Citadel's vaunted plebe system and through three academic years assisted in her discipline, direction and maturity. She finished the required curriculum and was handed her diploma by her dad—in an emotional and ceremonious tradition. She graduated magna cum laude—with highest honors. Despite the early graduation in 1999, she is proud to be a member of The Citadel's class of 2000 and remains inspired by those associations buoyed by classmates who are and were supportive.

In time, Mace focused her career to the digital explosion of the media world. Electronic media has changed the paradigm, and Mace saw the opportunities.

She and former South Carolina governor Mark Sanford's press secretary Will Folks own the provocative site FITSNEWS.com. Their self-description gives a range of popular interest.

"Unfair and imbalanced," FITS covers "politics, sports, pop culture and everything in between with a simple commitment to the truth and to keeping it real."[98]

But there is more. The Mace Group, LLC, is a burgeoning force in the world of political campaign strategies and support. The entrepreneurial

Nancy Mace has acomplished much more than changing a college. She has changed the world around her. *Courtesy of Curtis Jackson.*

Mace emerges here. She has assembled resources to support political campaigns and assist in public relations, fundraising and polling information. They have strategists, social media gurus, designers and crisis communications experts.[99] Her firm also works with small businesses and public-traded entities.

There is more. Mace's text messages are on the unlimited plan. She and two others began Citizen Hill, a Facebook application program to stream town hall meetings. It will prove to be an invaluable tool for those politicians, elected officials, industry leaders and college presidents to instantaneously touch their constituencies.

As if Mace were not busy enough, she has joined forces with local campaign veteran Andrew Boucher to offer professional campaign services for higher-level national candidates. Boucher served as national political director for former Pennsylvania senator Rick Santorum's Republican presidential bid.

"Pay attention: Nancy Mace will be at the forefront of the new economy for decades to come. She has established a tremendous and well-earned reputation for cutting-edge creativity and professionalism, and it is no wonder she is thriving in an industry where one's reputation is the most important asset an entrepreneur can have," Boucher stated.

So one would guess her priority would be placed within the web and political arena. Not so. She has a passionate devotion to family.

"Curtis and I believe in the value of what some might call extreme parenting…or sometimes referred to as 'attachment parenting.' It gives the children such positive psychological advantages and security. It's not often you see people carrying their babies on their bodies in a wrap," Mace detailed.

"It is literally the idea of spending those first three years or so in an attached way to nurture your child's physical and psychological growth. When they're babies, you literally have the child on your hip as much as they need to be. Both parents participate. You have them in bed with you until they start into their own bed, when they are ready, usually between the ages of three and five. You wear your children! You nurse longer, for two or three years. I call it a 'granola' way of parenting. From this close association you receive such positive results. They, ironically, become very independent and more confident in themselves. The process is so positive, and my husband, Curtis, could not be a better partner to have. Just last Saturday, I was gone for fourteen hours with my work. Curtis was there. He is a great father."

Mace continued: "During the week, when Curtis has his nine-to-five set of hours, I have them [the kids]—mostly. I get help from my parents or a sitter now. But the nature of what I do requires I have a very flexible schedule. It may have me out to some political events, especially in the early evening. I also may have events like last Saturday—when I had to be gone all day. The children get our focus. And you know that we, as parents, also get so much positive out of the experience."

These attentive parents recently built a home in the Lowcountry. They see Charleston as an optimum place to raise Miles and Elli. "We came from Atlanta, and there were some great advantages to being in a bigger city. But for us, Charleston seems perfect. My dad is originally from Hampton [South Carolina], and they live in Goose Creek. Charleston has such neat little locally owned restaurants and shops. The pace here is slower. I always felt that home is where your feet are, but Charleston, to me—and to Curtis—appears to be the best place for our children to grow, attend school and make friends.

"We have found so much here, and we enjoy the experience. Our perfect day is a Sunday. It's family day. Curtis and I love to have a great brunch. We love being outdoors with the kids. The beach is always a favorite. Oh, and I love to eat truffle fries. You can get those here. Coleman Public House might have the best ones. A place the kids love is Kilwin's on Market. They'll tell you the caramel apple is the best. There are so many great places to discover."

She's an adventurer. She recommended Bakehouse Bakery Café at 160 Meeting Street for coffee and an interview. She enjoys their chai tea latte. She tried the "everything" bagel. She noted other mentoring friends who frequent Bakehouse, like Mallory and Elizabeth Factor. In the process, Elizabeth Factor arrived. The ladies greeted each other warmly. They are part of the raging fire of brilliant femininity that has enriched and enraptured Charleston.

Would Mace make a great political candidate? She does have succinct views. She has a perspective rooted in a mostly libertarian ideology. She believes strongly in constitutional rights and the benefit of a free market economy. She expects government to spend at or below the rate that money comes in. She detests the "good ole boy" politics sometimes seen in southern legislative circles. "We're a strong 'red state' here in South Carolina, yet policies do not reflect that. When revenue is coming in at a 5 percent increase, you cannot raise the budget by 12 percent. We seem to be at the top of all of the bad lists and bottom of the good ones. So it may be a matter of finding the right people to get this turned around—true conservatives. I can help that process with what I do. Do I want to run for anything? I don't see me doing that."

The consideration may not always infer that the political door is closed. Mace is young. Her energy and eloquence match the description of what she would find in another potential candidate to extol and support. Don't rule her out. Ever.

Mace circulates. She is the maestro at her own concert. She knows exactly when to bring in the string section. The cello is closer than the trombones, but the music is still the main product. She has contacts all over the place.

"I feel that there are people essential to my progress and that there have been other key influences that have helped me along the way," she said. "For instance, Dr. Barbara Zaremba was invaluable to me at The Citadel. She was there for me. She passed away."

Dr. Zaremba died in May 2009.[100] After retiring from The Citadel, she became a private practice educational consultant in Charleston.

"I also had people I considered mentors, but they were more like cheerleaders. Tandy Rice in Nashville and Allison Dean Love in Columbia were certainly part of that. My classmates in the Regimental Band from The Citadel class of 2000 were so very supportive. They included me," Mace reminisced.

Being overly scrutinized at The Citadel was not easy. She saw much. The twenty-four-seven military college world had darker sides. Some she expected. Some she didn't.

"There was harassment of every type, but I was mentally prepared. Some was just immaturity; some was systemic in the mid-'90s. I learned that fair and equal were never the same things. For instance, the haircut standards made no sense for women when I was there. That's changed since. I was ordered to thin my hair because I have naturally thick hair. I know of no male cadet that was made to thin his hair. I also didn't like to see the female cadets buy into the 'good ole boy' attitude. Girls should be proud of who they are and not do things to try to be accepted by good ole boys. But the entire experience was just what I needed and at the time I needed it. Being a rebellious young lady, it changed me to a person well prepared for responsibility and achievement."

Mace smiled. She reflected the thought of her youthful perseverance and her personal goal of completion. Going forward, those qualities are more of what defines her.

Defining Nancy Mace will take a full lifetime and perhaps more. Her world is in front of her. She is courteous but direct; not content with the status quo or even the idea of status. She presents a wide array of interest to a wider audience—the city, the state and the nation. She keeps current on news, political theory and the elements that make media impressions—from Twitter to blogs to electronic town hall meetings. It is her world to seek and secure. She will define what course and degree of collaboration her own life will require to meet her threshold of meaning.

Indeed, the dynamite did not define Alfred Nobel.

Finding the Center of a Soul

Reverend Danny Massie

There is a heritage built of toil that comes from Mississippi. They are so much like us but perhaps have the subtlest of differences. It would be appropriate to describe the perspective of a native Mississippian as a charmed soul birthed in pragmatism. There are exquisite examples.

The singer Jimmy Buffett is from Pascagoula. Faith Hill grew up in a small town appropriately named Star. Elvis Presley hailed from Tupelo. James Earl Jones, the actor and voice of Darth Vader, was born in Arkabutla. Politician Trent Lott is from Grenada. Oprah Winfrey is from Kosciusko. Playwright Tennessee Williams, as it turns out, is not from Tennessee at all. He was born in Columbus, Mississippi. William Faulkner, one of the great southern authors, was born in New Albany. Others? John Grisham was born in Southaven, Eudora Welty in Jackson. It could reasonably be argued that Mississippians put the "person" in personality.

More proof? NFL greats Walter Payton, Jerry Rice and Bret Favre were all born there. They are statistically the best running back ever, the best receiver ever and the best quarterback ever. Others from the Magnolia State include historian Shelby Foote and musicians Tammy Wynette, Percy Sledge, LeAnn Rimes, Britney Spears and B.B. King. There are unique names of people and small towns. Conway Twitty was from a place named Friars Point. You know Diddley? Bo Diddley was born in McComb. Stella Stevens, Haley Barbour and Jerry Clower were from Yazoo City. Jefferson Davis (Warren County) and Nathan Bedford Forrest (Hernando) gave the state some historically compelling names.

Newscaster Robin Roberts is from Pass Christian. Actor Morgan Freeman was born in Charleston. Not this one—that one over in Mississippi.

Understanding the foundation of Mississippians would help one to appreciate Reverend Danny Massie, the pastor of First Scots Presbyterian Church. He's from Canton, Mississippi. His story is one that touches at the heartstrings of the entire community.

Dr. Massie's historical church dates to 1814. The original church on the site burned down. The congregation began in 1731 with an initial church building erected in 1734.

Dr. Massie decided as a young teen to join the ministry. He has shared the story to encourage others. "My minister and mentor, Dick Harbison, the young, dynamic pastor, encouraged me and supported me in these efforts, asking me to assist in the evening services at the church from time to time. He had become my hero, my mentor, and I held him in the highest esteem. A graduate of Washington and Lee and Union Theological Seminary in Virginia, a Rotary scholar who studied at St. Andrews University in Scotland and a native Mississippian himself, he came to our church right out of seminary and was there during my formative years of junior high and high school. I fell in love with his family, a pretty young wife and three precious children whom I babysat from time to time.[101]

"When I was in junior high and high school, I came to understand that there was not only a community connected to the cross, but there was also A CHOICE, A COMMITMENT ATTACHED TO THE CROSS. Of course, as Presbyterians, we speak a great deal about God's choosing of the elect. From Abraham on, the scriptures speak of God's choosing the unlikely, the ill prepared, the weak, the unqualified to serve his purposes. So as a young Presbyterian in love with the church, I relished in the thought of being among the elect, the chosen, if you will. But some might even say the 'Frozen Chosen.' But in my teenage years, I came to realize that the chosen must make choices of their own. Joshua instructed the Israelites before entering the land of Canaan, 'Choose this day who you will serve... as for me and my house we will serve the Lord.'"

Massie concluded, "So it is that the God who chooses us, undeserving though we may be, invites us to make a reciprocal choice ourselves. We must choose God. We must choose whom we will serve and how we will serve."

And serve he did. An unassuming yet engaging gentleman, Massie sports a healthy crop of gray locks, truthful blue eyes and a broad farmer's

The collection of humorous epitaphs is but one of the facets of Reverend Dr. Danny Massie's wide personality. *Courtesy of the* Post & Courier.

grin. He is the advising uncle who tells you you should eat more oatmeal and the old-timey doctor who spends a few extra minutes with you asking about your family. His smile is natural, as if he were looking for an audience to tell a wonderful homespun story. His accent is right. It fits everything else about him. He and his wife have four children and six grandchildren.

His reputation from the pulpit is that one should be prepared to be entertained in his own brand of self-deprecating humor. Humor defines the holy man.

"Humor is part and parcel of the Christian faith. Humor helps you relate to people if you have the ability to laugh at yourself. Comedians, especially stand-up comics, sometimes mesmerize me.

"I guess I had fantasized about doing some stand-up comedy over the years. I like to make people laugh and enjoy life. I like when people lay their troubles down and just relax and enjoy life. A little humor keeps everything else balanced. I believe humor is essential. Even Jesus used humor."

"Why do you look at the speck of sawdust in your brother's eye and pay no attention to the log in your own eye?" The passage is from the Book of Matthew, Chapter 7, Verse 3.

It illustrates that Christ used unexpected humor to make a point. Dr. Massie sees the verse as an insight to Christ being engaged in moments that would humor his audience.

To that end, the reverend has had a lifelong love of seeking gravestone humor. Even the First Scots churchyard has dozens of graves predating 1800. The humor that permeates life even pervades death. He offered several examples: "In Burlington, Vermont, there appears on a gravestone, whether she intended it this way or not:

She lived with her husband for fifty years,
And died in confident hope of a better life.

"Ernest Hemingway's tombstone reads:

Pardon me for not getting up!

"A gravestone in Aberdeen, Scotland, reads:

Here lies Martin Elmerod.
Have mercy on my soul, good God
As I would do were I Lord God
And you were Martin Elmerod.

"A memorial in the north of England I saw when visiting there said:

GOD GRANT THAT I MAY FISH
UNTIL MY DYING DAY
AND WHEN IT COMES TO MY LAST CAST
I HUMBLY PRAY
WHEN IN THE LORD'S SAFE LANDING NET
I'M PEACEFULLY ASLEEP
THAT IN HIS MERCY
I BE JUDGED AS GOOD ENOUGH to keep."

The odd collection of epitaphs Reverend Massie began years ago gave more material for his largely entertained congregations to enjoy. Massie has even written a touching epitaph for someone else. It was for his mother-in-law, Bennie Dumas Morrison, whom he deeply admired. She was from Prentiss, Mississippi:

She lived and loved and laughed
And helped others to do the same.

Dr. Massie, the Charleston spiritual leader, found his own profound belief in people through other baptisms that were anointed in the church's sacristy. He tells a compelling tale of his own birth of faith. "To provide a little background: My family struggled with some weighty matters during my childhood and youth. My mother, who was as pretty and intelligent as any women I have ever met, suffered terribly during all of those years with severe depression. Hospitalized in the state mental hospital on several occasions, she was plagued by this malady, and in those years there were few psychotropic medicines available for treatment. My father did not have sufficient financial resources to care for my mother, and so we were always in great debt. My father was too proud to declare bankruptcy and lost the business that he had loved and founded years before. My grandmother moved into our modest little home to help care for my brother and me. My father tried to drown his sorrows and disappointments in alcohol, which only added to our desperate plight.[102]

"And yet, something wonderful, even transformational, occurred in the midst of this misery. Members of our little congregation, Sunday school teachers, youth workers, Cub Scout leaders, baseball coaches stepped forward to become caregivers and to provide a network of support at work for my family and especially for my brother and me. They went out of their way over many years to befriend us and encourage us. They paid for us to attend church camps and conferences, which we could never have afforded. Our neighbor and one of my Sunday school teachers, Mr. Hodges, drove us to Sunday school and back when my parents were incapable of doing that. Another Sunday school teacher took a special interest in me and saw to it that each week I had memorized Bible lessons to recite in class. She had her husband give me a job as a teenager in his warehouse."

Spiraling staircases have made great use of limited space within the pursuit of ascent. They are seen in Charleston, and elsewhere, as part of church steeples, cotillion towers, lighthouses, fire escapes and even rooftop cupolas. Spirals also go downward from the top. Dr. Massie told the most personal story of how far they go.

He initially told the story from the altar as pastor of the First Presbyterian Church of Kingsport, Tennessee. It was done to illustrate the universality of need in the interim between two Habitat for Humanity homebuilding projects the congregation had adopted. Dr. Massie wanted to inspire the second, and though it was difficult to relate something so personal, he did so to benefit the cause.

Growing up in 1950s semi-rural Mississippi, Dr. Massie's father owned a seed-and-feed store that aligned itself with the farming community of Madison County. His business was steady enough to build a new house. He had taken it upon himself to craft a hand-hewn cedar fireplace mantel. The Massie family excitedly moved in when the house was completed. Within a year, the farm business of the area swooned into economic misery. Dr. Massie's father had generously extended account credit to the weary farmers, but the struggles became too great for the farmers to repay. Mr. Massie lost his store as a result. They lost their home, too. Young Danny Massie was only in the first grade. When they left the house for the last time, he asked his father if they could at least keep the cedar mantel he had built himself. His father had to explain that it was no longer his to keep.

The Massies moved into a small two-bedroom apartment. Danny slept in the same bed with his brother and later had to share that room with his grandmother, who had moved in. The apartment was old and dank with roaches and rodents. "A spark went out of my mother's and father's lives with the loss of our home. Although he never said so, I am sure the move was accompanied by a loss of much self-esteem, a sense of failure and the pain of embarrassment—none of which was warranted, but all of which was terribly real. My own feelings must have been but a dim reflection of what my parents were going through, but I was embarrassed to have friends come over to our place. I was afraid they might count the beds and realize there were not enough of them. Or the roaches might come out of their hiding places, or they might see my mother weeping or her still in her bathrobe. Or my father might come home having had too much to drink—a problem that was growing since he had lost his business, his home and, I am sure, his hopes.[103]

"Those were painful and difficult days; from which we later emerged by the grace of God, but not without individual and family scars. And not without memories imprinted indelibly on our minds about what effect inferior living conditions can have on both parents and children. I could not share this story without emotion and a few tears. But the congregation could not have been more supportive or responsive—and soon the money was in hand to complete our second Habitat house."[104]

Dr. Massie never forgot those times. The hardships gave him a poignant view of life's realities for himself as well as others. He knew the aspect and the effect. "Following the worship service that day—I was to learn later—friends in the congregation took upon themselves a secret, generous and loving project. They contacted the pastor of my home church in Canton and, through a review of the tax records, located where our home had been. They asked the current resident, James Fox, the son of the family that had bought the home from us, whether the mantel was still in the house and if it would be possible to buy it. It turned out that the mantel had been sitting in a storage room for nearly forty years, simply gathering dust. Fox could not recall the mantel being in the home; apparently his parents had removed it since its rustic style did not fit their tastes. He also said he never had understood why they had not disposed of the mantel, as his wife had requested on many occasions. My friend asking about the mantel said that he knew why they hadn't—there must have been a purpose behind the preservation of that mantel.[105]

"The house owner, Fox, not only generously donated the mantel, but he also arranged to have it shipped to Kingsport. At the close of our morning service on June 28, 1992, my son and one of the friends involved in the project marched down the center aisle of the church carrying the mantel, which weighed over one hundred pounds. Forty years had passed since I had last seen my father's mantel, when I stood with him in our living room that last time. And now it was being carried down the aisle of my church as a miraculous and loving gesture. It was no less beautiful than I remembered and even more valuable. Not only did the congregation present me with the mantel, but they announced that they had raised more than $3,000 to contribute toward a home renovation project in Madison County, Mississippi, in honor of my mother and father."[106]

Redemption! A restored soul! It brings the spiral upward again—a surge of happiness brought on by the emergence of goodness in others. An earthly salvation!

Dr. Massie's qualifications for the exigencies of everyday life are credentials forged in experience. He has been able to see the realities with the calm of a blue tick hound in repose.

The smiling reverend has extended his considerable oratorical—and writing—skills well beyond the pews of the Meeting Street landmark.

Proud to be an American? So is Reverend Dr. Daniel W. Massie. His sermon in the spring of 2009 on the subject—within the associative context of church "palpitations"—went viral:

Freedom was God's idea before it was man's. From the very beginning, from Eden on if you would, our connection to the Creator was not a chain or a cage but a willing bond of love and gratitude. The relationship between the Creator was characterized by freedom and based on trust. Adam was free to obey or disobey God, but he was not free to escape the consequences of his decision. This arrangement entailed tremendous risk on the Lord's part, because the risk of freedom is the bondage of sin. If we are truly free, then we are free also to become enslaved. And yet, it is not God who enslaves us. Rather, when we freely choose to violate the will and the ways of God and to discard the truths of God for the opinions of man, we will discover new, or rediscover, old forms of bondage.

Everybody serves somebody, and if it is not the living God that we serve, then we will serve a God of our own making and design. Yet if we do serve the living God, then we will not be afraid to challenge or confront those lesser gods that vie for our allegiance and threaten our liberty.

At its best, America has cherished a belief in freedom for all people, and this belief arises from our spiritual heritage. Freedom is a foundation truth that originates not with constitution, nor the abstract philosophical notions, but with the faith that founded and fuels this free republic. In 1789, the year our Constitution was ratified by the states, the second president of the United States, John Adams, wrote: 'Our constitution was designed for a moral and religious people. It is wholly inadequate for the government of any other.' Now some might challenge that statement, and many do today, but there remain many of us who hold to it still. And that is precisely why I am so concerned about freedom's future in this country. If we choose to abandon the moral and spiritual principles that brought about our existence, then our liberties as a people will eventually be lost. And why is that?

To begin with, history reveals that liberty and democracy tend to be short-lived in nations or societies where divine truth and Judeo-Christian values are either ignored or dismissed. This is because reason alone, philosophical principles alone, however noble they may be, cannot produce truth nor provide the foundation upon which liberty is built. As I indicated earlier, the Romans came to a point where they were more interested in their personal comforts than in their individual responsibilities. It was only a matter of time before they desired freedom from responsibility more than freedom for responsibility. As a result, the price of freedom came to be regarded as too great a price to pay, and the Romans increasingly looked to the state to provide or to require what they were unwilling or unable to provide for themselves. We would do well to remember this as a people for it seems we increasingly look to our local, state and federal governments in a paternalistic way to do for us what we are simply unwilling to do for ourselves. And yet there are always hidden costs and unexpected obligations attached to our expected entitlements and services.

There is simply no public freedom apart from individual responsibility. The more we look to the state to do for us what we are incapable of doing for ourselves, the more our personal liberties are jeopardized. The more power we transfer to the state, the less power we retain as individuals and the more difficult it is to reclaim what has been given away.[107]

Other excerpts from this introspective warning of factors that would decimate or even eliminate freedom in America were repeated, reprinted and retold to persons well outside the great harbor that sustains us. Dr. Massie had reached the heart and consciousness of a great many with the insight of a visionary. He has been cited across communities outside of ours.

His historic church is one of a handful of the oldest church structures on the peninsula. The congregation predates the country by more than forty years. The distinctively Scottish markings and the architecture, presumed to have been copied from a Baltimore church designed by Benjamin Latrobe, render the church an imposing street presence. To be sure, there were Scottish Presbyterians in Charleston from the beginning (1670), but they had no formal congregation separate of the English until a generation later. The Anglicans (Episcopalians) began the two most photographed churches of Charleston—St. Michael's and St. Philip's—where the Presbyterians assimilated for a time. There were other early Presbyterian congregations as the colony grew.

As in the times of yore, the sentiment of Dr. Massie has been to deliver messages that may be positive to most and sometimes pungent to others. The act of standing in front of hundreds to deliver a biblical message and its modern meaning has its drawbacks.

"I can remember repeating a topical message that had the word 'hell' in it. A lady, after the service, made a point to tell me the word was inappropriate. I respected that. What I have come to respect is the extraordinary graciousness of the Charleston community. It is unlike most others. We can disagree without being disagreeable. And you know what? I welcome another's point of view. It's healthy in religion as well as in politics.

"This is the most beautiful city in America. But with it you get some understandable difficulty in getting something passed. We went through that at First Scots. You have a maddening system here. You have the Board of Architectural Review, the Neighborhood Association, the Zoning Board, the Historic Charleston and the Preservation Society groups to contend. But the effect is that you have a city that everyone is proud to show off. There is so much to do here. So many people want to come and visit me here. We've lived in places where people didn't come unless they felt they had to! And I don't know how many times I've gotten something in the mail from somewhere else that more or less said, 'I'm moving to Charleston. Can you help me find a job?'"

The trend of so many young people being un-churched has been part of the challenge of traditional churches nationally and worldwide. Dr.

Massie sees it as a cycle: "Young people are brought up in one faith, then marry and sometimes move away. They spend time out of churches with the notion that their 'personal church' and peace with God is at the beach or on a mountaintop. But they don't take time to honor and understand God's teaching as part of their routine. It sometimes takes the birth of children to bring them back to church, if they come back at all. I always try to get young people to look at other churches. They may find something that suits them better somewhere else, but it is most important to come back somewhere, to be in a pew on Sunday. I don't believe that Christian followers have to have a certain label, they just need to love Christ."

Reverend Dr. Danny Massie, the humorist and the pragmatically charmed soul from Mississippi, invites all to his most interesting topical sermons each Sunday. Prepare to be entertained!

Arrival

WARREN PEPER

The wind had to blow somewhere. For Warren Peper, he remembers his North Charleston neighborhood near Park Circle where it seemed that the wind always blew in the same direction. It was the bearing that brought the obnoxious and disgusting fumes of the Charleston Paper Mill to his driveway.

"You could never get used to that curious white smoke," Peper recalled. "That smell was the immediate reminder of home to me as a teenager."

Peper came to Charleston at the end of a journey, that of his father's military commitment as a navy corpsman. His father became a Baptist minister and founded, with others through a progression of ministries, the mega assemblage of Northwoods Baptist Church. His father's late-career commitment meant the young Peper would have the benefit of uninterrupted high school and college periods for a well-adjusted entry into adult life. That suited him well because of his love of sport, especially basketball. His sojourn at North Charleston High School brought him other accoutrements: a college basketball scholarship, a bevy of lifelong friends and his wife, Judy. Sweethearts since high school, they were married in 1974.

"I was raised in a blue-collar working-class neighborhood. There was the navy yard, GARCO [General Asbestos Rubber Company] and, of course, that paper mill. Everybody seemed to be on a shift. There were times that you really couldn't move around in North Charleston. But the families all knew each other, and the playgrounds had fantastic coaches and athletes. There was definitely a sense of personal responsibility growing up in the more industrial environment we had back then. There were trains running through everywhere and the constant takeoffs and landings at the Charleston Air Force Base."

Peper, one of the finer ball-handling guards to come out of the metropolitan area, accepted the opportunity to play basketball at the newly ordained Baptist College of Charleston (opened in 1964). The college began as an affiliation with the South Carolina Baptist Convention. Peper played ball there from 1970 to 1974. The left-hander also displayed a knack for hitting deft bank shots when left open. Upon graduation, Peper transitioned to the media. His personable demeanor, innate humor and warm smile made him a natural for the camera.

The all-American story could have reached all of America. But Peper stayed in Charleston. He went to work after college at the local CBS affiliate, WCSC Channel 5 television.

"Carroll Godwin took a chance on hiring me. I had done an internship at Channel 2, and Red Evans, their news director at the time, had recommended me. Channel 5 was looking for help, and I started there the day after I graduated from Baptist College [now Charleston Southern University]. It was learning on the fly. Live television was like that then. You grabbed pieces of this and that and soaked up as much as you could. Eventually, I became a fill-in for sports. This worked for me because I loved sports, and I was much more familiar with the subject matter."

Peper did sports at Channel 5 for nearly thirty-one years. During that time, his popularity soared. There were murmurings of larger markets and bigger contracts offered to the locally iconic journalist. But Peper was committed to his wife, his family and the community that welled inside of him as his "home." Peper won Emmy Awards both as a sportscaster and as part of the news team at Channel 5 reporting the aftermath of Hurricane Hugo in late September 1989. During that most difficult time of recovery, it seemed that Peper worked multiple shifts to get the news and information to the Lowcountry. There were reports on the availability of supplies, road closings, shelter needs and safe drinking water. As the power trucks took weeks to get homes back on the "grid," Peper and company kept the spirit of community at the forefront. He could be heard on both radio and television.

Within the framework of his experience, he was able to cover major sporting events like the NCAA Final Four, the Masters and the Darlington 500. Through the years, Peper appeared in bit parts of movies that were shot in Charleston and once was even used in Hollywood in a walk-on role

A journalist well known among Charlestonians, Peper gives an insight on his Charleston experiences. *Courtesy of the* Post & Courier.

of a soap opera. Life imitates art. Everybody knew Warren Peper. The better career offers were there. Peper stayed with those he knew.

Irony bites through iron: "It was in 2004 that the station sold to other investors. My contract was up for renewal. They could hire new young people much cheaper. That appealed to the bottom line and would assist the station in squeezing out every dollar of profit. So, in a flash, I was expendable. My contract was not renewed. So, after thirty-one years, I guess you could say I was put out to pasture. I was literally on the street."

The loyalty he espoused was inconsequential to the bottom line. The group that bought the station did flip it to yet another buyer. Peper was, at the age of fifty-four, looking for new employment in a very constricted area of expertise: local television reporting.

A year later, Peper signed on with WCBD Channel 2. He was back on the correct side of the camera. At the height of the recession in 2008, Peper was laid off as his employers cited sagging revenues. But fortunately, Dan Herres, the president of the Evening Post Newspaper Group, and Cathy Wilkerson, the paper's vice-president, had other plans: "They didn't know what they wanted to do with me, but they told me they wanted me, and at that point, it was nice to be wanted." He was named to the post of multimedia producer. He produces videos on the website. He hosts a TV show and makes public appearances on behalf of the newspaper. He eventually was asked to write a weekly column, which he calls "I'm Just Sayin'."

The Post and Courier Building on Columbus Street has few windows on the first floor. The backdrop of Peper's private office on the second floor is the peninsula of Charleston, a view to the southeast. The spire-filled vista reminds one of the Holy City's naming inspiration. "I like it here. They are so nice to me. Some of the younger people call me 'Mr. Peper' as if I was some vestige of a past period of history. I suppose some of them are young enough to know very little of my background. Hey, that's okay. I'm fine with this opportunity, and I want to make the most of it. Writing columns is new for me, but I am able to do something I enjoy. I get to express myself as opposed to reporting an event.

"Walking through the newsroom, there are no teletypes clicking along like I always pictured. The constant phones ringing like we saw in the movies is not there either. There is nobody here I know of named 'Scoop.'"

Peper chuckled. "It is really a peaceful place to work."

He has gotten to see his children grow. He and Judy raised three: Mark, Brad and Anna. All have finished college—Mark at Wofford, Brad at South Carolina and Anna at Georgia Southern. Mark is a local attorney. Brad just graduated from MUSC dental school, and Anna works in Statesboro, Georgia.

"They had the benefit of Judy. I had unusual hours most of my career, so the credit for their academic work and completion of college should be because of the structure Judy was able to implement," Peper stated. "Being a father is a role that requires that you be the best you can be. You have to provide, and you have to lead. Now it's cool to watch my children become their own people."

Being a friend has its rewards, as well. There have been personalities Peper recalled that made a difference. "Charlie Hall. Wonderful man. I had a great relationship with Charlie. We were at opposite ends of the news desk. We often shared moments and our mutual love of Charleston. I was in great admiration of the way he carried himself. Early in my career, Charlie told me that he did not like sports especially, but he really liked the way that

I reported sports. He said that I made sports 'fun.' Coming from this great professional, it was the best compliment you could imagine.

"I remember Charlie telling me that other opportunities would come along and that I would not have to chase them. He had a profound impact on me. They [the station] used to run these little surveys for the local media. At some point their survey said that my popularity had surpassed Charlie Hall. Heck, I was embarrassed. This bowled me over."

Peper was not always just news, weather and sports. He became the news in the weathering of sports.

"I was able to play basketball until I was fifty without breaking anything. I did have that one bad ankle sprain," he winked.

In the mid-'90s, routine tests spotted a benign tumor on his lung. He went through surgery and happily returned to the sports desk.

"That was a scary time for me. In a way, it brought me back to some realities. We're only here briefly." Peper sensed that he would find another sport. He loved golf.

"I had played golf as an athlete, not as a golfer," he explained. "So here I was fifty, no experience, no lessons and very little time devoted. I decided to play at a competition level. I got better. I entered the City of Charleston Senior Amateur when I was fifty-three or fifty-four. I was nine shots back with one round to play. I got pumped up to try and become the low amateur among the membership at the Muni [Charleston Municipal Golf Club]. I started making a few shots and got in with a sixty-eight, three under par."

Lurking behind Peper were several veteran amateurs with local golf pedigrees. Tommy Ford and Bubba Hightower were in the final group, presumably matching each other shot for shot, trying to come home as champion.

"There were no scoreboards. I got word in the clubhouse that Ford was struggling. Doggone it if Bubba wasn't having trouble out there, too. This was the first amateur tournament I had really been near the lead, and when they came in with scores in the high seventies, I won. I was elated. I tried to call Judy. Then I called Mark and Brad. I was so genuinely excited. Well, it so happened that the tournament was in early December, and I was in the town of Mount Pleasant parade that same evening. I'm riding along the route waving to the kids when I see Tommy Ford on the sidewalk. Ford doesn't miss the opportunity. He yells, 'Hey, Champ! Way to go!'

"Where else could you find that camaraderie among competitors?" Peper asked rhetorically.

"There is a charm about this place [Charleston] that makes it extra unique," Peper intoned while glancing at the vista of the rooftops. "I was not born here. I was certainly not privileged by any stretch. I was accidentally connected. But if I ever left here, I would say this was home."

Peper continued a stream of thought: "It was in October 2004, just a couple months after I lost my job at Channel 5. I was reeling. Some folks from North Charleston wanted me to be the grand marshal of their Christmas parade. Mayor Keith Summey insisted that I be there. I sheepishly said, 'Have you not heard? I'm not really anybody, anymore.' You know what they said? 'You'll always be somebody to us.' It made me extremely grateful to those folks. I knew, no matter what, North Charleston wouldn't forget me. That was an uplifting boost when I most needed it.

"You know, sometimes when my kids were younger, we'd walk downtown. The kids would protest that I was out walking them down the old streets again. The downtown area is so walkable and interesting. You'd see something old and curious at every turn. I'd always sneak a peek down the alleyways or into someone's garden. I loved walking on King Street. There is no other street quite like it anywhere. And if I had friends here from off, I'd like to show them that 'hat guy' at the corner of Church and Broad. There's a cartoon-looking character painted on a wall that is made up of every kind of hat. You can't find that anywhere else but in Charleston.

"It's those little things we know about Charleston that make us the hosts. Others come here and feel that we are charmed because we live here year-round. We should never let them know anything different. It is ours to share."

The smell has changed to brisk sea breezes. Illinois-based KapStone Paper and Packaging Corporation recently purchased the Charleston Paper Mill (2011). There remains some minor degree of smell rendered by the manufacturing process there. But the odorous days of the 1970s are long gone.

Other nuances to the community have ensued. The colleges are bigger and more vibrant. The playgrounds are nicer, with safer equipment and more lighting. The local shops are stocked with local merchandise. The coffee shops have popped up on every block, it seems. The airport is in expansion mode. The magazines give directions to our restaurants. The event calendar has something for everybody every weekend. The cruise ships have found us.

Charleston has changed with Warren Peper. The paper mill, the newsroom and the networks—they've all moved to modernity. Yet the true identity of a community remains in the collective memories of its citizens. They can best appreciate where we once were. They know time and place have elevated us all. We like being identified as the time and place that produced Warren Peper.

The Principles of Leadership

Lieutenant General John W. Rosa

When John Rosa showed up at The Citadel in August 1969, he was a wiry-thin football prospect from a military family, lately of Jacksonville, Florida. His plans in life did not go far beyond the aspiration of earning a starting quarterback position as a sophomore running Red Parker's vaunted "veer" offense. The cagey left-hander did just that. The son of a navy master chief, Rosa had used athletics to gain something his father never had the opportunity to achieve: a college degree. Rosa was an exceptional student. He did become the starting quarterback, until the irony of a severe knee injury vaulted him to longer-term objectives. By 2006, Rosa was a retired three-star U.S. Air Force general and president of The Citadel.

The air force got it right. Rosa, of the same Italian lineage that the world knows as Ferragamo, Gucci, Prada and Armani, presents a dazzling figure of leadership. He is forthright, direct and controlled within a crisis yet charismatic, creative and clever. His sense of humor belies the seriousness of function he encounters almost daily. It seems to sustain his objectivity. Rosa has deep-set dark eyes, a thrush of gray within his thick oily black hair and the olive complexion of a shrimper in July. He is tall and athletic, with habits only retired fighter pilots would associate as "tame and relaxing." He has a Harley Davidson "Hog" motorcycle. He and his wife of four decades, Donna, take two weeks every other summer to traverse the precarious currents of the Caribbean in a fifty-foot sailboat. His navigational skills have assisted more than his own hobbies.

Rosa came as president of The Citadel just before the cataclysmic economic downturn that plagued every institution of higher learning in America. He went from a cruising altitude to combat mode almost instantaneously. It was a most difficult time to be a pilot. There were more obstacles and less ammunition than one would imagine for the fight he would not be able to avoid. Yet the Rosa leadership qualities brought The Citadel forward.

"There is a contrast from the military to academia that is stark. In the military, there are quick decisions that have to be made in any field of operation. In academia, it's exactly the opposite. You adhere to a slow methodical process to achieve objectives," Rosa explained.

"In moving academia forward, you may achieve growth in the right way for the right reasons. In our world at The Citadel, we are cultivating the four-year experience as a developmental program where each step is related to the next so that our young people leave here with the skills necessary to lead in an effective and principled manner. Our strategic planning is to focus resources during difficult economic times to prioritized areas. In all of this there is a changing of the culture. That's an inherently slow and tedious process."

Rosa graduated in 1973 and came back for class reunions. In doing so, he watched Charleston change to a better place. His return as college president in January 2006 brought reflective insight.

"It's night and day from 1969, when I first arrived here. Mayor Riley was elected two years after I left. But it's apparent to me that he was the catalyst that brought Charleston out of the mire and into prosperity. He's a great example of visionary leadership," Rosa noted.

"I was able to see some of the transformation of Charleston during my visits here over the years. In terms of community pride, Charleston has not changed. The people who have been here would never want to be anyplace else. But the visuals have changed substantially. The 'new' King Street, for instance, has a character unlike any other main shopping street I've seen in my travels. It's unique, and it has a great flavor of the city. That street in 1969 was a minus. Now it's the city's biggest plus. Having been away, the two things I've heard from others that talked about Charleston at Washington functions and even overseas has been the Spoleto event and the Bridge Run. Outside of Charleston, those two events were making a lot of good press. So the city was slowly improving during the last forty years to a point that it is now among the finest cities on the globe. Seeing what has been accomplished in higher education has improved as well. Look at MUSC, the College of Charleston and The Citadel. These three institutions have advanced beyond our recognition from 1969."

Can we do better?

"We never really reach the optimum. There are things that can help us progress even further. I have been a part of the Charleston Regional Development Alliance. There are issues with railway and port transportation, all related to growth. We need to share a vision and work toward a compromise by negotiating for the good of the community. By my nature, I am goal oriented. To not move toward a goal is a failure.

"I will retire one day. Charleston, of course, is the 'leading contender' of places I would like to live my retirement years. So I have a personal stake in all that benefits the entire community. I've always had a passion to travel, so life in the air force was fantastic. We had an 'exchange tour' in Scotland from 1980 to 1983. It made me appreciate being an American. Donna and I had a few weeks in Tuscany we deeply enjoyed. There were so many other great places we have been able to enjoy. In our thirty-two years of the air force career, there have been twenty-four or twenty-five moves. It was difficult to stay in one place. But travel is certainly something that Donna and I share as a passion."

Donna Kangeter Rosa is usually part of a sentence coming from husband John. They are inseparable. The general's wife is a Charlestonian whom he met as a cadet. She graduated from St. Andrews High School. The ever-ebullient Donna Rosa is an amazing complement to the president. She hosts cadet freshmen at her home each year to let them know they have a mother away from home. She gets involved in other community charities and has a special interest in protecting people from the ravages of sun-related skin diseases. She is a survivor of melanoma surgery and the attendant aftermath of treatments, including chemotherapy. Her life-threatening Stage 4 event made her ever mindful of others. She even provides SPF sun block lotions to football game guests. The Rosas have two sons: Jonathan, a graduate of Florida State University, and Brad, a Citadel graduate of 2003. Jon and his wife, Elisha, are raising the Rosa grandsons, Mikey and Matty.

"Donna and I" dominates John Rosa's lexicon. They have been married since 1973. Devoted to each other, the Rosas are in unison, engaged and set on the same objective. Donna has been able to reattach to her Charleston roots, her old friendships and her Lowcountry family. They have bought a

Lieutenant General John W. Rosa will leave a legacy at The Citadel for his ability to lead when leadership counts. *Courtesy of The Citadel.*

home on a tidal creek in Meggett, where their closest neighbor is another Citadel graduate. They hope to retire there in time, but not before the course they have set has been achieved. The Citadel Board of Visitors unanimously approved a five-year contract extension for Rosa in 2011. This will take him to a ten-year term, a profound endorsement of his guidance and leadership skills as The Citadel's president.

"We never contemplated anything beyond my goal of commanding a fighter squadron," Rosa confided. "So everything after that was at a point where we were ready for options that had us back into private life. I remember the two of us thinking that I had become a lieutenant colonel and gotten the squadron, so that anything past that point was gravy. I was ready to get out when I was promoted to colonel. I never thought about being a general. It wasn't a goal. Over that thirty-two years there were many times that Donna and I thought that it was time to go. But there were different airplanes, different countries and different assignments. We stayed. Looking back, my takeoffs equaled my landings. I never had to jump out! That's a good thing."

Rosa did have fate intersect with timing and placement. It was on September 11, 2001. He was working in the Pentagon on the exact other side of the building from where the hijacked commercial flight crashed. The death toll, including the sixty passengers, reached nearly two hundred.[108] The Pentagon was evacuated. The young brigadier general remembered the event vividly: "Our military is prepared. Our reaction was as instructed. Our fighters went up right away. All the contingencies were covered. America was under attack. Our command room went into full alert, and all of our defense systems were engaged. Ultimately it is what we train to perform. It was a somber time."

Rosa paused to reflect.

"Lives were lost. In a way, the reach for the normal was difficult after that. This is why I believe it is so very important to challenge this next generation and to promote the values we espouse in our military and in the processes of training that we must plan for a better Citadel. We are relevant. We must prepare our young people to expect greater challenges in an ever-changing political world."

Rosa's experience went beyond those days of horror in Washington. He was assigned to resolve a crisis at the United States Air Force Academy. He became the superintendent (analogous to president) in July 2003 with the promotion to lieutenant general. There, he had to change a culture that had impugned this great American institution.

"We realized that what we had here is a culture and a climate that had to change to better embrace the air force's core values of Integrity, Service and Excellence," Rosa told the *American Forces News Service* shortly after his arrival. "We're at the point where we've laid down expectations and guidelines. Our expectations are that we don't tolerate criminals, we don't sexually harass people, we don't sexually assault people. We are not going to tolerate it."

Indeed, Rosa took 165 recommendations[109] from a blue-ribbon panel and then brought in a training program designed to implement proper judgment and actions. The intense work performed changed the academy. This leadership development—his "Values and Respect Program"—became the template for other institutions. The difficulty Rosa encountered in instituting the new agenda was measured. After all, he was an outsider coming in—a Citadel graduate running the flagship institution of the United States Air Force. Those who contemplated the results of such successes that stand out on a résumé interpolated another result. Rosa was likely on his way to a fourth star.

When The Citadel came calling, the Rosas remembered their commitment to each other. They had found a way to come home and to marshal yet another challenge. Rosa's love of his college superseded all other career options. The Citadel had only been ten years into coeducation. The state-supported institution had been through a private fundraising malaise, and the facilities were dated. It would be a whole new set of objectives for the Rosas.

"The first thing you might notice in a state-supported college versus a federally funded institution is the dearth of funding. The federal institutions are well funded, and getting something into the planning cycle was done directly through the Pentagon. In state institutions, the process is of its nature, slower and much more political. When I arrived at The Citadel, we had almost $70 million in deferred maintenance—things that had to be done in a priority order. There are roof systems in need of repair, HVAC replacements and termite damage to mitigate. In the case of Capers Hall, it is a major academic building in need of a total replacement—that's been highly prioritized for a decade! And now that deferred maintenance number is well over $100 million. And there are other facets of which we needed to adjust our thinking and consideration to resolve. That transition from federal to state was anticipated, so it was a matter of adjusting to a completely different system with a different set of priorities."

Rosa measures everything. He does so to quantify progress and direction. He surrounds himself with capable experts—his vice-presidents who understand his objectives and methods. He meets with them weekly and expects results. Charts are used and relied on to give a visual of the slow steps he has alluded to in academia. He has had to maintain patience despite the ingrained instinct of a fighter pilot's need for speed.

Observing him in action is like observing a street-wise one-man band. The knee cymbals cannot drown out the harmonica and the banjo. Rosa's balance of intensity and persuasiveness never outdistances his innate sense of humor. The quick jibe lurks.

"Kids are different when they come here than they were forty years ago," he told the assembly of parents dropping off the class of 2015. "They look just like we did except they have these overdeveloped forearms." He demonstrated the quick thumb movements of both hands playing video games. "Our biggest toy was a backyard full of grass and enough room to set up second base."

The parents identified. Rosa went on to tell the story of using one of the campus's only pay phones on a Sunday shortly after his arrival at The Citadel in 1969. He was waiting in a line in alphabetical order behind his classmate and football teammate Keith Roden. Rosa's anecdote told of Roden asking his father about coming home. Others could hear his father's loud reply in the receiver.

"Have all the other freshmen left?" he asked.

"No sir," Roden replied.

"When they do, call me, and I'll come pick you up."

The parents clapped and laughed. They appreciated the personal and parenting stories Rosa told. They were immediately at ease with the crisp military demeanor that recapped the insights of his personal experience. Rosa became one with them immediately.

Roden stayed and became great friends with Rosa. He was the team's starting center and went on to a successful teaching career, in addition to becoming one of the finest football officials working the Atlantic Coast Conference.

The Citadel has an elevated place in higher education's modern impact on the kitchen-table budgets of American families. It's a deal.

U.S. News and World Report magazine publishes an annual review of colleges and universities across the country. It measures other areas than expense. It looks at the effectiveness of all teaching modules along with graduation rates and class sizes. The Citadel has routinely been at the top—multiple number-one designations—among all southern region U.S. colleges and universities. In the practical sense, The Citadel graduates its students in four years at a rate among the highest in the country. The unwritten benefit is that the traditional military college is an anathema to trends in other institutions pushing graduations over a five-year and even a six-year period. Those savings are considerable.

In addition, The Citadel publishes what Rosa terms an "All-In Cost." It's not the amount of tuition as other colleges show but the tuition, fees, meals, lodging, uniforms, haircuts and other tangible otherwise-hidden costs that parents might not fully perceive if they just looked at tuition as a measure.

"It's the amount the parents can write in one check," Rosa concludes. "We've been there. We wrote those checks from 1999 to 2003 for our son Brad."

That practical measure means that parents can be resolved that their son or daughter is at a place where they know where they are at night, know that the meals are covered and know that they have a required "Evening Study Period." If that weren't enough, they would be further eased knowing that they receive physical fitness training and ethics training and are immersed in a four-year leadership program. The Citadel even offers a minor in leadership.

That analogy does not escape those across the country looking for excellence in education at a more-than-reasonable price. The Citadel class of 2016, the largest in the college's history, with 779 freshman cadets, arrived in the fall of 2012. That follows five straight years of more than 700 freshmen—another record. It precipitated a full Fifth Battalion and the addition of another company, "Victor." The cadet corps is at the largest strength ever recorded in the history of the institution. The Citadel is thriving, and Rosa is still forecasting other metrics.

The aforementioned "Values and Respect" program that Rosa developed from the U.S. Air Force Academy experience morphed into an even more comprehensive required program the cadets take each semester of each year. It has been expanded beyond sexual harassment to other forms, to include physical abuse, drugs, alcohol and even the new wave of non-prescription stimulants. The training prepares the cadets for the high road of ethics and honor as the antidote for cultural pitfalls in society.

"Not to overstate the problems we have in society, but by my estimate, 90 percent of the serious problems we have with our cadets, including hazing and all of the abuses, are related to alcohol. That's a root problem that we have to resolve throughout society," Rosa contended. "It's why I wake up in the wee hours of a weekend hoping that all of our cadets reported back safely without incident."

Being responsible is something that does not automatically happen for all college-age kids. There must be an effective way to teach respect for property and other people. The Citadel has other programs, as well. The Krause Center for Leadership and Ethics was funded from a lead gift given by L. William and Gay Krause, The Citadel class of 1963. Those programs of community service and the commitment to the role of ethics have been a major asset to the college.

There are other initiatives. The Citadel *Blueprint* was developed by the college in conjunction with the Board of Visitors. The document is a template used to forward The Citadel's eight most important initiatives in priority order. It has progressed to its second iteration, *Blueprint II*. Everything The Citadel does going forward has to relate to the *Blueprint*.

Rosa initiated a plan for a private funding model. The Citadel is not "going private," as the model would lead some to believe, but it is planning for the times that funding from the state budget and the Committee on Higher Education (CHE) contracts or even becomes unavailable. The difficulty of state funding since 2007 has been that sometimes state budget cuts happen within a fiscal year. Those cuts can wreak havoc on a very thin college budget. And they have! So Rosa looks over his left wing and his right wing on each sortie to know that he's covered the unexpected. He plans for the unplanned.

The Rosas have experienced much in their tenure. There have been the crucial needs of fundraising, the oversight of "legalistics" relative to summer camp incidents that happened before Rosa arrived, the deft allocation of finances to critical maintenance concerns and the concert of reworking on-campus organizations into leaner and stronger support groups. He has the benefit of a loyal alumni base, moving the giving percentages of donors to an upward trend in a down economy. They like him. They support him, and they are willing to follow him into combat as wing fighters.

Donna Rosa intimates the sense that husband John is on a mission.

"He's determined," she smiles, "and you better believe he will organize ways to get the things he wants to accomplish done. John's wired that way."

There will be a different Citadel at its two-hundred-year anniversary in 2042. It will have some very distinct markings of a college that John Rosa fostered forward. Those with the knowledge of historical impact will cite the determination of a general for what he had put into action that changed a future result. He will be the man behind a working strategic plan...that worked. Rosa gave it an end date of 2042 in 2007. There will be that Fifth Battalion, a new building funded by a renewed and energized Citadel Foundation, which for the first time incorporated its director as a vice-president of the college. There will be an "industry standard" four-year program of enhanced ethics, along with gender and cultural respect that will be the shining template for other colleges. The college will have achieved its continued climb of high academic achievement, that apex having been first reached by the Rosa regime. The college will operate under a carefully planned private funding model. It will maintain its status as being among the best of colleges and universities, including the burgeoning regional influence of a most prestigious Citadel Graduate College. And importantly, Lieutenant General John W. Rosa will be the primary impetus that vaulted The Citadel to become the preeminent institution in the education of principled leaders across the land—and perhaps across the world!

Convergence

Joseph P. Griffith

There were times when some may have counted Joe Griffith out. They thought him to be a dreamer, out of touch and aloof. They were wrong. Griffith saw things that no others imagined, and he postured his life solidly behind his convictions. The city and the community grew out of his four passions.

He had a background that propelled his pride of effort and pursuit of meaning.

"My father, George Louis Griffith, had a small service station but died at age forty-two of cancer. My mother, Alice Schragge Griffith, was a seamstress. She died at fifty-five from leukemia. I was the youngest of the four children," Griffith reflected.

"During the Great Depression, when my family was struggling, I took a job at the bowling alley at the Charleston Rifle Club. I was only ten. The bowling alley had manual pinsetters, and they paid $2.50 a day for a good pinsetter. I convinced them that I could set two lanes at a time because I had very quick hands—and I could! So, I made $5.00 a day, and for a time our family depended on that money just to get by. I remember that my mother rewarded me by making me a maroon sport jacket. It was the proudest thing I ever owned."

Griffith is a calm and pensive conversationalist, warm within his thoughts. His melancholy is evident. There are weighty recollections. His brow tilts, and he looks up to make a point as if he had not considered a certain memory for decades. He has a proper decorum posture at once, as if advising a bishop, followed by an insight to his personal well of sorrow. He misses his wife.

Where he had arrived mirrored where he had been. He took on the mantle of youthful responsibility and never doubted himself. He had known hardship, prayer and vision.

In time, the industrious Griffith drew on those early days of responsibility to bolster his confidence and resolve. A fine student at Bishop England High School, he graduated in 1947 as a member of that historic high school's very first football team (1946). That athletic journey of sixty-five years for the high school blossomed in the fall of 2011. Joe Griffith saw it all. The 2011 Bishop England football team won the South Carolina High School League's State Championship, its first ever. That experience was especially gratifying for Griffith, who had two grandsons contributing to that effort, Griffie Loy (daughter Elizabeth and son-in-law Pete) and Parkwood Griffith (son Stephen and daughter-in-law Stacey). It was the high school's unprecedented 100th state championship in all sports.

"Remembering those early days, without resources and without even a field to play on, this was an especially happy moment for me to see my grandsons as contributors," Griffith beamed. Grandson Griffie Loy scored the game's only touchdown in the Bishops' 10–0 victory over perennial state power Central High School. Of note, Griffith chaired the committee that moved the high school from downtown Charleston to an expansive parcel on Daniel Island, giving the football team its very first practice field in 1997.

Griffith's prowess as a Bishop England student and wholehearted immersion into the spirituality of Catholicism impelled him to attend a seminarian college: St. Bernard Abbey in Cullman, Alabama. It was a serene setting for Griffith and the foundation of his deep devotion to his faith. The abbey was founded in 1891 and operated by Benedictine monks who attach their lineage to 1,500 years of prayer and work.[110] Indeed, their Latin motto is *Ora et Labora*,[111] which means the Benedictines have been performing prayer and work since the Romans were speaking in Latin phrases. His four years there were influenced by the most pious man he had ever met: Father Bede Luibel, who later became the abbot (1952) of St. Bernard.[112] Right Reverend Bede Luibel passed away on March 27, 1986.[113]

"I wanted to become a Catholic priest and had no intention otherwise while I was at St. Bernard's," Griffith recalled. "But I observed a man that was so close to Christ and so perfect in every respect that I knew I could never be like him, Father Bede. Father Bede was everything I was not. And he was such a great lasting influence on my life beyond. When I realized what it would take to become like him, to have standards so high as his were, I got discouraged. I could be a priest, but I could never be a priest like him. I graduated and later joined the army."

While at St. Bernard's, Griffith befriended another seminarian, Oscar Lipscomb. They have stayed in touch for a lifetime. The archbishop of Mobile, Alabama, from 1980 to 2008, he is now retired.[114] He was the first archbishop of Mobile.[115]

"He sends me a fruitcake every year during the Christmas season, and we usually get in touch," Griffith said. "I have been able to build on the friendships and the experiences of St. Bernard's year by year, and I am very proud to have studied at this unique and wonderful abbey."

Griffith's life in the secular world began inauspiciously. He spent the next two years in the army, hoping to return to Charleston. In addition to his spirituality, three other great passions emerged. The next was the stuff of legends.

"I had a friend from Estill, South Carolina, Davis Powers. He had a chance to go out on a date with a beautiful girl, the runner-up in the Miss Georgia pageant." Griffith thought back.

"He wanted me to get a date to accompany them. The only girl I could think to ask was Bette Smith, though I really didn't think she'd accept. She said, 'Yes.' We took a 1954 canary yellow Ford convertible out to a place near Folly Beach and had a lovely time. That was it. It hit me. I had found the love of my life, and I knew it right then. While I was still in the army, my mother had come down with leukemia. She decided to give me her engagement ring. She had met Bette. She said, 'You go ask that girl to marry you.' We were at our house on Coming Street that evening. I had no wheels, and we used Bette's car. We were going out with Jim and Caroline Condon. After the date, I asked Bette to marry me. I was prepared for anything, but she honored me by saying yes. That was in December 1954. We got married on September 10, 1955. I got out of the army in December 1955.

"The wedding was the last event I recall that my mother could physically stand up," Griffith lamented. The Griffith matriarch, Alice Griffith, passed away in January 1956.

Along with his two sisters and an older brother, the Griffith family persevered.

With Bette and nothing but dreams in his pocket, he sought his next passion. In short time, he embarked on a real estate career. Within a few short years, he and Bette moved to a nice suburban home on James Island.

"It was at this time that I was inclined to go into business for myself. But I had no money. Nobody was lending money, either. I had a great friend in

An entrepreneur, Joe Griffith facilitated Charleston's suburban expansion by creating neighborhoods. *Courtesy of Helena Griffith Bastian.*

Bill Ehrhardt, a fine man and a great lawyer. Bill believed in me and lent me $3,500 to start Joe Griffith Realty in 1957. He saw the vision I had. The World War II baby boomers were just coming on, and I saw the need for Charleston to move beyond the bridges east and west. I developed an ability to look at a piece of land and visualize what could go there, residential or commercial. I started developing neighborhoods like Parkshore, Cross Creek, Plantation Estates and, later, Snee Farm. I had some great investment partners like Falcon Hawkins, Fritz Hollings and my old friend Bill Ehrhardt. Everybody told me I was crazy and that these places were too far out from the peninsula. But some of the same people saying that ended up building houses there."

The closeness of Mount Pleasant to the downtown area made sense on a map. But there was a compelling objection. When Griffith started negotiating for the Snee Farm tract in 1965, there was only one bridge to Mount Pleasant: the John P. Grace Memorial Bridge. The Grace Bridge was completed in 1929 and only had one narrow lane each way for 2.7 miles. The 7 percent incline was difficult for stick-shift automobiles, especially if a wreck stopped the traffic. Wrecks were all too frequent. Large trucks and even farm tractors in the oncoming lane contributed to a fairly common fear espoused by a large percentage of the peninsular population. There existed a reasonably significant segment of Charlestonians who had never driven across the Grace Bridge, though they had a driver's license and a reliable vehicle to take them. The development of Snee Farm was not only across the great and scary monstrosity but also nearly 5.0 miles farther out into the country. It was thought to be Griffith's folly. With the new Silas Pearman Bridge[116] on the way, Griffith gambled.

Griffith did the unthinkable. He not only advanced the idea of large residential lots but also developed a championship golf course that included serpentine panoramas throughout the nine hundred acres. The site accommodated 1,020 homes and another 304 villa units. With the help of others, he attracted a national amateur golf tournament, the Rice Planters in 1970, to augment interest in the property. The lots sold. Larger semi-estate homes were built. A clubhouse and a neighborhood pool followed. Later, the expansive neighborhood promoted a remarkable youth swim team. Tennis courts were emplaced. One could fish in the meandering lakes. There was something for everyone at Snee Farm. A major success was snatched from the predisposition of failure that so many pundits had predicted. The Griffith name was golden.

"Dad did something else in the Snee Farm development that became a part of Mount Pleasant's future. Both entrances incorporated roundabouts. He knew that roundabouts were extensively in foreign countries. Dad always felt they were aesthetically better and more efficient than stop signs and traffic lights," noted Stephen Griffith, who serves as secretary-treasurer for Joe Griffith, Inc., "and now, Mount Pleasant is famous for using roundabouts in many other locations."

Snee Farm itself appears to owe its name to a corruption of British lettering.[117] The Old English "f" that was evidently meant to designate a "fee farm," or one traded as a tariff concession, was miswritten as an "Sn" in later years.[118] The fee farm became Snee Farm. Griffith's attempt at a modern suburban neighborhood also encountered an ironic event. They found the skeleton of a ten-thousand-year-old mastodon near what is now the third hole while excavating the golf course.[119]

Charleston was discovering Joe Griffith.

His business grew in a fast-paced manner. He was a full-service realtor—one who could connect a buyer to the lot, to the builder, to the house and even to the lender. He worked tirelessly. He and Bette were building their family in the same pace of life—Joseph Jr., Helena, Louis, Stephen and, finally, Elizabeth, nicknamed "Lil Bit." In time, Griffith developed over forty neighborhoods in vectors around the metropolitan Charleston area, in addition to several landmark commercial and retail parcels. Joe Griffith defined Charleston real estate for a full generation. The suburban pedigree of the Holy City was the foresight of this faith-filled and determined Charlestonian. He had arrived.

His largesse became part of the community's growth. The passions— wife Bette, the real estate business and his devout Catholic faith—were now intertwined. The crowning passion was his attitude of assistance. He got involved. He contributed mightily. He devoted his considerable energies to those less fortunate or to a burgeoning community need. Griffith became one of the community's greatest philanthropists—ever. Giving back served his sense of purpose.

"One of my great early influences was Joe Riley Sr. He was involved in everything and gave both his valuable time, leadership and financial support to so many things that you simply could not count them. I wanted to be like him from the time I was a young adult. All the things I aspired to be, he was. He set a great example for everyone, especially his son, who has gone on to do so many magnificent things in his career as mayor. I could only try to do a part of what Joe Riley Sr. had done. But Bette and I had no second thoughts about filling community needs if and when we could."

Griffith kept adding addendum pages to his impressive résumé by adhering to his value system of giving back. He chaired or presided over more than two dozen organizations from the country's largest Exchange Club to the MUSC Foundation Board to the chamber of commerce. He became president of the Hibernian Society; a founding member of the Spoleto, USA festival (in 1977); and the founder of the Southeastern Wildlife Exposition (1982), as well as chairman of the board of First Trident Savings and Loan. He worked tirelessly on the boards of the Charleston Symphony and the Coastal Carolina Fair. He chaired the boards of two local industrial companies whilst raising a family and lending his talents to a multitude of charities. His wife, Bette, was no less active and engaged.

The balance in Griffith's life had always been there. He enjoyed the support of many friends and associates—Joe McInerney, Ed Mullan, Michael Knapp, Claude Blanchard, Bobby Scarborough and Ed Naylor. They all have passed away. The others—Bernie Puckhaber, Fritz Hollings, Leonard Fulghum, Bobby Molony and Henry Berlin—were vibrant personalities within a wide circle of Charleston's phoenix-like transition to a world city.

Griffith found the balance by being consistent. He went to his office on East Bay Street to explore future potential developments and then to lunch meetings. There followed out-of-office meetings and, invariably, an evening meeting of a local board. He had moved to the historic home at 117 Broad Street. This house once belonged to Edward Rutledge, the youngest signer of the Declaration of Independence and, later, a governor of South Carolina.[120] Griffith enjoyed his closeness to his business, his community endeavors and the church he attended for daily morning Mass across the street. The Cathedral of St. John the Baptist was his spiritual refuge.

By 2001, the Griffiths had moved to a quieter home off Mathis Ferry Road that enticed them with a sunset water vista of the Wando River. The children were grown and now engaged in their own lives. The fifteen grandchildren had a new place to enjoy the famed Griffith hospitality. Their annual Christmas party was the talk of Charleston. To be invited was the honor of acceptance. The Griffiths were still repositioning much of Charleston to an upward band of livability.

In the impressive rendering of his service to others, Griffith was always at the very front of his Catholic faith. He befriended the priests, the monsignors and several bishops who had taken up residence next to his 117 Broad Street home. He and his constant companion, Bette, went to Rome on four pilgrimages, including the occasion of the elevation of his good friend Archbishop Joseph Bernadin to cardinal in 1983.[121] Griffith discovered new avenues to help others nationally and internationally— all from his muted and humble perspective of his childhood, the son of a Depression-era seamstress. He still maintained the optimism and mindset of a pinsetter in a bowling alley handling two lanes at a time.

The assistance Griffith administered as a consultant to three bishops in Charleston and his indefatigable efforts in support of Catholic missions and projects earned him two of the very rare designations conferred by the papacy. The Holy Father, Pope Paul VI, accorded him the title of knight of Malta. Later, the pope accorded Griffith a second title, as a knight of St. Gregory. No other known member of the Charleston community has ever been accorded these international designations.

Griffith, pensive and always near to his cherry-tobacco pipe, finds these accomplishments to be treasured but never to be dwelled upon. That area had always been reserved for his wife, Bette. When Griffith would approach her birthday, Valentine's Day, a wedding anniversary or Christmas, a simple bauble or bracelet was in order. He enjoyed surprising this svelte and stately lady with something unique, unpretentious and yet dazzling. There was always the look in her azure eyes that enhanced her deep affection for him and his constancy. He was thoughtful, romantic and timely. Their lifetime together was nothing short of idyllic. They danced life in a slow minuet, never wanting the music to cease.

Griffith's world changed when Bette became ill. She had beaten thyroid cancer with surgery and treatment in 1965, only to contract breast cancer in 1999. The years of her battles were chronicled by all who knew her kindness, her pleasant demeanor and her selfless concern for others. She would recover intermittently and then decline, sadly. The Bette Griffith before cancer was never replaced by another persona. She remained forthright, faithful and fearless. The period of her passing in the summer of 2004 brought a deluge of condolences to this seminal Charleston family. Her loss was felt well beyond.

A love of the ages had passed after forty-eight years of marriage. The late afternoon of her funeral service was accentuated by the beauty of a rainbow that bent horizon-to-horizon across Charleston Harbor. It seemed to emanate from the Griffith Mount Pleasant home and terminate on James Island, the site of her Holy Cross Cemetery interment. It was a time of reverence for an awesome God. Who is to say that the most beautiful natural rainbow that ever graced Charleston Harbor did not come that dusky summer evening as a sign from a loving God? All was right in heaven. And who is to say that Bette Griffith did not gaze down lovingly on her family and friends in the mist of a retreating shower? Who would not ponder the exquisiteness of that magnificent spectrum in solemnity without a small prayer of thanks?

"I attribute all the goodness in my life to my faith and to my life's companion, Bette," Griffith lamented. "I miss her every day.'

Speaking about his wife, Griffith is slowed and in solemn grief, eyes washed in memories. It is in these moments that time stops.

"She was the love of my life. She was the reason I tried to be the best husband and father I could be. She gave me happiness and joy. God had blessed me with Bette," Griffith spoke in intimate, reverent tones. "I cannot go a moment without thinking how deeply she touched my life. I was undeserving of her and my life can never be the same. I hope I am worthy to meet her again one day." One could readily feel the breadth of his sadness and reflection.

There remains a devotion of the Charleston community that celebrates the Griffith legacy and Bette's fight. The Medical University of South Carolina, where Bette volunteered countless hours to help others, dedicated the Bette Smith Griffith Pavilion in 2006. It is part of the Hollings Cancer Center. Her portrait adorns the expansive lobby therein. The center serves more than seven thousand cancer patients each year.

Daughter Helena Griffith Bastian expressed the family sentiments with intense insights: "During that short time that she had with us, she taught us a lot. She taught us how to face the challenges life throws at us with grace and dignity. She taught us how to have faith in God and her family and friends. She told us how to give back to the community, and giving back meant giving others in her same position a leg up and giving them the confidence that they can make it.

"I didn't realize how important those lessons would mean to me until 2007. I, too, was diagnosed with breast cancer. They caught mine a lot sooner." It was the same type and location that her mother had. She has been an advocate of the Lowcountry Susan G. Komen affiliate and Hollings Cancer Center and their commitment to education, research and providing resources for early diagnosis. Bastian's dream, as was her mother's, is to end breast cancer forever.

The legacy of the Griffith children remains. All have an instilled gene of faith, compassion and service.

The *Ora et Labora* theme still holds Joe Griffith's life together. He works in other spheres and prays devotedly. He loves people and gives time to others when he can. He offers a calm and sensible mentorship to the continued success of his adult children. They make him quite proud. They return that sentiment to him exponentially. To a generation of Charlestonians, he is "Papa Joe," the man who changed much of what the Holy City looks like from the sky.

The four passions have converged and then divided. Griffith's time is spent with his fifteen grandchildren and a few old friends. He has found another pace. It is methodical. He brings his morning paper to a Mount Pleasant roadside breakfast eatery, the Boulevard Diner. The wait staff there knows him and expects his routine 8:30 a.m. arrival. It is usually after attending a daily morning Mass. His table for two is always reserved. But there is only one. He has his pipe at bay. He scans the paper and sorts the important items. He eats, leaves a gracious tip and departs back to the Wando River. He awaits God's plan for his final convergence. It will be that glorious day when his passions are together again—Bette, his generous spirit, a perfect home and God to watch over it all.

The Griffith name has become a signature Charleston moniker. It conjures the vision of a great man, his charming and beautiful wife and a family adept at participating in the meaningful progress of a community. The patriarch is a part of our heritage, whether related by blood or friendship. He remains poignant, brilliant and resilient, true within his convictions.

In the Here and After

MARK SANFORD

A broad stroke of life was painted on the canvas by the master. It was enriched by a brilliant swath of kaleidoscope colors that amazed all who viewed it. They found inspiration and meaning. It remains an unfinished painting with great promise to a world of art critics awaiting the master's return.

It is an unfamiliar story with an unknown ending. Master artists know the cause of the pause.

It's the week of Easter. Pollen tints the buildings, porch furniture and vehicles into subtle greens. Azaleas have decorated all of Charleston. It seems to be the first act of another promising tourist season in the Holy City.

A trim and handsome father stops for lunch to fulfill yet another promise to one of many old friends. Some friends are still available. Some are not. It is part of the struggle he has encountered. His dreams were washed like pollen from the piazzas. He has been the new political definition of "anathema" for three years. He blames no outside person or circumstance. He takes full responsibility for his every action—something he has taught his four boys throughout their upbringing. He is a realist. He is in a mode of muted avoidance of public life. He is abject in his humility. He is sincere in his deep and profound devotion to his Christian faith. It has sustained him. His bright stare and pensive introspect relive the past, suspect of the future. He was once a United States congressman. He was a two-term governor of South Carolina. In so many ways, he has risen to a higher purpose. Yet, he hasn't quite recognized his own timely relevance to so many other public causes. The one role to which he has redirected himself in his daily devotion is profound. It makes him happy, if only momentarily. He is "Dad."

Mark Sanford is a proud father. His oldest son, Marshall, is a fine student at the University of Virginia in Charlottesville. He visited Marshall for Palm Sunday weekend. His second son, Landon, will be off to college in the fall of the year. He might decide to join his older brother at UVA, where Mark Sanford obtained his master's in business administration at the famed Darden Graduate School of Business in 1988. His two younger sons, Bolton and Blake, are growing up quickly. Too quickly. Sanford fears that he will not see them as much in the coming years. When his former wife divorced him in 2010, it was very public, and it has made access to his boys less frequent than he would like. It has been his deepest pang in his ordeal. He perseveres cautiously.

"I am so proud of the boys, but it can never be as it was. My life is about them now. We have times together that I cherish—water activities during the warm months and some together time on the family farm near Beaufort during the cooler months," Sanford intimates. "Before you know it, they'll be adults and the time that I can be there for them will have dissipated. So I really focus on them now."

Sanford is, as his closest friends note, a much warmer and caring person. Through his struggles for his own post-fifty identity, he has gained new perspectives.

"I am much more spiritual than I was before. Part of the past mindset was that I thought I could solve any and all problems. Now, I realize that I can't. I need godly help and inspiration. I pray more," Sanford shared. "There are other areas that I feel I have been able to gain a better perspective. I was rightly much judged by many others. It has hit home. Was I judgmental, too? I know I was. The experience has taught me in new ways the importance of empathy with others in the highs and inevitable lows that come with life and the wisdom found in 'Judge not, that ye be not judged.'"

In the area of lasting friendships, Sanford laments that he lost some. "I do not blame friends that have fallen away. I am happy with the trusted friends and family that have stuck with me through my flaws, sins and controversies. I am a perfect example of imperfection. Yet, those that see me for what I am, warts and all, have meant more to me than they can ever imagine."

Sanford is indeed relevant. In fact, he may have been a decade ahead of his time. His surprise win over a sitting governor in the South

Carolina gubernatorial election of 2002 made headlines across the country. The dashing young fiscal conservative—some would argue his libertarian bend—fostered a refocus to practical governance. He performed the business management surgery that was well overdue. He sold the state jet and cut an array of government extras within months. He set the stage in leading by example on spending on the very night of his election as he pushed back on state police protection, citing it as unnecessary and costly. He surrounded himself with like-minded spending contraction theorists. His frugality made him a hero to some and an adversary to others—especially those in the

Mark Sanford has retired from politics but remains relevant in his simplistic view of how government should work. *Courtesy of the* Post & Courier.

legislature he felt were doing the same old things the same old ways. In retrospect, many of those adversaries may now agree that he might have been a clairvoyant.

Sanford vetoed bills that would have benefited himself but cost too much for a small state like South Carolina to consider. On one occasion, he vetoed a beach renourishment bill. His family home on Sullivan's Island was a dune away from the beach. It mattered not because it did not appeal to sound economic reasoning for the state's entire citizen base.

Sanford promoted the need for austerity and common sense. He insisted on paying back state reserve funds first when there were budget surpluses. He supported state vouchers for public education to foster market principles and better performance. He looked for ways to streamline some of the replication expense of higher education by introducing several cost-saving proposals. He scrutinized public utilities. He considered several initiatives, including partial reforms to healthcare and Medicaid, infrastructure and finance. There was no area of his oversight that was not studied for its efficiencies and potential contraction of expense. He remained true to his personal adherence of fiscal conservatism.

Now, Sanford is a page in a study of economic reform and political history. He assumes that this page is not a positive reflection of his personal life and value system. Will there be other words written? Will there come redemption? Will the phoenix rise?

Listening to his resonant and charismatic acumen for all things political, Sanford hits higher notes than any of those finely coiffed politicos seen on television as presidential candidates. It's late. It's the warm spring of an election year. There is a larger-than-expected support base of his political viewpoint that laments his public service departure.

Mallory Factor, a FOX News analyst, put it in perspective: "Right before his fall, Sanford was a great hope to many who believed that he might be the person to lead our country to fiscal sanity. It was a crushing disappointment when this bright light of the conservative movement failed to live up to all the dreams that had been placed upon him. But Sanford has been extremely diligent in making amends. And who is to say that there couldn't be a place for him in the future of our state and our nation still? Sanford sees where this is going. He hopes that the mandate of the voters will be to cut needless spending, reduce debt and reemphasize constraint."

Sanford has stayed constant in his overview: "Too often people in government are tone deaf to the real hopes, fear and needs of those who work and pay the bills. In South Carolina, this is pronounced. Our system is dysfunctional. Here government usually works from a central motivation of those elected, and this leads to a very fractionalized system that doesn't work for the taxpayer. We don't have traditional checks and balances, and so personalities too often drive the ship in Columbia. The founding fathers wanted the opposite, a system of laws and not men. We need the people who cast votes to understand how dire our situation really is both at the state and national levels—and to make noise!"

Sanford is passionate and direct. He has spent his adult life reading works that espouse the precepts of the U.S. Constitution. He is convinced that those who developed this document did so for prosperity and posterity. He sees that there are those who have an agenda to diminish or even destroy it. He has studied history and quotes those who have edified the American way of life and fought for our liberties.

"There will be a multitude of financial adjustments for the American public in the years ahead because you ultimately cannot continue to live spending on your son's or daughter's dime. That's true whether you're a student, a business or a country. There will be more tax, less in benefits, more in the way of inflation and less in the way of purchasing power. Historically, political systems break when they don't fix basic math problems."

By example, Sanford mentioned an appropriate study on the matter, *This Time It's Different: Eight Centuries of Financial Folly*, by Carmen Reinert and Kenneth Rogoff.

The authors build the case study: "Throughout history, rich and poor countries alike have been lending, borrowing, crashing—and recovering—their way through an extraordinary range of financial crises. Each time, the experts have chimed, 'This time is different'—claiming that the old rules of valuation no longer apply and that the new situation bears little similarity to past disasters…[The study widens by] covering sixty-six countries across five continents; [by] using clear, sharp analysis and comprehensive data, Reinhart and Rogoff document that financial fallouts occur in clusters and strike with surprisingly consistent frequency, duration and ferocity. They examine the patterns of currency crashes, high and hyperinflation and government defaults on international and domestic debts—as well as the cycles in housing and equity prices, capital flows, unemployment and government revenues around these crises.[122] Financial math always works. And it will certainly work in this instance with horrific consequences for the American way of life."

In so many look-back ways, Sanford has been right and sound in his assessments: "South Carolina should be much more of a magnet for capital investment. It is what we tried to accomplish as for the first time in South Carolina history we were able to lower the income tax rate for small business, partnerships and LLCs. But we wanted it for everyone, much like what is done in states like Florida or Texas. It is helpful as out-of-state business to look at South Carolina. But importantly, it is good for in-state businesses—large and small. Small businesses are the engines of job creation in this state, but our current incentive system more rewards elephant hunting—and there are not too many elephants out there [referring to large national and multi-national companies]. Our bread and butter should be small business. That is where we can optimize growth and gain the most benefit in creating and adding to the wealth of our state."

One would have to believe that Sanford is more relevant today than perhaps he was on the inside of the political spectrum. His insights are long-term fixes based on time-valued principles of the marketplace. He had long been an advocate of streamlined government and minimum federal and state intrusion. Currently, when one of every six jobs in the United States is a government function—whether federal, state or local—and nearly 50 percent of eligible taxpayers do not pay any federal tax, Sanford may have been so far ahead of his time that he might have seemed to some to be aloof. Pundits may have thought of DaVinci, Einstein and Locke in the same manner. Sanford gets it, and he can eloquently detail it to others.

"America is on a path that we cannot possibly sustain. To change it, we all have to change. And we will need leaders who are willing to stand on the timeless principles our founding fathers birthed this country on," he added. "Standing up, when it's not popular, will be difficult."

Sanford did so time and again. His sometimes-legendary rails with the South Carolina statehouse became uniquely comical, though they were not meant to be so. He once carried two piglets to the entrance of the House chamber to emphasize his dissatisfaction with "pork barrel" spending. Legislators didn't much care for the piglets, named Pork and Barrel, but the public got it.

When disagreements occurred, Governor Sanford invoked the strategy of President Theodore Roosevelt, a Bull Moose Party ploy to take matters to the people when the opposing party legislature did not accept his point of view. It was Roosevelt who made political use of the "bully pulpit." Sanford did much of the same but was in disagreement mostly with majority party allies. They did not always buy into Sanford's ascetic fiscal plans. It was as if Sanford already knew that the system was heading into arduous realities.

The gangly former governor never really acclimated himself to the loft of stilted popularity. He remained within himself, assured but free of a high-minded alter ego. It was his humility that endeared him to the Charleston culture as a young man. He recalled the fond memories of Charleston past.

"Home at the time was the farm, and I remember coming here for dances when I was in college. You wouldn't see as much of these formal traditions elsewhere, and I attended a few. Inevitably, in them there would be these conversations that fit a fine novel with such unique personalities. People like my old friend Johnny Zervos would have sooner taken a spaceship to Mars than ever leave Charleston. Incredible people live here. There is such a sense of place, and accordingly the old saying was that in Atlanta, a conversation would start with 'What do you do?' In Savannah, it would be, 'What do you drink?' In Charleston, it always came back to a tie to place in those days. 'Who's your dad?' or 'Who's your mom?' were really nothing more than reference points for the *where* in 'Where are you from?'"

The genealogy stayed thick. The friendships were even thicker. Sometimes fitting into Charleston's vaulted and venerable society meant embracing it for what it was and what it meant to others.

"People here had an incredible pride in the lifestyle they knew they had here. There was an especially pronounced pride of place and a way of life that I remember fondly. Now Charleston is more cosmopolitan and transient than the Charleston I knew back then. But there was definitely a larger-than-life component to some of the great personalities—maybe based on the many years of isolation, or perhaps it was self-imposed isolation in Charleston's case. Now there are national brands and national outlets where there used to be local flavor and color. Yet the uniformity or commonality that is in the rest of America is not as much seen here because of people like Frances Edmunds. The first thing visitors may notice is that there are no skyscrapers. Thank Frances Edmunds for that."

Sanford's journey included time in the commercial real estate world, where he began his reputation in the community. When familiar icon Arthur Ravenel Jr. decided to come home after eight years as the First Congressional District House representative from Charleston, Sanford vied for the seat, though he was unknown in political circles. He was able to get into a runoff with the favorite, Van Hipp III. When Sanford won, it was off to Washington—for six years after winning two subsequent reelections. It was there that then fellow congressmen Lindsey Graham (R-SC) and Steve Largent (R–OK) first experienced the famously documented Sanford frugality.

"We had become good friends in D.C. We always tried to get together and had a habit of catching a few new movies. We'd rotate getting the drinks and popcorn. One evening, it was my turn, and when I went to the concession counter I noticed a jumbo special—a big tub of popcorn and a super drink for a fraction of three individual orders. It was more than I could resist! When I got to the seats where they were, they grumbled a bit when I handed them the big tub of popcorn to share. They were uncomfortable but putting up with it. When I handed them their personal straws to the large drink, they began to push away and run like rats on a sinking ship! I really caught it from them! Graham and Largent went back to get their own drinks."

Sanford's Washington days found him rated among the top 5 percent of voters on largely conservative issues and even sometimes as a maverick.

He never accepted the status quo and often voted his convictions, even as a lone dissenter. He abhorred "pork" spending and was careful to review all items attached to seemingly innocuous and bipartisan consensual legislation. In time, he kept his "term limits" promise and happily moved back to Charleston when his third term expired in January 2001.

His term as governor from 2003 to 2011 was marked by many controversies over budget issues, heated rhetoric and political philosophy confrontations. He was not the "good ole boy" governor who sometimes had rubber-stamped legislation in the power-imbalanced hierarchy of South Carolina politics. When his personal life wavered and the difficulty of an emotional and very public divorce was imminent, Sanford became a target for some and a tabloid entity to others. He became the country's loneliest governor.

"When Jenny decided to move back to Sullivan's Island with the boys, I was left there in this fifteen-thousand-square-foot mansion by myself until my term expired," Sanford indicated, more aware of the emotional loneliness than the physical fact of his circumstance.

"I knew that I had no one to blame but myself, but it didn't change the difficulty that came in that chapter of life. And despite calls for me to step down by some that had wanted me to step down for years before I had given them ammunition for the call, I felt strongly that we had work our team needed to finish. There are times in life you need to stay around to make lemonade as best you can from the lemons you have poured on the floor. The easiest thing would have been to walk away, and I got within inches several times."

Sanford stayed. He made few public appearances, and he remained vigilant in his watch over what he considered effusive statehouse spending. He then faded into the next stage of his life with the ever-evident eye of public scrutiny about his personal life. He understands that people can be both hurtful and forgiving. He does not seek publicity, endorsement or edification. He enjoys the higher and now more meaningful value of friendships and the treasured relationships that are special—his four boys. He is inspired more now, by reading and by spending moments in reflection of his lifelong blessings and God's grace and forgiveness.

He is still Mark Sanford, a compelling and magnetic communicator to those who want to understand the precarious times of the special country we live in, the incredible foresight of our founders, the opportunities of a market economy and the need of oversight to preserve these things for our children and grandchildren.

The broad stroke of vibrant kaleidoscope colors remains on the canvas to view for its brilliance and meaning. It took a master artist. There is still other paint on his palette.

The PGA of Roger Warren

The world audience of the combined four major golf tournaments routinely exceeds 1 billion viewers. The Professional Golfers' Association of America (PGA) of 2012 was estimated to entice 580 million television golf fans from Albuquerque to Zimbabwe. So, to whom did the PGA turn to host the fourth and final major of 2012? It chose Kiawah Island's Ocean Course and its president, Roger Warren. It marked the third time that the eyes of the world were turned toward the view of Kiawah Island. Warren's eyes were on much more.

There's the course itself, its condition and ambiance. There are the corporate sponsors—and their hosting of the "tent people." There's the television cranes and towers, the players' accommodations, the parking and shuttle transportation, the rules officials, the concessionaires, the first aid stations, tight security, traffic control, the hundreds of volunteers. There's caddie stuff and inside-the-ropes stuff. There's well more than meets the eye. Warren is a pro at this.

Warren served as perhaps the most unlikely president of the Professional Golfers' Association ever from 2004 to 2006. His story is like getting a hole-in-one on a scorecard that records a stroke compilation of 110. He accomplished this most unlikely prestigious position notwithstanding the very long odds of his journey. Born and raised in Galesburg, Illinois, Warren spent thirteen years coaching and teaching at a junior high and then at the high school level. He coached basketball. He remained in coaching for an additional five years before immersing himself in his new career. He was late into the golf administration game as a thirty-eight-year-old applying for credentials to become a PGA club professional. The credential was needed to qualify for the day-to-day administration of the twenty-seven-hole layout at nearby Village Links at Glen Ellyn Club, a public golf course. Within fourteen years, he essentially ran golf in America!

"I started to play golf seriously in my early twenties and simply loved the game," Warren explained. "It was easy to see that the sport that I enjoyed so much had an administrative side that had challenges. And it had people like me that loved to play come to the club every day. So I decided to completely change directions and try to make a new career of golf administration.

"The Village Links at Glen Ellyn gave me my first opportunity. My parents, George and Rosalee Warren, set examples for me growing up. They emphasized hard work, honesty and treating people like you'd want to be treated. I also met people later like Alex Stupple of the Chicago Golf Club, a mentor, and several others in the profession that elevated my career by their advice and friendship. Alex talked about the game in such a way that it made you look forward to play. He was most instrumental in helping me to learn to love the game of golf."

Warren became familiar with golf as a twelve-year-old making a few extra dollars picking up balls at a driving range. He even drove the tractor. In time, he learned how to play the game. Warren began college at Western Illinois University in Macomb, about thirty-five miles from Galesburg and thirty miles from the Mississippi River. He successfully walked onto the Leathernecks basketball team. The basketball coach was impressed by his determination and recommended the athletic Warren to the soccer coach. He transitioned to the world game and became the team's starting goalie. The college had much for which to boast even before the emergence of PGA president Roger Warren. WIU alumni include several notable Major League Baseball players (Chris Short, Gene Lamont, Rick Reuschel) and NFL football players (William James, Rodney Harrison, Jason Williams), in addition to Mary Matalin, a renowned Republican strategist married to James Carville, renowned Democratic strategist.[123] The college enrolls more than twelve thousand students.

Like his athletic transition from basketball to soccer, the metamorphosis from high school teacher and coach to PGA professional took much resiliency and vision. He still coached basketball while running the Glen Ellyn course for nearly five years. It was quite a busy time that also included his course work necessary to achieve his PGA certification. He and his wife, Mary, persevered.

They remained dedicated to the tasks at hand with an eye open for the opportunities that appeared—all in a most timely manner.

Warren had made a name for himself beyond Illinois. But it was within the framework of the Illinois PGA that he arose.

Warren was elected to the board of the Illinois Section of the PGA in 1991 and became the section's secretary in 1992.[124] He moved through the chairs to become the section president, a two-year term. Warren was also a member of the Golf Professional Training Program (GPTP) faculty for three years. In 1996, he served on the task force that developed CareerLinks, the PGA of America's job identification service. Warren's golf shop at Seven Bridges Golf Course in Woodridge, Illinois, was named one of "America's 100 Best Golf Shops" in 1991, '96, '97, '98 and '99 by *Golf Shop Operations* magazine. He was named the Illinois PGA Section's Merchandiser of the Year for Public Facilities in 1992.[125] By 1998, Warren had run for national secretary of the PGA and lost. But he ran again in 2000 and won. From there, he ran for and won a two-year term as vice-president and then president of the PGA of America from 2004 to 2006. Voila! There you have it!

Roger Warren shouldered the responsibility of hosting 2012's PGA Championship at the Ocean Course. *Courtesy of the* Post & Courier.

"Only in America!" Warren recalled. "Now, as prestigious as this would be and as meaningful to my career—the position of a lifetime—there was no salary. It's a volunteer position. There is a wonderful administrative organization that runs the business at our offices in Palm Beach Gardens [Florida]. In essence, I represented the nearly twenty-eight thousand PGA professionals at golf clubs all over America."

His organizational experience was "on-the-job training," and his strongest suit became the interaction of working with people—especially golf people: "I enjoy people who love to laugh. People tend to take themselves too seriously. This becomes more interesting in dealing with well-known golfers as you see them in their more personal moments—and see their genuine nature. Laughter does that. When we had the Ryder Cup at the K Club in Ireland [2006], the players' wives and some of the players were taken to a place to learn how to fly fish. One of the player's wives did a wide cast and hooked my cheek. The incident may have seemed serious to others, but it certainly wasn't to me. The hook was carefully removed, and all you could do was laugh about it."

Warren endeared himself to the golf world. He was hooked, after all. The opportunity to come to Kiawah Island as director of golf arose, and Warren immediately fell in love with Charleston. By 2005, he had been made president. And he was accorded yet another title as "honorary president" of the PGA. He brought distinction to the golf world and even more celebrity to Charleston, now proclaimed proudly as his home.

There were too many reasons to make Kiawah and Charleston home: "The people here are so special. They are genuinely the friendliest to be found anywhere. I have never been any place where the caring nature of the people and the concern for other people is so real. And the weather is fantastic. I love downtown Charleston. The restaurants like Fulton Five, SNOB, 82 Queen, Fig—I've never been to one I didn't like. I play golf on the weekends here and work out. I'm doing the 'insanity' workout now.

"And what really excites me is flying into Charleston after I've been away. You see the old houses, that great bridge and the downtown area. It's perfect. My wife and I love to walk downtown. It's a comfort that always gives a good feeling. It's not a fluke that Charleston is rated the number one city. It represents everything good about southern hospitality. I am always proud to let people know about Charleston in my travels because it is so very special."

The worldview of Charleston was refocused in mid-August 2012. Every golf fan might have had a chance to see course architect Pete Dye's Ocean Course at Kiawah. Many had seen it before. There was the 1991 Ryder Cup when the course first opened. The close match had been deemed the "War by the Shore," and a victory was sealed for the Americans when the Europeans missed a sliding six-foot putt on the final hole. Then there was the 1997 World Cup of Golf—played on the same wind-challenged 7,676-yard layout. The Irish team of Padraig Harrington and Paul McGinley won it. In each instance, the dramatic protagonist was the Ocean Course. The wind that wails in the omnipresent syncopation of beach waves parts the sea oats and sways the hardened growth of the otherwise sturdy oaks. The course is what God makes it on any given day.

"That 1991 course had more sand than is present now. There is more of a grown-in feel," Warren explained.

"The fairways look more 'perched' now, the result of the erosion of wind and water. It makes the target more defined. We also changed the grass surface from Bermuda to a hybrid paspalam, a salt-resistant grass. Interestingly, Dr. Ronnie Duncan of the University of Georgia developed this hybrid from grass that grew naturally on Sullivan's Island. Now this grass is used at many seaside courses with excellent results.

"Pete Dye has been back here multiple times in preparation for the PGA event of August 2012. He had made other subtle changes to the course that gave it more flow. The mounding that was slightly altered for the tournament, for instance, has given the course a better playability beyond the event. The second fairway is now tilted back to a better position. Throughout the course, the bunkers better define the line of play. So I think the course will continue to show beauty, challenge players well and gain an even better standing in the golfing world. It was one of the most challenging venues ever for a PGA or any championship for the most simple of reasons. On seaside links, wind is always a major factor. We will always have wind to make players think, to create approaches and to measure clubs."

The aforementioned Pete Dye has long been both admired and admonished for his uniquely challenging golf course designs. The term "Dye-abolical" refers to his use of bunkering and even railroad ties incorporated into famous golf venues across the United States—and beyond. In addition to the Ocean Course, Dye has designed Harbour Town in Hilton Head, among 5 others he's done in South Carolina. He has also done the TPC (Tournament Players Club) at Sawgrass (Florida), Whistling Straits (Wisconsin), Crooked Stick (Indiana) and PGA West (California). In all, Dye has designed over 120 golf courses. There are as many actual encounters with Bigfoot as there are passively easy Pete Dye golf layouts. There are international travel experts set on the opportunity to lure avid Pete Dye fans to the dunes of South Carolina. It will be to experience the nuances and frustrations of Kiawah's now-famed Ocean Course. There is something to be said about the quest to conquer the biggest beast on the beach.

You might even get to see Roger Warren measuring the break of a birdie putt.

Warren will be the brilliant man whom you'll remember with the microphones pushed below his jaw line during the 2012 PGA Championship. It would not be because he shot a sixty-five or double-eagled the sixteenth hole. His importance will rise to what he performed behind the scenes to promote the real star, the Ocean Course at Kiawah Island. In doing so, Warren elevated golf across the world while simultaneously lifting the entire Charleston community to an even greater height.

The youthful Irishman Rory McIlroy, only twenty-three, won the 2012 PGA Championship by posting a score that tallied a record eight shots better than second place. Given that the Ocean Course befuddled the entire field on the Friday round with thirty-mile-an-hour winds, hoisting scores to an average of four over par for the entire field, McIlroy's command of the event was all the more amazing. He was the only golfer who made it look easy.

"I was four over through thirteen holes on Friday. It had all the signs of a round that could get away from you. I dug in there deep," said McIlroy, who finished at 13 under 275. "I definitely feel like I'm getting better at handling conditions like that and being able to just know when a 74, 75 is a decent score and move on and know that the next day should be a bit better."[126]

The Ocean Course brought Charleston and Kiawah Island to a world that finds the universality of golf a reason to broaden the interactions of humanity. They play. They doff their caps, and they shake hands.

On any given day, the scene at the eighteenth green will show the players of the last group placing the flag back into the hole while removing their caps prior to the traditional handshake. Golf is a most courteous tradition. It is usually a day well spent. The foursome will imagine the camera pulling back to a wide angle. As Charlestonians, we will all be in that visual. It will be our Kiawah, our Charleston and our Roger Warren who administered it all to that vast admiring world.

The Most Interesting Man Alive

DR. HARVEY SCHILLER

T hink Indiana Jones. Lord Byron. James Bond. Sir Walter Raleigh. Still, you have not reached Dr. Harvey Schiller. Simply, he is the most interesting man alive.

He flew missions in Vietnam. Others did that. He retired from the United States Air Force as a general officer. Impressive, but there are other retired generals. He became the commissioner of the Southeastern Conference, America's premier NCAA football conference. Well, there's just one of those at a time. That's pretty special. He became the president of a sports network and then president of an NHL (hockey) franchise. He started another network. He became the executive who changed World Championship Wrestling. He advised George Steinbrenner, longtime owner of the New York Yankees. He worked closely with entrepreneur Ted Turner. He was a director of the United States Olympic Boxing Team (director of Los Angeles Olympic Boxing Competition) prior to becoming the secretary general and executive director of the United States Olympic Committee. Impressed yet?

"Three hundred million Americans take ownership of that team. Not winning the Olympics is not an option," Schiller smiled. "Those 300 million bosses watch, and you better not fail."

Schiller received his undergraduate degree in chemistry from The Citadel. His roommate was All-American Paul Maguire. The legendary coach Al Davis recruited Schiller and Maguire to play football at the military school. Maguire went on to a career in professional football and a post-football career as a television color analyst. Schiller received his master's and PhD in chemistry from the University of Michigan. He did research there prior to appointment by the president as permanent professor at the United States Air Force Academy.

It was the chemistry that worked best in Ann Arbor to find his lifetime bride, Marcia. They have been married for fifty years and are now South Carolinians, living at Kiawah Island.

There's more to know about this Zarathustra, the omnipotent one, the golden boy with the silver harness. He is a marathon runner and adheres to a physical fitness routine. He rarely drinks, never smokes and loves food from the blue-plate restaurants that offer fresh vegetable side dishes. He is tall and athletic, tanned and self-confident. He is your best dinner guest. His stories are front page but in the back of his mind. His sense of humor is both academic and alleyway. He epitomizes the foreseeable end to an adventurous journey. He did it. You wish you had been there. He was.

He did minor things—for him—that would be career highlights for the best of us. Schiller was chairman and CEO of YankeeNets, owners of the Yankees, Nets and Devils; a director of the Boys and Girls Clubs of America; and serves on boards with Mesa Air Group (airlines) and the Competitor Racing Corporation. He is in the New York Athletic Club Hall of Fame, as well as The Citadel Athletic Hall of Fame and The Citadel School of Business College Hall of Fame.

He served as the executive director of the World Racing Group, Inc.—"The Greatest Show on Dirt." He serves as chairman of the board and chief executive officer of GlobalOptions Group, Inc., one of the top risk mitigation firms in the United States, as well as vice-chair of the Diversified Search group. He was chairman of Assante, U.S., a major player in the financial and life management field of products and services. He famously suspended "Mr. Ego," Eric Bischoff of World Championship Wrestling, live on television as president of Turner Sports Network. He attended the Armed Forces Staff College for the military. He completed Army Airborne parachute training and is a distinguished U.S. Air Force pilot. He knows how to drop in.

He served the U.S. State Department as advisor for alternate games (1980 Moscow Olympics) played in Nairobi, Kenya. He served as vice-chair of the Host Committee for the 2004 Republican National Convention in New York City. He served on a White House commission—for President George W. Bush—on presidential scholars.

Multiple times, Schiller has been accorded among the Most Powerful 100 People in Sports by *Sporting News* magazine. It's just a part of what he does.

He is a board member of the Baseball Hall of Fame in Cooperstown, New York. He was president of the International Baseball Federation. He served on the NCAA Executive and Championship Committees. His oversight of wrestling, dirt track racing, baseball, hockey, football and the Olympics would seem to be enough. He recently agreed to be the vice-chairman of the 2013 America's Cup, the world's premier sailing race.

It would seem that he enjoys the challenges of high-profile tasks. It may be because he is not afraid to fail. He is more focused on effort.

"I most cherished my time in the military because it was service to the country. It meant much to me and still inspires my career after the air force. The common thread of my career is 'service.' Even in the business world, the idea of service makes it all worthwhile," Schiller explained.

There may be a manual on service that Schiller read that had pages missing for others of us mortals. The most interesting man has the most interesting stories for every step along the way.

Take Ted Turner, owner of CNN, TBS and the Atlanta Braves. Schiller was privy to Turner's verbal sparring with FOX Television's Rupert Murdoch.

Dr. Harvey Schiller is among most accomplished people in any sphere. He lives at Kiawah Island. *Courtesy of Marcia Schiller.*

Turner famously challenged Murdoch to a boxing match. Walking down one of New York's wide avenues with Schiller at his side, Turner asked, "Do you think I can beat Murdoch?"

Schiller deftly replied, "You might want to put me on the undercard!" It was an implication that someone from the Turner organization needed to ensure potential attendees of a victory.

Schiller would seem to most observers to be the straighten-out-the-mess chairman who comes in, identifies the mission and has the solution charted before the directors have their coffee. He's a doer. It's his modus operandi.

But Schiller is also a time management expert. Yet his personality is wide beyond a schedule. His interests include even the outlandish. Citadel roommate Paul Maguire explained: "Four of us were in an alcove [large corner] room during our senior year. We all had a weird side of mischief. But Harvey was the chemistry major and the best student in the room. You never suspected him of anything. One of our roommates, Freddy Williams, used to be able to nap for ten minutes and wake up like he'd been out for hours. It was uncanny. He'd come in and spring to the top bunk, right over Harvey's, and you could swear he had fallen asleep on the way up. Harvey saw this every day. So one day, while Freddy was at class, Harvey carefully removed the wire spring support beneath Freddy's mattress and placed it behind the full press [metal closet] where nobody could see it. He then balanced the mattress back up on the edges of the steel bed rail. When Freddy came in and sprung to the bunk, he landed in the middle and fell all the way through to Harvey's bunk. You should have seen the look on Williams's face! I have never laughed so hard at a prank as I did that one. Williams was livid. Harvey and I were rolling with laughter. I still hold that prank as one of the great memories I have of my time at The Citadel. People look at what Harvey's done in his career and presume that he's all business. Harvey's sense of humor can match anybody's."

Roommate Maguire was drafted at the end of his senior year by the Los Angeles Chargers[127] of the American Football League. They became the more familiar San Diego Chargers[128] within his first year. Maguire became an All-Pro linebacker and punter. He is one of only twenty players to play all ten years of the AFL existence prior to its merger with the National Football League (1970).[129] He also played tight end at The Citadel and led the nation in touchdown receptions in 1959.[130] He and Schiller have remained close personal friends since their four years at The Citadel.

"Being great is not always being happy," Schiller intimated. "I have met many great people that were not happy. So, to me, the goal is happiness, not greatness. That goal has been foremost in what I have tried to do in my own life. You'd be surprised how simple life gets when you find happiness for your family, your spouse, others around you as well as yourself. Greatness is what others may assign, but happiness is up to you."

In the plan of happiness, Schiller is a PhD. He built a home near the beach at Kiawah Island. He reattached to many Charleston friends and his college. He flies out to New York City weekly to proctor his corporate startup, GlobalOptions Group, an international company specializing in information and risk management. Schiller is the CEO. His children, Derek Schiller and Erika Schiller Tucker, are both married and near enough to keep the extended family and the three grandchildren near the circle of happiness. Marcia keeps the schedule and serves as one of Charleston's most engaging conversationalists.

"She saw things in me that I didn't even see in myself," Schiller offered. They are an inseparable couple.

Marcia Schiller, lithe and lovely, has been the silent part of the Schiller dynamic for a lifetime. She has not kept a scorecard of his victories but has supported his career decisions as a seamless transition, remaining one in mind and perspective. The road traveled has been exciting, adventurous and fulfilling.

"Harvey has accomplished many things in his life, but nothing is more important or rewarding to him than his family. We first saw each other in a lecture hall at the University of Michigan…and it was love at first sight. Going into the military taught us to depend on each other and hold our family close. The family was a team, and we lived, supported and nurtured that team. Harvey is our biggest cheerleader and the one who continually sets the bar higher for us and for him. He is our rock. We all depend on him for his love, wisdom and sense of humor. We are where we are because of him, and he is where he is because of us—we are one."

Daughter Erika, a striking visual compilation of her parents, presents another perspective: "I could not be more proud of my dad and the many outstanding accomplishments he has realized in his life. His success has inspired me to push myself to continuously strive for excellence. I am always amazed by his ability to keep his love and commitment to our family above all else. The humility and grace he shows to everyone who are lucky enough to cross paths with him is a valuable life lesson. I am motivated each day to emulate his spirit for life and will always appreciate how fortunate I am to be my father's daughter."

Schiller's active lifestyle seems to have no far horizon. He enjoys the experience. In May 2012, The Citadel honored Schiller with his second honorary degree, only the second time that has happened in the college's 170-year history. Schiller served as the graduation speaker for the cadet corps. His advice was a blueprint from the rearview mirror of his experience.

"I never dreamed of being a pilot and hadn't even flown on an airplane, much less logging thousands of hours in defense of this country in both war and peace. They wouldn't even allow me to take chemistry in high school—my grades were so poor. And I went on to earn a PhD, teach and to do research. Careers at the highest level of sport, marching in front of our Olympic team in Barcelona and having a family to be proud of…you see, it's not always what you see in yourself but what other people see in you…We're a generation that turned sand into silicone…There are lots of mountains to climb, but here's a little fact: the mountains don't get any higher. The human spirit can transcend all that."

Indeed, Schiller had transcended more than the imaginable. And he was back, fifty-two years later, setting a course for 484 members of The Citadel class of 2012. Being back brought some reflection.

"I have rings from the Olympics, the World Series and several other meaningful venues. But the ring I treasure most is the one I received from The Citadel in 1960," Schiller noted. "There, I learned things that made for lifelong differences. I saw things in myself that I didn't know were there. There were lessons of leadership, academic performance, integrity and honor, interaction with the faculty and staff, time management skills, special friendships, memorable personalities, the inspiration for going to graduate school and the start of a career in the air force. None of these things were on my mind or in my forward view when I arrived there in August 1956."

Schiller returned to see the world he once knew. He noticed the change in the community as he began to recapture the youthful enjoyment and enthusiasm he found decades before.

"Charleston was definitely a different place than it is now. When I left out of those gates, there was no appreciable tourism in Charleston. Charleston had a village-like atmosphere, like a condensed city into a small area. There were some areas I wouldn't go," he said with a grin.

"There was some comfort in being a cadet. The local restaurants and shops treated you in a different way. Now, it's all about tourism. It's really an incredible transition. It's called 'growth.' It is culturally more attractive and more diverse. The biggest change is the idea of discrimination from the 1950s and 1960s. It was inherent, it seemed, and now I feel it has been mostly eliminated. It makes this community much better.

"When I come home to Kiawah now, Marcia and I like to take a nice morning walk on the beach. On Saturdays we go downtown for the farmers' market and eat lunch at one of the local places. I like to drive through The Citadel before I go back home. Later, I look forward to Marcia's fried chicken. We'll watch the sun go down, and sometimes we go for a swim. That's really a wonderful day."

Invariably, Monday comes too soon. Schiller's incredible life experience includes interaction with the names that had defined a generation in the world of sports. There's Ted Turner and the late George Steinbrenner, both owners with a flair for drama: "Two completely different styles, but both very competitive gentlemen that wanted to win. I had confidence in their vision, and they allowed me the latitude to do what I do best. I am very thankful to both. I also have a great big place in my heart for college football and especially those of the Southeastern Conference for giving me my first real experience in high-profile sports. That job got me to others. The Olympics were always a huge but rewarding challenge. I just love sports, and I had been fortunate enough that people trusted me in positions well within my abilities to assist and deliver results.

"But I guess you could say my favorite is baseball. Just look in any airport departure gate, and you'll see many partial newspapers, most all with the sports sections missing. They're mostly reading about baseball. Baseball is the only sport that is in the newspapers every day. It's because of the statistics, the contracts, the drafts, the personalities, the player combinations, the managers, lineup changes and the need for teams to fill voids. It is never out of season. Baseball requires daily attention. People cannot get enough."

Schiller's son Derek would agree. Derek Schiller serves as executive vice-president of sales and marketing for the Atlanta Braves. Derek, tall and athletic, has a wealth of on-the-job instructions that came from the attentiveness of his father.

"As any child who has a parent that has accomplished greatness can likely attest to, there are many lessons that are learned beyond just the traditional father-son teachings. In my dad's case, I learned to always strive to be a better person and to never stop learning. I can easily look to my dad to see someone who has not been satisfied with past successes as an indication of his future desire to achieve even more. In my career, I was fortunate to have him help open a door for me to the business world of sports. While I have accomplished much on my own in this business, it is those lessons of constant improvement that have been the foundation of my own success. In our personal life, he has been a great father, but he has improved to become an even better grandfather to my own children."

Schiller's stint with the United States Olympic Committee lasted two decades in different capacities. He started as the director of the boxing tournament for the 1984 Los Angeles Olympics. His leadership graduated him to other positions through several summer and winter competitions until he became the executive director of the Olympic Committee in 1990 for the Games in Albertville (1990), Barcelona (1992) and Lillehammer (1994). Schiller served in several other capacities prior to his appointment as the president of the International Baseball Federation (2011). His insight into the Olympic benefits of baseball as a sport has been compelling, though the 2016 Olympics in Rio de Janeiro will not pick up the competition.

Schiller was generous in his disappointment: "We want to congratulate Rio and the IOC on today's selection. As the 'national pastime' of so many Latin American countries, the upside from a grass-roots brand and marketing perspective to have baseball in the 2016 games grows exponentially now, and we will remain steadfast in our belief, despite the IOC's announcement…that baseball should now be strongly reconsidered for readmission to the program in 2016. Baseball is growing quickly in Brazil, and there is no sport that could bring more attention, marketing assistance and consistent exposure over the next seven years as a partner to the Olympic Games. We are hopeful that the efforts of the IBF [International Baseball Federation], along with our partners at MLB and COPABE [Confederación Panamericana de Béisbol], and the support we have gotten from the Organization of American States, will be revisited in the coming days. Baseball has done all that was asked, and will do whatever is necessary to both be included and be the best Olympic partner of any sport."

Baseball had been on a trial basis over the last few Olympics but was not picked up for the London 2012 Games or Rio de Janeiro in 2016. Besides facilities, there are expense issues and the soft emphasis of other worldwide grass-roots participation.

When—not if—baseball becomes an exciting Olympic standard, the entire baseball world will owe a maximum-decibel symphony of seventh-inning-stretch applause to Dr. Harvey Schiller.

Schiller's legacy with both the U.S. Olympic Committee and the International Olympic Committee could not be greater. In 1994, he was the recipient of the rare and highest honor—the Olympic Order—bestowed on an individual by the International Olympic Committee.[131] His work with both the United States and International Olympic organizations has not ceased. He is still the world's most viable Olympic consultant.

There are yet a few other categories in which Schiller may well qualify as the most, the best, the finest and the greatest. He may be The Citadel's greatest living alumnus—a very distinguished accolade for a college that supplies many general officers, CEOs, authors, religious leaders and national political figures. He may be the ultimate world authority on information and risk management. He could be the most forward thinker on major sports franchises and their media marketing accessibility. He is likely the most prolific CEO of diverse business and entertainment background extant. He measured it all to fit into one lifetime. Nobody else could have done it.

Simply, he is the most interesting man alive.

Remembrances of Henry Picard

THROUGH CONVERSATIONS WITH BETH DANIEL, DR. HASKELL ELLISON, TOMMY FORD AND FRANK FORD III

There are two truths about golf in America. It started in Charleston. The area is rich with names of those who played it well.

One Charleston golfing family can claim more than one hundred amateur championships. Another female professional golfer from Charleston is among the greatest to ever play the game. Golf in Charleston has sewn together another great history and with it more art than artifacts.

They remember us for starting the Civil War and forget that we started a much more significant "civil peace" in Charleston. Historians have no doubt that all golf of the Western Hemisphere started in the Holy City. Golf clubs were delivered to Charleston in 1743 for the express purpose of playing the greatest course in America: Harleston Green. It was the only course in America. That expanse of grass—its natural progression was to become America's first country club—became the home course of Henry Gilford Picard, a man we should never forget.

But first, we must speak of the "first."

The ultimate identifiable golf course worldwide was (and still *is*) in St. Andrews, Scotland, with evidence that golf was played there in 1552.[132] Finding just one of the lost balls from that era may fetch a fortune and a free stay at Macdonald Rusacks Hotel on the famed seventeenth road hole!

Though Charleston's Harleston Green course has been speculated to sprawl over to present-day Beaufain Street, the only known remnant—a park area—is best identified by a much-later pillared ruin of the old

Charleston Museum at Rutledge Avenue bordered by Bennett, Ashley and Calhoun Streets. In time, it became the first country club in America (1786). The Country Club of Charleston, originally named the South Carolina Golf Club, had moved. The third location of the club, now on James Island bordering the Intracoastal Waterway, features the design of renowned golf architect Seth Raynor (built 1924). There is no argument that the original organization (1786) of the currently monikered "Country Club" predates all other country clubs in America.

Golf Styles Media Group explained: "It is true that the South Carolina Golf Club was chartered in Charleston in 1786 with Rev. Dr. Henry Purcell, the rector at St. Michael's Episcopal Church, as president and merchants Edward Penman and James Gairdner as vice-president and treasurer. We know this from newspaper and almanac accounts, but we also know that the club had no formal course."[133]

Oh, they needed a formal course. No wonder there was confusion! The charter held. The name changed twice. In any event, a six iron from Harleston Green today might strike any number of hospitals.

Yet, those who refuse to bow persist. Another St. Andrew's Golf Club in Hastings-on-Hudson (near Yonkers), New York, proclaims itself the oldest golf club in America.[134] It claims 1888. But in 1884, a gentleman named Montague laid out a six-hole course on his hilly farm acreage in White Sulphur Springs, West Virginia. That club, the Oakhurst Links, predates the New York course. Because Oakhurst disbanded in 1910, the New York club pronounced itself the oldest golf club in America in continuous operation.[135] Technicalities aside, those Yanks have not been paying attention. The Country Club of Charleston, through the reanointments, beats them both by one hundred years. Our bluebloods beat their bluebloods, and that's that.

It is again historically documented in public website form. Try "Finley on Golf." It is researched quite well: "The first golf played in North America that is documented was in Charleston, South Carolina. A Charleston newspaper, the Gazette, made mention of scheduled events of the South Carolina Golf Club and referenced its first year as 1786. We can assume that golf was played for several years prior to that date. Being a major East Coast port city, many of its merchants were Scottish who obviously had access to clubs and balls shipped back to Charleston from abroad. One such Scot, David Deas, who ran a store on East Bay Street, received a shipment in 1743 from the Port of Leith, Scotland, which included 96 golf clubs and 432 balls. The written accounts of

The best of the best, Frank Ford Sr. and Henry Picard brought the game of golf to new heights in Charleston. *Courtesy of Tommy Ford.*

this golf association portray the organization as primarily social—which certainly seems appropriate for this gay, port city. The group would meet periodically at Harleston's Green, in the area between what is now Calhoun and Bull streets, east of Rutledge. They would dig a few holes and hit the little ball around. These gatherings were mostly an opportunity for the ladies and gentlemen to join together in fellowship, to spin yarns and enjoy good food and drink. Their 'club house' was William's Coffee House where they held their meetings. There is no evidence that a regular, permanent site course designated for golf existed at this period of time in Charleston. A similar fraternity of golfers was formed a few years later in neighboring Savannah. We can therefore assume with some certainty that the first golfers in America were South Carolinians, many of Scottish descent, playing the game only 12 years after the signing of the Declaration of Independence or perhaps, sooner. We can imagine these early golf outings would resemble chipping and putting contests."[136]

There you have it. But there is a broader message to be explored. What did we do with the sport? We can explore this through another history of significance. Charleston was the preferred home of an often overlooked but fine professional golfer of the 1920s and beyond. He was also known to be one of the game's great gentlemen: Henry "Pick" Picard (correctly pronounced pe-CARD). Picard was a tall and athletic player. He worked as a pro at the Country Club of Charleston from 1925 to 1934, or from around the time that the new Seth Raynor–designed course opened (early 1925). He returned to Charleston at every opportunity, including a stint at Yeaman's Hall Club in 1950–51, until permanently retiring in the Holy City in 1973. He considered himself a Charlestonian. He bought a home in Wappoo Heights in the early 1930s and kept that home for the duration of his life.

Picard was one of the "cumyas" who found Charleston's warm weather and welcoming country club to be a hospitable home for his game. Born in Plymouth, Massachusetts, Picard remained in Charleston despite a Depression-era setback that meant that the country club could no longer pay him. He and his then-pregnant wife, Anne "Sunny" Addison Picard, found another way to stay. Private investors from the country club noticed Picard's proficient talent, his regimented work ethic and his desire to join the touring professionals. They backed him. Over the next eight years, Picard won twenty-four tournaments, including the 1938 Augusta Invitational (renamed the Masters in 1939).

"I guess when they started the coat thing [the first winner to get a green jacket was Sam Snead in 1949], all of a sudden it got bigger than anyone could have imagined," Picard stated to Rick Lipsey of *Sports Illustrated* in 1995. "When I won I think they had to take up a collection from the members to pay me. And the prize money was $1,500. Now it's the best tournament in the world. Going back to Augusta for the annual champions' dinner is the highlight of my year. It's the only time I get to see all my old friends."[137]

Picard won the 1939 PGA Championship, then in a match play format. He bested Byron Nelson in a thirty-six-hole final. He won seven tournaments that year and the money title, at $10,303.[138] Picard was one of a handful of the finest players of his era, with Nelson, Ben Hogan, Gene Sarazen and Sam Snead. Picard played for two winning Ryder Cup teams, teaming with friend Johnny Revolta in the four-ball matches. He only recorded one loss (in a four ball, 1937) and was never bested in the singles play.[139] As his career peaked, the world spiraled into war. By the war's end, Picard was nearly forty. The many canceled major tournaments decimated what was an otherwise promising career. But Picard had other talents. He was considered the best teaching professional of his day. He gave lessons to both Hogan and Snead, once proclaiming that the lessons he taught Snead were "the most expensive he ever gave." They enabled Snead to win too often while Picard was still making a living on tour. In all, Snead won a record eighty-two tour events before his retirement.[140]

The excitement of playing for prize money and the lure of regular pay from country clubs was normally a compelling contradiction during the Depression. There was not much money to be gained in either venue. A typical 1930s PGA tournament paid out less than $10,000 to the entire field. Travel was not only expensive but also arduous. Amateurs like Bobby Jones kept their status, usually having another career that fed their families. Jones was a lawyer who "retired" from competitive golf at the age of twenty-eight in 1930.[141] Club pros got regular pay in addition to fees for lessons and a few tips. They did not have to contend with barnstorming time away from their families. Picard was one of many who were able to balance this lifestyle. Unlike the majority of the others, he excelled at both.

He gave other lessons but not always on the course. He became a trusted friend. His Charleston colleague Frank Ford Sr. was the greatest amateur of his era in South Carolina. Ford lived to be one hundred. Ford and Picard played matches with and against each other over a lifetime of friendship. They played against people like Sarazen, Hogan, Snead and even Bobby Jones. The benefit of that camaraderie reached to Ford's children and grandchildren, arguably the greatest golfing family the state has ever known.

Sports Illustrated framed the dynamic: "Frank Ford Sr. won 18 club championships [some in other parts of the state]; his sons, Tommy and Billy, have won 10 more between them; and Frank III [grandson] has taken another 16...[The senior Ford] played patriarch to a four-generation clan of hotshots with more than 100 significant championships to their credit. What the Wallenda family is to the high wire and the Gambino family is to crime, so are the Fords to golf in the Carolina Lowcountry."

Even great-grandson Cordes Ford, a Charleston lawyer, tied the unofficial course record at the challenging Raynor layout with a sixty-two. Picard also recorded a sixty-two. Tommy Ford has recorded two sixty-threes. Not to be outdone, the Ford women were also prolific. Frank Sr.'s mother won the first Ford family championship. His sister, brother and wife won others.[142]

The Ford family included, the Country Club of Charleston became a center for the once-isolated gentry. It was here that the short strides up Charleston's burgeoning rise were measured. There were bankers, lawyers, college presidents, retired generals and owners of small businesses. The club featured others: beer distributors, concrete providers, road builders, local merchants and insurance executives. The swaying slopes and flat-bottomed bunkering that Raynor set into otherwise flat surfaces challenged them all. As the resident pro, Picard could make their enjoyment greater by what he knew best—every nuance of the game of golf. He lived the game.

He also simplified the game to others from all walks of life. Dr. Haskell Ellison saw it firsthand: "Henry was a man of few words. He was direct. But he had a huge heart. Everybody that met him benefited from his friendship. I met him as I walked past the emergency room at old St. Francis Hospital. I knew who he was and asked if I could help him. He had nicked himself in his garage golf shop and needed a tetanus shot. He used to modify equipment for people and just loved crafting the old clubs. After the booster shot, he asked me to stop by and let him look at my swing. He lived over in Wappoo Heights. I called and stopped by a few days later. We became fast friends since that day. He invited me to play golf with him, and as good as he was, he was never intimidating or anything like that. If you were struggling, he'd stop and show you something to help. You felt privileged. After all, he straightened out both Ben Hogan and Sam Snead."

Picard, called "Pick" by his friends, was nicknamed the "Hershey Hurricane" by the greatest sportswriter of the age, Grantland Rice. He was also called the "Candy Kid." Hershey, Pennsylvania, is the chocolate capital of America. It is where Picard worked for seven years during the height of his playing career, from 1934 to 1941. Picard was known on the tour as a straightforward but benevolent teaching professional. He was very demanding and expected that what he taught would be practiced. Failure to practice lost the right to learn. He even taught the young Jack Grout, who later became the teacher of the greatest to ever play the game: Jack Nicklaus.

Picard had learned about helping others from a seemingly unlikely source. Walter Hagen, the carousing highest-profile professional golfer of the 1920s, was thrashed by a lanky young Picard in an eighteen-hole playoff at the Greensboro Carolina Open. Picard won by ten strokes, the first time Hagen had ever lost a playoff. After the match, Hagen took Picard aside and told him, "You can be one of the greatest golfers if you work hard on your game. Don't hit the ball so hard."[143] The *Milwaukee Journal* reported his large fan

Dr. Haskell Ellison gave Henry Picard a tetanus shot and they became lifelong friends. *Courtesy of Tommy Ford.*

following during the last round of his 1938 win at Augusta National: "It is true that perhaps outside of Bobby Jones, the galleries here wished for nothing more than a triumph for Henry Picard...Henry gives more than 1,000 lessons a year officially, we hear, and another 1,000 unofficially to the kids."[144]

Dr. Ellison shared that his humble kindness was seen well outside of golf. "He was known for his quiet generosity. There was a Dr. Reynolds that was in medical school at MUSC years ago. His family was unable to continue paying tuition. The young student was broke and ready to return home. Henry found a way to help him, and most people that knew Dr. Reynolds learned that Henry paid his way to finish. Henry never said a word about it. That tells you something about the character of Henry Picard. That was the way Henry was.

"Even when Ben Hogan was struggling with his game in the early 1930s and wanted to quit, Henry pulled him aside and encouraged him. He was fading the ball on every shot. He fixed his swing and told him to hang in. He told Hogan he'd back him financially, but it never became necessary. It's a matter of record that Hogan credited Picard with saving his career. He helped him again years later by adjusting his hand over a bit when Hogan had developed a big hook."

A 1989 article from the *Chicago Tribune* gave more insight. Hogan dedicated his first book, titled *Ben Hogan's Power Golf*, to Picard. "I thought he was entitled to that dedication," Hogan said. "He's a wonderful man. He dedicated his life to golf...I wanted to do it for him.[145] We were in Oakland, California, and he surmised that I was in a bad financial position, and I might have to go off the tour. He came to me and told me if I needed help just ask him, and he would help me."[146]

The Country Club of Charleston celebrated Picard's contributions to both golf and the Charleston community on April 6, 1959, the Monday after the Masters. "Henry Picard Day" was one of the greatest golf days the city had ever experienced. A high-profile match was played among Picard, Hogan, accomplished club pro Al Esposito and Frank Ford Sr. Over two thousand onlookers followed these expert players around the course. A formal dinner followed. Speakers extolled Picard's considerable contributions to the world's most aesthetic sport. The proceeds went to charity. By every measure, the event was an abundant and fitting tribute to a man of profound significance well beyond golf.

However, tragedy struck in the aftermath. William H. "Billy" Picard, a top amateur golfer and oldest son of the former champion, was killed in a head-on collision near Kingstree, South Carolina, on his attempted long journey home the next day. Billy Picard was one of the best amateur players in the country. He graduated from The Citadel in 1950 and, after a stint of military service, finished in the top 10 percent of students in his Harvard Law School class. He was a legal counsel for Alcoa in Pittsburgh. He and his brother Larry had followed the foursome around the country club the day before. The young promise of life was dashed. Billy Picard was only twenty-eight.[147]

"He was returning to his home. They were staying at our house at 88 Murray Boulevard. The body was laid out in our parlor, and the whole city mourned," Tommy Ford recalled. "It was a devastating time for Mr. Picard, as I recall. His son had a wife and two children. I'm not sure Mr. Picard ever got over that tragedy." The very private Picard grieved this loss profoundly.

In later years, wife Sunny became ill and needed nursing care. She was moved to a facility that could better assist her daily needs.

"Henry was by her side every day at five o'clock, even as she was fading. That was their time together," Dr. Ellison recalled.

Sunny predeceased him, dying in 1993. Henry Gilford Picard died at the age of ninety on April 30, 1997. He is buried at Live Oak Memorial Gardens, next to Sunny and his son Billy. Son Larry had put together a commemorative scrapbook, dedicated to his brother Billy, detailing the career of their father. The scrapbook included handwritten notes and insights into the game of golf. The script being most legible, they are treasured keepsakes that bind a deep friendship: "How do you describe a friendship? We got along well. He was a true friend," one note read.

The words slowed and drifted to an unspoken reminiscence. Larry's composure was interrupted. It was a moment he genuinely reflected. The large black scrapbook was there. Pages were turned. Each memory brought another. The pause was in reverence.

"Henry was my friend," another note memorialized.

Beth Daniel, who grew up through the youth program at the country club, had her own proud relationship with "the gentlemen's gentleman" that she described to others. She learned the game from the club's excellent professional, Al Esposito. But Picard was always there. Picard knew the difficulties of the tour and the importance of preparation.

Daniel won thirty-three LPGA tour events, including seven in 1990 when she was named the Associated Press Female Athlete of the Year. She is a member of the World Golf Hall of Fame. Daniel knew that the career of Henry Picard had been much overlooked. Statistics did not gauge his impact on the teaching side of the game. He had twenty-six career victories but was robbed of the chance for more because of World War II. Daniel made sure that veterans' committee voters noticed Picard's wide impact on others. She did not need to persuade but rather remind. Picard was voted into the World Golf Hall of Fame posthumously in 2006, as Daniel recalled.

Beth Daniel, in the LPGA Hall of Fame, attrributes much to the tutleage of Henry Picard. She gave his PGA Hall of Fame induction speech. *Courtesy of the Post & Courier.*

"I received a nice letter from a man in North Carolina that knew of my golfing relationship with Henry Picard. The letter had all of Picard's records and statistics attached. It appeared to me that he was certainly most deserving, so I made a few calls to others to make them aware that I supported his nomination. It was easy to forward the statistics because I had them from the letter I received. Since Mr. Picard had passed away, his vote would be in the veterans' category. He just missed getting voted in the first year [2005]. He made it into the hall the following year [2006]. Well, you know I was elated. He had meant so much to me personally."

It was in the eloquence of her memories that Beth Daniel performed the presentation of Picard to the World Golf Hall of Fame on October 30, 2006. Her remarks cited his impact not only on her but also on the game of golf: "I knew Mr. Picard from the time I began to play golf as a little girl in Charleston until his passing in 1997. Nearly fifty years separated us in age, yet the game of golf, as it does with so many strangers-turned-friends, brought us together. Now, he was quite the figure at the Country Club of Charleston, tall and handsome, always wearing his cotton dress shirt and tie, even in the one-hundred-degree heat. To a little eight-year-old kid just learning the game, this legendary golfer was an imposing figure. I was definitely intimidated by him. In fact, there were times when I would see him coming down the path looking for me, and I would hide behind the big oak tree by the first tee. You see, he would always ask me a question about golf like, 'How do you hit the ball high?' 'How do you hit a fade?'—something usually related to the swing—and then he would walk away. At eight years old, I didn't have the answer to his questions, but I knew I had the rest of the day to work on it. And he knew I would go out and hit ball after ball all day long and figure it out. That was his way of building my work ethic, helping me to develop my shot making and instilling in me a purpose on the golf course and a love for practice. At the end of the day, he would find me again. If I got the answer wrong, he would explain why and help me understand that particular lesson, how to hit it high or how to hit a fade. But if my answer was correct, he would simply say, 'Thank you,' and walk away.

"One day, I went to my golf bag, and I discovered it was full of brand-new balata golf balls. You have to understand, as a kid, I played with whatever golf balls I could find, so I felt like I had hit the lottery. When I realized he was the one who had done it, I gathered up the courage to thank him. He just looked at me and said, 'You should be playing with the right kind of golf balls,' and walked away. That was it. That was his way.

"Years later, when I saw him, I asked him about a few things, and he mentioned he no longer received golf balls. I remembered what he did for me so many years before. I called Titleist and had a gross sent to his house.

"As my career developed, I got to play golf with both Mr. Picard and Mr. Frank Ford. They both had a fine knowledge of the game and especially the short game. They'd say, 'That looks good' and 'You should try this.' You bet I listened! These were two wonderful gentlemen.

"That place [the country club] had something for everybody. You could even learn from the caddies there. I'd sometimes sit by that big oak by the first tee just to hear what the caddies were saying. Horace, the caddie master, would check on my putting. He was really helpful. The ladies there had a strong Ladies' Association, and the Junior Golf program for both boys and girls was simply outstanding."[148]

Daniel organized a benefit tournament for several years that she named for Ford and Picard. She brought in fellow LPGA professionals each year, like Liselotte Neumann, Jane Crafter, Meg Mallon and Betsy King. The two legendary gentleman golfers drove the course together and greeted the players. It made the event all the more meaningful.

"They were great ambassadors. They were not playing anymore but still quite interested in the game. They'd ask how I was doing. They'd ask about my irons, look at my swing. They were at home on any golf course and just loved being around golfers. And just to see Mr. Picard brought me back to those little girl days. He knew the game, and you respected every word he said."

Tommy Ford, another in the finest line of Charleston's amateur golfers and Frank Ford's youngest son, recalls the unusual ways that Picard taught the principles of the game: "I needed a chipping lesson because I was having trouble controlling the golf ball around the greens. He agreed to meet me one afternoon. He turned me toward a large oak tree, just a few feet away. I wondered what he was doing. He threw some balls down and told me to hit chip shots at the tree. I wasn't even sure that he was serious, but I did as he directed. Sure enough, I took the club back and stopped it abruptly on the downswing, conscious of not injuring my wrist by hitting the tree. The clipping of the ball

Tommy Ford has earned a reputation as one of the finest gentlemen in the game. He is also one of the best golfers. *Courtesy of Frank Ford III.*

put backspin on the shot and gave me the feel of control. It was a brilliant lesson, though unorthodox. But it was typical of Pick."

Tommy Ford has won seven club championships at the Country Club of Charleston, the Senior Azalea and the Super Senior Azalea. But the best comment on the next generation of Fords that Picard knew was said almost forty years ago. When Ford was twenty-nine years old, Picard told him he had never seen anyone who could hit a three wood better.[149]

"If you want to find the best person, the best past president, the best greens committee chairman, it's Tommy Ford," said Country Club of Charleston director of golf Hart Brown. "And he has the best golf swing in the club, bar none."[150]

Ford had many occasions to learn from Picard through Picard's golfing relationship with Ford's much-accomplished father: "The pro, Al Esposito, taught us the full swing. There was nobody that had that part of the game more down pat. Even though my father was among the finest short game players anywhere, he rarely gave lessons but was most gracious to everyone in giving tips. Dad could spin a wedge shot close from off the cart path pavement.

"Picard loved to teach the short game. He had every shot and every technique. He was especially a fine putting instructor. There was no part of the game that he did not teach well.

"One of the golf stories I remember is the one about Picard going to Forest Lake Golf Course in Columbia before the Masters. He was hitting a bunch of long irons into the tall pine trees when the pro came out. He asked him what he was doing. Picard told him that he was practicing the high soft two iron that could climb over pines. That's the way he thought and practiced to play at Augusta. He worked on specific shots for specific courses. He won the tournament the next week, as the story goes."

A high soft two iron? Would such a shot even be contemplated given today's technologically advanced equipment and penchant for specialty clubs like hybrids?

Frank Ford III, the namesake grandson of Picard's golfing friend, also crowded

In admiration of greatness, Frank Ford III has emulated his grandfather and Masters Champion Henry Picard. His amateur record is unsurpassed. *Courtesy of Tommy Ford.*

the prodigious Charleston family's trophy case. The country club's flagship amateur tournament, the Azalea, is considered among the best in America. It attracts an international field. Frank Ford III has won the Azalea six times. Ford most recently finished third—at the age of fifty-nine—in the 2011 Senior British Amateur played at Royal Portrush, Northern Ireland. He has won six City of Charleston Amateurs, three State of South Carolina Amateurs and numerous four-ball championships and senior amateur titles.

The accomplished stockbroker may not be easily impressed about golf exploits. But then again, he saw something that would have impressed even Hogan and Snead.

"When Henry Picard was sixty-seven years old, we had arranged to play one summer day. We had a foursome with younger guys and Mr. Picard. We had planned to play thirty-six holes that day from the very back tees—or as we called it 'one foot in the rough.' He said he'd play all thirty-six. He had that broad-brimmed white hat and that long-sleeved white shirt. Charleston is always sweltering in the summer. You know what he shot? Sixty-eight, sixty-seven. He shot sixty-eight, sixty-seven over thirty-six holes in the Charleston heat at the age of sixty-seven! That was just amazing! And during the round, he showed me something I never forgot. He would hit his clubs the opposite of the wind. If the wind came from the right, he'd fade the ball into it; if it came from the left, he'd draw into it. I had to ask him why he did it backward. His answer was that he used the wind to control the ball, not to carry greater distances. That made perfect sense. I never forgot the lesson.

"He had an eye for things. Now, you would pay a fortune to go get videotaped to see what Pick would already notice just by looking at you. One day, he watched me for a minute and told me I needed a different shaft for my irons. I had Hogan Apex irons with a four shaft. I didn't think anything about it. In a few weeks, I had a new set of irons delivered to me with Hogan Apex 5 shafts. I had no idea they were coming. I played with them, and sure enough, they fit me better. Another time he told me that I would need to change my swing because I couldn't use my legs as well as I got older. He convinced me I needed to do it. I did. He was right again.

"He had this habit that, when you demonstrated a result that he was trying to lead you to, he would simply say, 'Thank you.' It meant 'mission accomplished' and that the time he spent was not wasted. There is no better story about this than when I was playing in the last group for the 1986

Azalea title. On the par-three seventeenth, I was three up. My opponent was on the green. I hit into the short-side bunker. The pin was tucked close. My opponent could birdie; I was looking at bogey. But Pick had just given me a bunker lesson before the tournament and had me practicing a weak left wrist and more aggressive swing on those short high bunker shots. He and my grandfather were walking along behind the match. I had one foot out of the bunker and concentrated on the lesson to try to get the ball up quick and stop. I pulled it off. The ball landed and trickled to eight inches. The next sound I heard was Pick from behind me saying, 'Thank you.' After that tap-in and my opponent's miss, even I couldn't blow three shots on the eighteenth!

"What a heritage to have! Granddaddy [Frank Ford Sr.] was the best amateur around. Pick was a hall of famer and a gentleman champion that taught other great golfers—like Snead and Hogan—and even Beth Daniel. He was widely admired. And they were both right here. If ever Charleston had a 'golden age,' it was those two guys at this old country club."

Our golden age is longer than that of those other delusional claimants up north.

A merchant ship brought golf clubs and golf balls to Charleston in 1743. It's indisputable. Henry Picard brought the intricate lessons of the game of golf to Charleston in 1925. We should all say, "Thank you." That is equally indisputable.

Driven by an Idea

Pat Caddell

A t the age of twenty-six, Pat Caddell was in a room with presidential candidate Jimmy Carter, his wife, Rosalyn, and advisors Hamilton Jordan, Griffin Bell, Bert Lance and Jody Powell. Caddell was the whiz kid, the only one amongst them not from Georgia. They were looking to him for political savvy and direction. It was 1976.

Caddell read the numbers as a pioneer in the somewhat new science of political polling data. He also knew much about what the public wanted. He knew how to make the public comfortable with this refreshing candidate from the Deep South, when other pundits wrote him off as being regionally crippled. A southerner could not win the White House in 1976. By their nature, according to other political gurus, "any candidate from the South had to be a racist."

Caddell knew better: "I always read a lot. C. Vann Woodward wrote a book entitled *The Burden of Southern History*. Southerners had one advantage in the racial upheaval of the 1960s that northerners never quite understood. They may have had cultural adversity, but the whites and the blacks were from the same land. They understood that the land was a unifier. Van Woodward saw this. Also, the South was the only region in America that had the benefit of the experience of defeat. They were able to eventually resume life beyond the loss of the Civil War. It was devastating, but they persevered. So southerners understand that there is a downside to losing a political disagreement that changes a culture. Where there was once prosperity, poverty followed. You saw this in Charleston perhaps more than in any other southern city. Take that thought to today. Most of this country thinks that we are charmed and that we cannot fail. The South knows better."

C. Vann Woodward taught history at Yale University and became one of the country's leading authorities on southern history. He lived into his nineties and was described as a "master of irony and counterpoint."[151] The theories on cultural bias and race relationships that Vann Woodward represented in the 1970s were thought provoking. Caddell read him as a viewpoint of his interest in voter tendencies.

Born in Rock Hill, South Carolina, Caddell was a graduate of Harvard University by way of Bishop Kenny High School in Jacksonville, Florida. His father had a career in the United States Coast Guard. He spent several of his younger years in Charleston before his ultimate homecoming to Hanahan in 2006. He is here for the duration.

Caddell is beyond smart. He is much like the top physician in the hospital monitoring its most important patient ever. That patient is America. It has his full attention.

"When I explain my stake in this period of our history and—most importantly—the predictable results, I pull out this picture," Caddell noted as he showed the cellphone photo of three young grandchildren together in his driveway.

"That's Olivia, Patrick Travis and Janie Kate, my grandchildren. They are six, five and four. One day, if God allows me the time, they will be young adults and they will ask me, 'DaDa, how could you have let this happen?' I want to make sure that I do everything I can to educate the real stewards of this great country, its citizens. You've heard the term 'American Exceptionalism.' It says that we are different than every other country and that our system works and that we will always survive crises. There are some great traits among Americans, but we should realize that we are not exempt from history."

Caddell's conversational skills are compelling. His breadth of knowledge as to historical, cultural, military, economic and social issues includes quotes from the most pertinent person related to the current topic. He can go back centuries: "Abraham Lincoln said at one of the train stops on the way to his 1861 inauguration, 'I am a mere sentiment of your will.' Do you know how much the country has changed since then? Elected officials rarely express the sentiments of a voter's will these days. They seem to forget that it's the people that got them there. And the people are starting to see this. This must advance their will in the form of revolutionary ideas. The country must unite back behind the values by which we identify ourselves. There will be a renaissance. It must come in order to move the country forward."

A third party? Maybe.

"We have two parties in America. I call them the party of the corrupt and the party of the stupid. I worked for the Democratic Party. But I have no real affiliation with anyone by my own rules. I belong to the 'Memory Party.' That's the party that remembers what we're all about. It understands the reason for the Declaration of Independence and the U.S. Constitution. The Declaration is our soul. It cites 'deriving their just powers from the consent of the governed.' What happened to that? The constitution is our expression. It gives extraordinary latitude to one group that has managed to overstep its intention. That's the press. The press forms more judgment by swaying opinion against one or for the preference of another. They are the one institution without checks and balances. And their reasons are usually fraught with corruption. They give some easy passes to some, and others are hounded by innuendo. The press was not meant to have the enormous impact it enjoys at the expense of the people.

"There are two things we should be aware of: urgency and identity. We must know who we are and what our values are—and we must be able to recognize what's most important. That's what's urgent. If we can get together, both parties, and settle the big things, then the little things will be easier. But our identity—what we're all about—should help us define the solutions to the big things. These are the things that matter to our citizens, our security and our economy. We cannot afford to delay decisions on the most urgent matters, much as we are doing currently.

"A third party almost worked in 1992. Ross Perot was polling well ahead of Bill Clinton and George H.W. Bush. He was way ahead in major states like California and Florida. It was a sign that the people were aligning into revolution. Historically, an idea revolution starts a significant time before an actual revolution. The Stamp Act of 1765 was ten years before the actual fighting at Lexington and Concord. The American ideal had already existed under England's rule. Colonial Americans thought themselves different and more independent from 1670 to 1770. The revolutionary ideal had been here for many years. When they dumped tea into the harbors at Boston and Charleston, it was done independently, each without the knowledge of the other's protest. It was the people reacting to the unfairness of a distant ruler. But the Revolution did not start until ten years later. In a way, Ross Perot was the Stamp Act of 1992. The people—and I think it's a large majority that are neither Democrats nor

Pat Caddell seems to be the ultimate authority on presidential campaigns. He has managed six of them. *Courtesy of Fox News.*

Republicans—had had enough of the usual. So Perot became viable, and though he did not win, he changed the entire system. Maybe the Tea Party is the next change in ideals. It is certainly a movement to bring the power back to the people. I believe we will see this as soon as the next presidential election cycle in 2016.

"In another way, the experience with Jimmy Carter was a reaction against the normal. Carter was honest. One of the compelling moments was when he stood up and said, 'I will never lie to you.' This was after the Watergate scandal and the Vietnam War. Everything in Washington and New York was a lie. There was no question that Carter had strong moral principles. I saw it firsthand when my good friend Bob Shrum went on the attack with a public press conference against Carter. Everyone was looking to Carter for a response through me. I walked into the hotel suite. Carter's in his stocking feet, sitting relaxed. I simply told Carter that I couldn't go out and attack Shrum out of respect for an established friendship. I could have been fired. Carter asked, 'Does anyone know of a good speech writer?' Then he laughed. He told me that he admired my position and that it was not anything to worry about. We simply moved on without a response because Carter was principled in the way he protected the value of my friendship even with someone that came out against him.

"History was served. Carter won."

Propitiously, Caddell met others during the experience. It may have been more timely that others met Caddell. One was Warren Beatty: "I had started out as a high school senior in Jacksonville completing a project based on a Walter Cronkite initiative of finding out people's leanings prior to elections. I tested it and predicted by the measure I'd sampled that a particular candidate—Fred Schultz—would win a close race in Jacksonville for the statehouse. The media caught it. Schultz won."

Caddell was asked by Schultz to serve as an intern in Tallahassee, the state capital. There, he learned much from Schultz about ethics in politics. "Fred Schultz was a mentor to me and left a great impression. He was honest and always truthful. He emphasized that I should get the best education first and then start a career. Though he was a graduate of Princeton and wanted me to go there, I went to another Ivy League school: Harvard.

"Later, while finishing my degree at Harvard in Cambridge, Massachusetts, the McGovern people hired me to do some polling work based on the Schultz experience. I became a part of the McGovern campaign. Though McGovern lost, those around the campaign found that I could predict results and monitor people's feelings about the issues. It built my reputation quickly enough that Carter hired me for his 1976 run. During that time, he visited all of the southern governors. All of them were Democrats in 1972, when McGovern ran. When Carter went to Arkansas, their governor asked him if I could come along because he wanted to meet me. When I got there, another of his guests was Warren Beatty. We struck up a friendship. From that friendship, Beatty brought me in to look at some Hollywood projects."

Caddell became lore. The brilliant mind applied to politics could equally be applied to the genre of political productions. He became a major part of the cerebral insight built into movies like *In the Line of Fire* and *Air Force One*. He was the consultant for the hit television series *The West Wing*. Caddell's wealth of knowledge had crossed from reality to the surreal. He lived in California for a time: "It was a needed sabbatical. No bugs, no humidity. Santa Barbara is one of the world's magnificent places. There's great scenery and agreeable weather. It was a nice time for me. I even taught a course at the University of California at Santa Barbara, 'A History of American Presidential Elections.' I recharged my batteries."

But Caddell is a Charlestonian. Both sets of his grandparents are from Charleston. One set, Leon and Emma Burns, lived on Nassau Street for nearly forty years and had a corner store there. Leon Burns worked on the John P. Grace Bridge during its construction from 1927 to 1929. The Charleston roots run deep.

"Grandpa Burns could speak Gullah as well as anyone. He had that little store and worked it through the Depression and beyond. I lived there as a young boy in the 1950s and enjoyed my time with them, my mother's parents, and listening to all of the old stories. I was here for the Centennial Celebration of the firing on Fort Sumter held in Charleston in 1961 and also for the 150-year celebration in 2011. Not many can say that! My other grandparents were also enjoyable. They would talk about my great-grandfather as a Confederate soldier being able to go home to plant crops during the Civil War and missing the Battle of Chancellorsville. But he got back in time to participate in Gettysburg. He was one of the lucky ones to survive it."

Caddell's ability to recall battles, strategies and results hinted at his profound interest in the nation's most calamitous period of strife. And yet he is able to draw back to a wide-angled view of the result and enunciate conclusions. "The Civil War is one of the few wars in world history that had a sudden stop. Most civil and regional wars seem to transition from direct confrontation to guerrilla warfare that can last for decades—or even centuries. Look at the Middle East, Northern Ireland and so many other examples. In that regard, the United States was able to recover and rebuild with the matter settled. That is so very unusual in history."

Caddell is of Irish stock. He appreciates his Irishness. His thick hair and grandfatherly crop of facial growth would seem to have postured him as a character actor—the scientist, the taxi driver or the dean of the English Department. His gift of eloquence was earned. He is well read and well opinioned. He would be your worst nightmare in a political debate—and sometimes we all see that. Caddell serves as an often-summoned personality on several news shows, most notably as a frequent contributor to FOX News. He books Delta direct flights to New York, the Charleston airport situated just fifteen minutes from his Dominion Hills home. At FOX, Caddell is the centrist voice of reason, neither liberal nor conservative. His pedigree of party politics is most compelling.

Andrew Boucher, a Charlestonian who served as the national political director of Republican presidential hopeful Rick Santorum's campaign, expounded on Caddell's impact on national party politics: "Pat transcends the traditional party system; he's not cheerleading for anyone. As a result, he has a well-deserved reputation as a fearless political truth teller, even when those truths hurt. In the business of polling and public opinion, there's no higher compliment."

Indeed, Caddell is in great demand. His cellphone number is a cherished privilege given only to family, close friends and key national personalities. Otherwise, he would not have time to himself and his daughter and grandchildren. His daughter, Heidi, lives in the house that his parents bought, just seven doors away. His father's failing health was a reason for Caddell to have experienced Hurricane Hugo in 1989.

"My father had pancreatic cancer. I was here with him daily. As the hurricane came in, we had decided to stay. There was really no good option of moving my dad. So we sat it out. As fate would have it, trees hit every house on our street from the tornadoes that came through. But no tree hit ours. You could not hear anything during the storm. The winds were terrifying. By three thirty in the morning, the winds were still strong, but the worst was over. We went to bed. I went out the next morning to see the devastation. It was something I just could not believe. Every house had major damage, except ours. The memory of that time with Dad was special. My father passed away a few weeks later."

The remembrances of his dad, the Charleston childhood connection, his times with his grandparents—all are part of the reason Caddell describes himself as an "ersatz Charlestonian." His heart is here when he is not. But it was his daughter and her three children who eventually pulled him back permanently. They are his life: "This is home. In an ironic sense, that hurricane improved Charleston. It may have spurred the spirit of the community and the rebuild process to our overall benefit. This is a community of genuine people. They're truly gracious, generous and helpful. The romance of happiness is instilled in Charleston's people. Here you have both historical and cultural ambiance with a genteel society, not overly pretentious. There is even charm in the arrogance. It's telling the world, 'We're in a great city, but you can come here and see for yourself.' And the cuisine…well, there's just no place like it. Every restaurant downtown is outstanding. When I travel and I tell people I'm from Charleston, they immediately show a genuine interest. Either they have been and loved it or they have us on their 'wish list.' Either way, it's a very positive conversation-starter. The idea that the people that give out the award as the 'friendliest city in America'[152] retired the award after thirteen consecutive selections of Charleston tells you that this place is really special."

The 2012 presidential election loomed. Caddell has had a history of seeing the future. He remains disarmingly frank: "This is a tough one. Neither campaign is compelling. On the one side you have a sitting president that has failed at his job. On the other you have an opponent that cannot seem to connect with people. And it's the people who must get past the silly stuff and realize what is urgent. They'll decide.

"This country is center or center-right with an instinct toward progress. The American melting pot is a myth. Ideas unite us. There are important things to fight for; 75 to 80 percent of Americans don't care as much about ideology as they do about the identity I spoke about earlier. We have to define who we are. Once we know that, we can better deal with the selection of people to represent that ideal. I always ask just two questions when assessing any candidate for any office: 1) Is this person a patriot? 2) Is this person of the highest character? We should all look at candidates from that viewpoint."

Pat Caddell can go home to see his grandchildren after returning from New York or Washington, or even Hollywood. He can tell them that he speaks truths, he exposes corruption, he argues for the words our forefathers meticulously chose as our course. He is a patriot with character.

The Classmate Generals

MIKE STEELE AND JOHN SAMS

E ven the similarities are dissimilar. In 1952, two seven-year-olds go to the second grade together at Hooper Alexander Grade School in Decatur, Georgia. One is William, though he prefers his middle moniker, Mike. The other is John. They remain classmates until the end of the fourth grade. Their families both move to other points of the compass. In a world of seven billion, what are the chances they would ever see each other again? The circumstances that followed were mathematically incredible.

Move forward to August 1963. A class that will feature an internationally regarded author enters The Citadel in Charleston, South Carolina. The two second-grade classmates are back together. One is a tall athlete who merits the role of catcher on the baseball team—along with the aforementioned author and team third baseman, Pat Conroy. His height predetermined his company choices—either Tango or Alpha. He reported to Tango. The athlete stood six feet, three and a half inches, and the corps of cadets still operated on the General Mark W. Clark–invoked "parade-sizing." The shorter cadets went to Second and Third Battalions, the taller recruits to First or Fourth. Listing six feet on the college application guaranteed the latter, unless one listed a propensity for playing a band instrument. Band Company was unto itself, regardless of height.

Lieutenant General William M. Steele reflects warmly. He is immediately likeable. He prefers "Mike," is gangly and tanned and engages conversation with a smile that is not expected from the loftiness of his wow-résumé background. He is the retired commanding general of the United States Army Pacific. He knows what is happening in China and Indonesia. He is skilled at making large decisions that affect the global community. He understands every detail of strategy, from Cold War politics to economic sanctions. The decal on the red Corvette that he waited a lifetime to buy has three stars. He folds into it happily for his ride home to Seabrook Island.

The other class of 1967 "knob," being shorter and, as he would say, "much closer to the perfect height," reported to India Company in Third Battalion. He hardly noticed his friend, whom he'd last seen in the fourth grade. Knobs at The Citadel hardly notice anything since they are commanded to look straight ahead at all times. Any deviation from that order would surely invoke an upperclassman's ire and query. "Sams, *smack*, what are you looking around at? You wanna buy this place? Huh? *Smack*, pop off!"

"Sir, no sir. Sir, no excuse sir!"

The career of cadet recruit John B. Sams Jr. had started. He would not be buying The Citadel. He would simply be adding to its value.

Lieutenant General John B. Sams Jr. is a pensive and introspective delight. He thinks through a question before engaging an answer. The answer will be better than the question. Sams wore his three stars as the commanding general of the Fifteenth Air Force, with global air mobility oversight and seventy thousand men and women under his authority and guidance. Like Steele, one would be surprised to learn of his easy and paced rapport.

Lieutenant General Mike and Pam Steele had a choice of retirement settings virtually anywhere on the globe. They chose Charleston. *Courtesy of the Steele family archives.*

The youthful exuberance of Lieutenant General John Sams has made him a great resource for the military as well as Boeing, Inc. *Courtesy of Susie Sams.*

Their Citadel experiences were shared—apart.

By Parents' Day in October 1963, Sams would advance with the rest of the survivors of those first grueling eight weeks. He'd take an oath on the Parade Ground and become a cadet private. On down the line, nearer to the World War I–period cannons, Cadet William M. Steele would take the same oath simultaneously. In time, they would rediscover each other from their common beginnings.

"My time at The Citadel was invaluable to my career. I learned how to balance the military with academics and athletics and to deal with the problems that would arise inherently from conflicts, especially to scheduling," Steele noted. "I gained a sense of value and principle—what you really stand for—and what defines your character; what you live by. Relationships were established by character. Like The Citadel, military relationships are lifelong. What forms your character is important in both relationships."

"Mike recognizes that on the Board of Visitors and utilizes that thought," Sams added. "Boards can be so productive and yet sometimes get mired. Sometimes you get to solutions before you identify and understand the actual problem. It is best to be wide and deep in your thought process before engaging and offering a quick fix."

The youthful-looking Sams, who could well represent an age of fifty or fifty-five, is actually sixty-six. His light blue eyes match The Citadel's football uniforms. Sandy haired and actively engaged, Sams paused to tell of his India Company and corps of cadets experience.

"The Citadel has been a multitude of little things that mold and form young people. We all came in stressed and concerned in 1963 that we could stand the test. We were taught to work hard to succeed, to graduate in four years—and that was a firm expectation. In fact, that expectation came from the administration, the professors and the upper-class cadets. It transferred to become the mindset of your classmates.

Everybody wanted to walk that stage in four years—and anything extended beyond that would be a failure. There were so many other maturation principles like attention to detail, an affinity to perform at the peak, duty and responsibility, assistance to others and honor. Honor is above everything."

Steele observed: "After four years at The Citadel and thirty-five years in the military, there are many correlations you can draw upon. Managing complexities was part of both. There were so many others. Reliance upon others to perform, results-oriented strategies, the ability to be flexible, et cetera."

"It was here at The Citadel that I first realized that authority does not always translate into respect. Respect must be earned," Sams interjected. "There were lessons that had to be heeded. I was a cadet that came with a purpose in mind. Actually, there were two reasons to be at The Citadel. I wanted to be a pilot. This was the avenue for that. Secondly, my parents and grandparents were from Mount Pleasant and Awendaw. I was close with them."

Steele and Sams. Sams and Steele. In time, they would both go forward and change the world. And somehow, they did that together but separately.

They are both alumni-elected members of The Citadel's trustee board, the Board of Visitors. Steele commands the college's strategic plan and has mentored the development of The Citadel *Blueprint*, a look forward in three-, six- and ten-year layers. It is a working plan that adapts to changes. Sams serves diligently on the strategic planning committee in addition to other roles supporting the college's audit, finance and education committees.

They've both traveled quite impressive roads from their mutual beginnings in Decatur, Georgia. Somehow, their roads kept intersecting in the most astounding places.

Mike Steele took a contract to join the United States Army during the height of the Vietnam War. He would enter as a second lieutenant and spend 1969 and part of 1970 with the Twenty-third Ranger Battalion in the highland jungles of Southeast Asia. Tall and energetic, he had to learn to be shorter.

Overhead, army captain Steele might have heard C7-A air support for a few months in 1970. It may have been his second-grade and Citadel classmate, air force captain John Sams, who flew more than one hundred missions and upward of seven hundred hours in Vietnam. He would eventually command the First Airborne Command and Control Squadron. The history major was out making his own history.

"The military learned a lot in Vietnam. The value of 'unit integrity' comes to mind. We went as individuals to replace other individuals. Relationships became bonding, but we then came home as individuals. Now the army rotates units rather than individuals. People go and come back together," Sams explained. "Fundamentally, the unpopularity [of Vietnam] was taken out on the troops. Lesson learned. Today, the nation values more what the services are asked to do."

"Our military is the best the world has ever seen." Steele noted. "The enlistment standards are higher than they've ever been. It's an all-volunteer military. That alone raised the bar. The presumption was that the draft would produce a better cross-section and a better force. I initially believed that theory, but I was proven wrong. The opposite is true. All volunteer forces have performed at a higher level than at any time in our history. We are better in every way than when I entered the draft-oriented military of 1967.

"In a global conflict, if a return to a draft would become necessary, we would not be able to sustain the standards that are in place today."

Sams and Steele had mutual reasons for their mutual observations. They served in separate services together. Literally.

Sams said, "We had both just made major general and served under a marine corps four-star, Jack Sheehan, a fine man who was commander in chief of Atlantic Command. We were to report to Norfolk at the Naval Operations Base. We both moved to Dillingham Drive. That entire street is lined with flag officers—all admirals. Mike and I were, to my knowledge, the first flag officers living on that street that were not admirals.

"But we were there for a military reason that was hush-hush at the time. They brought in an air force two-star and an army two-star to tackle a larger-than-expected humanitarian assistance program in Haiti. Mike and I became part of that team under General Sheehan. Mike had just finished serving as commanding general of the Eighty-second Airborne Division with the mission to parachute assault the division into Haiti to depose the country's dictator, General Raoul Cedras. The division was turned around in flight when Cedras agreed to depart Haiti."

"John had just completed serving as the commander of the Tanker Airlift Control Center, the organization responsible for the airlift of the Eighty-second to Haiti!" Steele recalled. "We had several occasions to travel down to Haiti. There was a crisis there that the world knew little about. Many of the Haitian refugees that did not come to the Bahamas or to the U.S. on a flotilla of shoddy rafts had headed to Cuba instead. We had a big problem at Gitmo [the U.S. base at Guantanamo Bay]. We had to relocate nearly sixty-five thousand Haitians. That's where John and I had to formulate a plan. We went down to Gitmo and were told essentially, 'You can only be reassigned from Atlantic Command after you relocate the refugees.' We had to get inventive with the four hundred Cuban hard criminals that Castro let out of the jails that were now our problem, as well."

This is the moment that Sams and Steele came face to face with Raul Castro, the current dictator but second in command at that time.

Sams continued, "We worked out a plan that the Cubans accepted. We dealt with a Cuban brigadier general."

"Named Perez Perez," Steele interjected, recalling the unusual repetitive name. "Perez Perez was that general's name. From General Sheehan's perspective, we were on our own to get the job done—two guys from The Citadel. Our job was to relocate the sixty-five thousand refugees and find a home for the four hundred hard-core criminals—many of them convicted murderers and rapists. We arranged to meet with the Cuban leadership on Gitmo to discuss these criminals and agreed there were to be no photos, no media and no records. We went out in the pitch black of night. The Cubans were clear about this, and we had to be careful, too, because we had no official relationship of any kind with Cuba. We reached an agreement to hood and shackle ten of the prisoners every Monday, walk them out to the boundary wire and hand them over to the Cubans."

Steele added: "We had myself, General Sams, General Sheehan and a few enlisted men out for the transfer. They had several foot soldiers, General Perez and another man standing next to him. It was Raul Castro. We made the transfer as agreed. The very next morning, I got a call from the army chief of staff, General Gordon Sullivan. I was summoned to the Gitmo Command Center. The morning edition of the Washington Post had a photo of our whole group. Unfortunately, the only nametag that could be read was 'S-t-e-e-l-e.' Obviously, they were aware of our dilemma and orders. But they didn't expect to see us with the Cubans on the front page of the morning paper within hours of the transfer. The Cubans must've had a photographer behind one of the trees or in the bushes."

"Well, they wanted results. And Mike and I gave them results. All four hundred prisoners were transferred," Sams detailed. "We also took care of the other situation in Haiti. By mid-1996, our task was completed."

But there was this other incident that happened along the way.

"Actually, the other Cuban incident was much more serious," Sams confided. "There were these Cuban American pilots on small private planes that used to drop leaflets in Havana from the Miami area. This was all citizen-produced political stuff, not associated with anything the U.S. was doing. Those crazy pilots were taking a major risk. Well, in time, one of the small planes was shot down. Now we have an international incident. There was a lot of heat in Washington. Both Mike and I were there and were ordered to try to resolve the issue. But we really were on a very thin diplomatic line. We moved in with aircraft carriers and destroyers. It was quite serious. I was appointed as the negotiating lead with Mike offshore three miles awaiting the results. He had the heavy response of the United States military forces to command. I'm not sure the Cubans knew just how precarious this negotiation was. I made sure they knew we were ready to command severe retaliatory action. In essence, they shot down a private U.S. citizen. After some very testy talk with the Cubans, we were able to resolve it. They were not to shoot down any future private flights under any circumstance. They agreed to that if we would agree to amend our laws to disallow American citizens to fly their private aircraft over Cuba. We had a copy of a newly passed federal law in their hands within twenty-four hours. The aircraft carriers and destroyers off Cuba returned to U.S. waters. A dire situation for the Cubans was averted."

The Citadel Class of 1967 almost went to war with Cuba! Top that, Conroy!

"I was promoted and reassigned to the Army Pacific Command and parted company with my good friend once more," Steele said. John was promoted about one week later and reassigned to become the vice-commander of Air Mobility Command, Fifteenth Air Force. "John retired in 1999, and I followed suit in 2001. What were the chances we'd both come back to Charleston?"

Those chances were actually quite slim. Mike explained: "Charleston was not on my list. Not that I didn't have a great appreciation of Charleston, but Pam and I made a list picking our top five places to retire. Pam did a lot of research, and Charleston definitely made her top five. I was thinking Hawaii, among other places. A lot depended on my post-army career and the access of a good airport. Now, it appears to me that I should have placed Charleston as number one."

Pam and Mike had been together since high school. Their children had grown. They looked for the best of all worlds. As a retired lieutenant general, his expertise in many areas is sought by private industry. Steele continues to perform consulting work where needed, sometimes in the Far East. His air mileage is considerable.

The retired air mobility expert Sams went to work with Boeing Company in Seattle, Washington, in 2000. His first job with Boeing was in Charleston, where he became the director of Boeing C-17 Field Services.

"The job was perfect, since we were able to return home to the Lowcountry after thirty-two years all over the world."

Charleston Air Force Base is the largest base of deployment for this incredible aircraft. Sams became responsible for the placement and distribution of the C-17 *Globemaster III*. He also consulted on worldwide infrastructure into the air force equipment inventory and provided engineering and logistic support for the aircraft. Subsequently, Sams moved to St. Louis to head the Boeing U.S. Air Force Tanker capture team before being promoted to vice-president and leading the U.S. Air Force portfolio for Boeing. While has tasks were in St. Louis and Washington, D.C., John and Suzy continued to live in Charleston, with Suzy taking him to the airport every Monday morning at 4:30 a.m. and picking him up each Friday, usually around 10:00 p.m. That's quite a commitment for a retired general, but Sams found these challenges fit his energy and personality well. After six years and the completion of several major initiatives he wanted to see to fruition, Sam retired from Boeing in 2008.

But Sams and his wife, Suzanne, had Charleston roots. Suzy (née Searson) Sams grew up on St. Margaret Street, near The Citadel campus. They met and started dating after his graduation and married while Sams was in pilot training. His parents moved back to Charleston, the home of his entire family as well, so Sams was able to get a snapshot of Charleston each time he visited—every year or so. For the Samses, coming back to Charleston was in parentheses and understood all through their twenty-seven military career moves.

"But really, Suzy loved to travel. Still does. So it was really more me convincing her to return to Charleston. Now, she's content. She has really enjoyed the community and the wonderful people here," Sams related.

Suzy Sams recounted the decision: "While John was always intent on returning to Charleston, I was more open-minded, since we had lived in so many wonderful places…and met so many terrific people and community leaders all over the country. You might say I had underestimated the value of being close to family and realize we made the correct decision. Now, I seldom want to leave, unless we leave to visit with the children and grandchildren… all five grandchildren!"

They had monitored intermittent inspections of Charleston's progress through the years. Sams explained: "I noticed the great change after [Hurricane] Hugo. I saw the damage and the piles of debris when I visited in November 1989. Coming back often was encouraging. Today, this community is different. It was 'small-town America' before. I don't remember ever seeing more than two theaters. Now, it's a vibrant community with exciting local and regional events. It has all the benefits you can imagine, yet the traffic is still not as bad as you'd see elsewhere. There has been positive and planned growth."

Steele and Sams were both in Charleston during the aftermath of Charleston's most devastating storm. But neither knew it.

Steele recalled the bridge between his Citadel experience and coming back as part of the Hugo response experience: "When I first came before reporting to The Citadel, I remember the College of Charleston was small with mostly girls. I remember the great benefit of the beaches—mostly all residential. There were so many young people, but I remember thinking that they didn't really seem to have an appreciation of their own history, which I had studied in high school. My next return after graduation in 1967 was from Fort Benning, where I was the deputy commanding general [a brigadier] and was deployed here for recovery after Hugo had hit. The commanding general at Fort Benning was Carmen Cavezza, Citadel class of 1961. We set up command in Johnson Hagood Stadium. I took a reconnaissance helicopter early on to Folly Beach. The pier was gone. Based on the senior class parties I had been to at the Folly Beach Pier, perhaps that was a good thing! The devastation here was very similar to a war-torn landscape. It was shocking."

Steele shifted to his ultimate return to Charleston: "The next time that I came back was in 2001. Pam and I had made up our minds on Charleston, and we were looking for a place to retire. Pam and I met in 1958 and dated since the ninth grade. She knew more about Charleston than I did."

Pam Steele recalled the experience in pleasant tones: "Although Michael and I were so very fortunate to have lived in and visited some of the most beautiful and amazing places all over the world, when it came time for retirement from the army, we decided that the 'rest of life' was about being in close proximity to family. So we crossed Hawaii, a true paradise, off our list and set out to explore Georgia, Florida and South Carolina. After two weeks of 'recon,' we arrived in Charleston and knew we were home. Captured right here in this city of beauty, charm, history, wonderful people and The Citadel, we found the best of all those places where we had lived and visited. And, yes, we even found our tropical paradise: Seabrook Island."

"By 2001, this whole community was a showplace," Mike Steele noted. "We loved everything we saw. Most of that change from 1989 to 2001 has to be attributed to leadership. I'm sure Joe Riley was a great influence in that regard. After Hugo, money flowed in when it was hard to come by. King Street changed especially. The sense of community became stronger and more prideful. The houses on the battery, devastated during the hurricane, looked magnificent—like a postcard. Charleston was better than it ever was."

And now it is a destination city preferred by travelers from all over the world.

Sams and Steele have found another avenue for their teamwork. As they approached their mutual responsibilities in the prosecution of their volunteer commitments for a college trustee board, they found many insights. They were elected—independently, two years apart—to the aforementioned Citadel's Board of Visitors. This governing board has three alumni-elected members, along with nine other positions available through various legislative and gubernatorial selections. The two generals combine a pool of experience rarely seen—even on the boards of major industry.

Sams puts his role at The Citadel in perspective: "The fundamental challenge is the financial vitality. We, as alumni and as board members, must provide the proper use and distribution of resources to the prioritized needs. The goal is to assist the president in the pressure of day-to-day fundraising. Additionally, we must provide the policy leadership for a positive environment so our president and his staff can run the college. What makes The Citadel unique is the blend of military and academics to promote principled leadership. We are doing that. Nobody really speaks about the quality of academics like we should, but that certainly is a very strong feature of our experience here, and especially for the cadets of today. We're blessed to have great leadership in our administration, especially that shown by Lieutenant General John Rosa, our president."

Steele sees his role as vital because of the vision General Rosa and others on the board have acknowledged. His chairmanship of strategic planning has been an exemplary study to other board members. He puts his heart and soul into every dynamic: "Finances are key to keeping the college healthy. The challenge is to change the business model, or better yet, to transition into an independent business model. Somewhere along the way, there was continuity in leadership by placing resources where they were most needed, despite the very difficult economic environment. We must always have a view of where we are going next year and the year after that. Planning for contingencies is essential. President Rosa puts it all in perspective by gauging the *where* and the *why*. He profoundly understands priority and the crucial importance of strategic planning. We are so very fortunate to have him here at The Citadel."

There is a trio of three-star generals sitting in that boardroom. One is the president. Rosa came to The Citadel in January 2006 from his last active duty role—as superintendent of the United States Air Force Academy. His abilities and leadership have surely benefited The Citadel. Both Steele and Sams are particularly appreciative of his insight and guidance.

The fortuitous timing of having Sams and Steele back together has benefited a college and a city. The long-ago second graders have known each other for six decades. Their intertwining paths have resulted in major impacts for the United States military, for the world community—and now for Charleston.

They meet for lunch every Monday when they're both in town and are now working together to promote a solemn memorial for The Citadel's alumni war fatalities. They share a mindset. They motivate, they calculate, they postulate and they provide meaningful experience and assistance. They share a suite together at the college's recently renovated football stadium. They have elevated every station of their own incredible lives. They are inexorably linked.

"The common experience that allows us to be close after the long absences has been a lifelong trait," Sams offered. "Mike has been truly a lifelong friend."

Steele added, "Our friendship is an example of great Citadel relationships. It was certainly comforting to see John arrive at Norfolk late in our careers. It seems we've been friends forever. John never has a hidden agenda. He is always grounded in truth. There has always existed a deep trust between us."

"A lifelong friend whom I have admired and have maintained mutual respect. That respect was earned," Sams concluded.

Steele and Sams. Sams and Steele.

Where the Marshes Meet

COACH RALPH FRIEDGEN

R alph Friedgen has coached football in the same way that George Patton commanded the Third Army in World War II.[153] His objective meant defining his enemy and developing a strategy to prevail in the most consistent manner possible. Like Patton, Friedgen could be considered unconventional and brashly outspoken. Lieutenant General George S. Patton moved swiftly, commanded successes unmatched in all of history and captured more prisoners along the way than had ever been recorded in the annals of military warfare. What the public knew about Patton was that he was not McArthur or even Eisenhower. Nor did he want to be.

Sound familiar?

Ralph Friedgen got results. He knew more about offensive football than anyone of his generation. He has been cited as among the most talented geniuses the game has ever produced. He's played a major role in an NCAA National Championship and a Super Bowl. Yet those inside the profession failed to gain enough insight to notice this large man who could coach large. He was hired as a head coach much later in his career than his talents would have predicted. He took the college of his playing days and made it into a national power. He did it all with a bombastic spirit and confidence that inspired his team but sometimes rankled those at the scene of the battle—the capricious press and impulsive administration. They controlled much of public opinion but could never control Ralph Friedgen. He was always his own man.

It was just after Friedgen had been voted as the Atlantic Coast Conference Coach of the Year for the second time that new Maryland athletic director

Kevin Anderson announced that the program would buy out the last remaining year on his contract. Friedgen dutifully coached his seventh bowl game in a ten-year span, unprecedented for Maryland football. His team beat East Carolina University 51–20, rolling up bowl records for yardage gained. It was an appropriate final show. Friedgen's last season at Maryland shows nine wins and only four losses.

For the record, if Maryland were to win nine of thirteen games every year, the Terrapins would place in the top ten of every Division 1 college football program—for all time![154] Instead, Maryland football rates as the number fifty-eight program at a 53 winning percentage.[155] Friedgen's ten-year record at Maryland was 75-50, for 60 percent. The man has definitively elevated a generation of Terrapin fans' expectations.

Friedgen has always been committed to the action, dedicated to the command of the battle. He's a winner.

"I coached defense so that I could learn to counteract every offense and then find the offense that could test the best defense," Friedgen related. "As a matter of fact, I tried to gain experience from every area of position coaching to better understand all of the different schemes I would encounter from every conceivable system. That's how you learn."

General Patton studied the great cavalry commanders of the Civil War. His ancestry was rich in military service. His Confederate grandfather died in battle. Patton studied the battle movements of the Greeks and the Romans while at West Point. He became a student of the battlefront. Likewise, Ralph Friedgen learned football from his father, a coach. He commanded the battlefield as a high school quarterback, earning a full football scholarship to the University of Maryland. Given his sturdy build and knowledge of the game, he was shifted to running back and then, with success, to the offensive line. He met and learned from other coaches. Ralph Friedgen became versed in the language of the gridiron.

He started his full-time coaching career in Charleston.

"I moved here in February 1973. Frankie Beamer and I were both hired as full-time assistants by Bobby Ross. I had been working as a graduate assistant at Maryland, making $150 a month. Not a week, mind you. That's $150 for the month!" Friedgen detailed. "Frankie made the same $150 when Coach Ross brought us on at $11,000 a year. That was more money than I thought I could ever spend."

Frank Beamer stayed with Friedgen and head coach Bobby Ross at The Citadel but left for Murray State as an assistant and then head coach. After four years there, he landed the top job at Virginia Tech. Beamer's college coaching record through the 2011 season stands at 251-121-4.[156] He is considered among the very best in the college coaching ranks.

They both arrived at The Citadel excited about the opportunity. Coach Jimmy "Red" Parker had been hired by Clemson University after a fine run of success at the military college. Bobby Ross, a Virginia Military Institute graduate who had a distinguished athletic career there, was hired to continue the Bulldogs' success. Ross had a brilliant mind and a burgeoning future. Along with the youthful Friedgen and committed Beamer, Ross brought in another promising young coach: Jimmye Laycock. He retained the wide receivers' coach, Cal McCombs. All four of these Bobby Ross assistants went on to become Division 1 or 1A head coaches. In addition, three of his players from that first year in 1973 became coaches: Ellis Johnson (Southern Mississippi), David Sollazzo (University of Massachusetts) and Keith Jones (U.S. Naval Academy).

Friedgen's engagement to Gloria became possible when Ross offered him a then-healthy paying job in December 1972. Gloria, a cute and outgoing brunette, caught Friedgen's eye and gave timely direction to his life. They met while Friedgen was in graduate school. When he and Gloria married, they moved into cramped Citadel campus housing—a small apartment just steps from the practice field. They spent the next six years at The Citadel. It was from careful savings that Gloria and Ralph Friedgen bought his permanent Charleston home overlooking the Intracoastal Waterway on the backside of the Isle of Palms in 1977. It was a project when he bought it but is now a showplace, complete with a top-deck view of the world beyond. Their architect suggested a roof perch at the maximum height allowed by zoning. From it, an observer can see ships on the horizon in one direction, as well as the night lighting of the Arthur Ravenel Jr. Bridge in the other. The much-modernized home has been the one constant the Friedgens have maintained throughout his coaching career.

Well, there was this other constant. Ralph Friedgen could coach. His first permanent coaching position with Bobby Ross produced results, and those results were critically measured.

Ross happily recalled his associations with Friedgen over forty years.

"An outstanding football coach with no weaknesses—knowledgeable, demanding, fair, hardworking, loyal, good communication with his players—just a few of the good things I could say about him!"

Ross, widely respected in college football and professional football ranks, added, "He is also a dedicated family man. He and Gloria raised three outstanding young girls who are all doing quite well. A while back, Ralph

Retired University of Maryland football coach Ralph Friedgen enjoys his time at the Isle of Palms with his wife, Gloria. *Courtesy of Kelley Friedgen.*

was named 'Father of the Year' in the D.C., Northern Virginia area. That's quite an honor."

The Father's Day Council of Washington, D.C., named Friedgen Father of the Year in 2007. The proceeds of the dinner event that followed went to the American Diabetes Association.[157]

It's a good bet Friedgen topped a few congressmen, some White House occupants and a bevy of political columnists. He did so because the efforts he put into football were just part of his passion. He doted on his three lovely daughters. There's daughter Kelley, a fine health law attorney now at Genentech in San Francisco. The middle, Kristina, a University of Maryland honor graduate, is a drama teacher and director at Good Counsel High School in Maryland. Then there's Katie, the youngest, a Phi Beta Kappa honor graduate from the University of Maryland. She was magna cum laude and gave the graduation address. Katie is immersed in the world of art as a webmaster for United by Blue in Philadelphia. The photo of them that sits by the Friedgen front door on the Isle of Palms is impressive. It would give every dad in America the right to brag.

Wife Gloria began her thirty-year teaching and coaching (volleyball, basketball and track) career in Charleston at Fort Johnson High School. Her teams won two South Carolina state championships in the 1970s. At first, she taught physical education. After eleven years of following Ralph to four states, she was able to teach within her trained discipline of biology. The Friedgens have been married for thirty-nine years.

"Gloria gets sentimental about Charleston. She just loves it. She always got excited when we came here. I think she is in her best element here. And the girls always loved it when we spent time here over the years," Friedgen assessed.

"Every day in Charleston is a new adventure. I remember starting to power wash the house. I guess I had the machine turned up too high, and it took the paint off. So I started repainting the house. My neighbor, Steve Stephens, brought a drink over and told me that I was working way too hard for an Isle of Palms resident. It's so very laid-back here. And Gloria and I used to sit out on the porch and watch the traffic, but the IOP Connector has changed that. There are not nearly as many cars coming down this way anymore. It's quieter."

Daughter Kelley recalls the Isle of Palms with fondness: "Although we have been fortunate enough to have lived in many different and wonderful places, the Isle of Palms is the one place we've always called home. My sisters and I now all live a plane flight away, but when we turn onto the connector, we roll down the windows to smell the air off the marsh, the mix of salt, sea, pluff mud and sun that means we're close. And we smile when we come to the crest of the bridge where before us is the ocean, to our left the Intracoastal Waterway and to the right Hamlin Creek. We can't wait to go crabbing off the dock and out in the creeks, to play in the tide pools, to bike to Sullivan's and grab a bite at Poe's or grab breakfast at the Sea Biscuit. We've too many memories here to do them justice in just a few lines, but I think it's telling how year after year, we gather as family to sit on our porch and watch the sun set, see the moon rise and watch the lights from the city flicker in the distance. Charleston and her islands have called us home."

Gloria added her own thoughts: "The ocean is the very best therapy that exists. Walking the beach or just watching and hearing the waves roll in is so peaceful. I do get sentimental about our home here. The girls have always loved Charleston. There are so many wonderful pictures of the past in my mind. And Ralph and I have so many wonderful memories together.

"We're always doing something new. Several of our anniversaries have been spent in Charleston. For the nineteenth, we took in downtown Charleston, dined at Louie's Charleston Grill and stayed at Charleston Place. For the thirty-seventh, we dined at the Charleston Grill. For the thirty-eighth, we started the evening relaxing at the piano bar at the Mills House. We used to go to the Mills Hyatt House when we lived at The Citadel, then to Charleston Cooks on East Bay Street for a cooking and dining class. We've got the thirty-ninth anniversary coming, and I'm sure we'll do something very special here in Charleston. Why go anywhere else?"

There are not many tougher football coaches in America. Now that Friedgen's retired, the sentimental stories are telling. He is not only a great father but also an outstanding husband.

The Friedgens are "empty nesters" with a wealth of expandable time to do all of the things they wished to do for so many years. They have a few routines and a few quick changes of plans daily. They attend the daily 7:00 a.m. Mass and early 7:30 a.m. Mass every Sunday at Christ Our King Church in Mount Pleasant. They enjoy the time to travel, sometimes to their lake house in north Georgia at Lake Oconee and sometimes to visit their very accomplished daughters.

Friedgen has other interests and captivations as well.

"History has always fascinated me, especially Civil War history. There is so much right here. I have made trips to my favorite sites—to see the *H.L. Hunley*, to Antietam Battlefield and to Gettysburg," Friedgen recounted. "You can't walk down the street in Charleston without feeling you are back in that time period. It's hard to believe that the Union bombed Charleston for something like 488 straight days. This really is living history.

"I play a little golf here and there and enjoy it. But I also like to fish. It's so easy to just walk down to the dock, get in the boat and cruise around these waterways and creeks. There are so many places where you feel like you're the first person that's ever been there. And it's so quiet sometimes that all you hear is the wind and the seabirds. These marshes are places of new surprises all the time. I have seen eagles in flight and watched dolphins playing. It's a new adventure every time. The ride to the Bull's Island entrance is something to see. And I have ridden south some days for hours just roaming around and seeing something beautiful around each bend."

Friedgen just got a permit to move his dock out an additional thirty feet so that he no longer needs to time the tides to get out and back in. He feels that will help him plan his excursions better.

His philosophy on life tilts the arrow toward "Enjoy." He and Gloria love to saunter to one or two favorite breakfast restaurants on the island. They usually walk back through the neighborhood just five blocks. The walk is another adventure that Gloria finds enlightening: "There are mostly year-round residents down our end. The whole area is quiet, and you rarely see much traffic anymore. It's a wonderful walk."

Friedgen has friends from all over the country who call or stop by. Coaching for more than forty years at the top levels has made him a fine conversationalist. He stays in touch with his mentors and friends.

"Bobby Ross is a very good man. If anything, he is an even better person than he is a coach. He is a hard worker and fierce competitor. What I learned from him is that you always prepare and organize to the extreme. Really, if you could live without it, you shouldn't coach. It's not for everyone. In season, it's eighteen hours a day, seven days a week. Bobby Ross knew this well.

"Frankie Beamer is not only among the finest coaches alive, but we are very close. We even went to Lamaze class together awaiting the birth of our first children. We shared offices at Maryland as graduate assistants and then at The Citadel. I coached with him at Murray State. He learned organization from Bobby Ross. And like Ross, he always surrounds himself with great assistant coaches. He is a fine motivator to his players and to his assistant coaches. Yes, you have to motivate your assistants, as well.

"I remember when Beamer's wife's father had to co-sign a lease so that Frankie could get an apartment on the $150 per month he was being paid as a GA [graduate assistant] at Maryland. Now that's going back a few years.

"Bill O'Brien, now the head coach at Penn State, was a graduate assistant under George O'Leary at Georgia Tech, and then I hired him to join me at Maryland as the running backs' coach. He is bright and an emotional leader. I wish him well. That other O'Brien in ACC coaching, Tom, lives here on Daniel Island. He coaches at NC State. I see him here every once in a while.

"I've been lucky in the coaches that I have been around. I spent four years as a GA. Jerry Claiborne, head coach at Maryland in 1972, gave me my last GA job. I graduated in 1970 and met Gloria while earning my master's degree. It was under Coach Claiborne that cemented my love with the idea of coaching football. My father was a coach, and he knew football. So there was already an inclination."

Indeed, Ralph admired so much of his father's coaching insights. It was his dad's balanced offensive philosophy to which Friedgen most adhered over a career: "Good football teams could beat you in several different ways. My father believed in having multiple formations with the ability to throw and run effectively. Dad taught me to call my own plays on the field. Since then, I have appreciated that mindset, especially as a coach."

Thinking like a quarterback has been what has sustained his creative devotion as a coach to the twists and wrinkles that disguise several traditional offensive sets: "I also became a big believer in assistant coaches being able to coach every position, much like I did coming along. How else will you learn how to beat the different looks unless you've coached it? That's how I learned is by coaching defense to stop an offense and by coaching offense to beat a defense."

Two other Charleston names have been in the Friedgen view over the years. Former Citadel head coach Charlie Taaffe was Friedgen's offensive coordinator at Maryland for four years. Taaffe was recently inducted into The Citadel's Athletic Hall of Fame as an honorary member for his achievement—especially during the 1992 season. Taaffe's Bulldogs rose to become the number one "1-AA" football program in the country, finishing the season at 11-2. Another Citadel head football coach, Ellis Johnson, played for Friedgen while an undergraduate at The Citadel. As USC coach Steve Spurrier's defensive coordinator, Johnson helped the Gamecocks rise to new heights in 2011. He has since been hired as head football coach at the University of Southern Mississippi.

"Ellis has had a really fine career. I somehow knew he would be a good coach. He went off to West Point one year and then came back to The Citadel, I remember. We've seen each other some over the years, and I'm really happy for him," Friedgen added. "Coaching is a knowing fraternity. We each understand what it takes. We recognize the hours and the commitment. We feel for each other when there's a coaching change. We are all in the same business, go after some of the same recruits and know the same high school coaches."

So many of the coaches come to Charleston to find top players: "You know, the Charleston area and the state of South Carolina have a wealth of players here. I remember when I was at Georgia Tech, and we had Joe Hamilton and Harvey Middleton. I think they were both cousins with Pierson Prioleau at Virginia Tech and Courtney Brown at Penn State. They were all from this area—Alvin, South Carolina, near Macedonia

High School. Joe Hamilton was as good as I had ever seen. He won the Davey O'Brien Award and finished second in the Heisman Trophy. And Courtney Brown was the top player in the NFL draft. That was a great place to find football players!"

"I still follow everyone. I've been asked to take a few jobs back in college coaching, but right now, I am content. I might change my mind next week," Friedgen postulated.

But then again, the tides might be right tomorrow for an exploration of the islands going toward Georgetown. He has earned the choice.

The Artist Within

Charlotte Aimar Simmons McQueeney

There is an artist within each of us. My mother knew this.

Though our individual perceptions may differ, the colors are no less vibrant. Mom's palette was always bright with mixtures and shades only she could apply.

Those hues had strengths and energies that came out of creative reserves that astonished us all. The steadiness of her hand, the pensive focus and the lift of her graceful brush carried us—in spirit, in joy and in the unwavering optimism of hope. It gave us a view of the surreal—beyond the current day's adversity or even the indiscretions of time.

She was but a child bride, a girl who loved my father unendingly. Their marriage of sixty-four years had the challenges that life heaves forward in waves. They raised nine children with examples of love, personal responsibility and an abiding faith—these among the constants in an otherwise frequently bare cupboard. It was not easy.

My father predeceased my mother by fifteen months—a blink in time. Mom rallied for a while from a seven-year battle with cancer, the bulk of that time while selflessly taking care of my dad. She never complained and asked for little help. There were times when I came by to see my disabled dad sitting in his recliner with a requested meal Mom had fixed when she was much too sick herself to eat. She had lost her hair twice in the collateral consequences of chemotherapy. I saw my mom fight the inherent depression of her state of health immediately after my father's passing in March 2011. Without him, her loneliness was certain—and her joy muted. She missed the great artist within him.

In the width of her career as wife, mother, artist and friend, she never was able to inspire anyone we know of to resent her. She was too grounded, too sweet and kind, too genuinely loving of others. It is such a rare trait. Accordingly, she never spoke unkindly of others. She only saw the great artists within. Though my dad would sometimes wonder what she saw in an occasional new friend, even he was content that her gentle demeanor made whoever crossed her path better for the experience of her companionship. And she had great friends as a result. The vestiges of old friendships had passed with time. She was cloistered within her generation, with the happy memories of good health, her large family and her grandchildren. The majority of her artist friends had previously deceased. The nostalgia merged through moments like the fusing of cumulus clouds. They were the past and the present together.

She wore a miniature Citadel ring with pride as the mother with the most cadet graduates in the 170-year history of that institution. She was humbly delighted that she had an aggregate success attributed to her. Yet she never sought attention. It was not her way.

Her paintings of The Citadel were made into prints that are both exquisite and timeless. They were a small sampling of her portfolio. There were other examples of her wondrous talent. She drew pastels of Charleston's everyday life spanning nearly seven decades. There were oil landscapes of sea oat gateways to beaches and the forgotten days of the shadowed Charleston streets. She drew the flower ladies, the basket weavers and the many churches; the shrimp boats, the wrought-iron gates and the rickety old country barns. She found the insignificant places like row houses and palmetto-laden marshes. She painted egrets and elephants, lambs and giraffes. There was art always within her innovative soul.

She designed unique and distinctive pottery and conquered crafty projects like the decoupage of lampshades and kilning of hand-painted tiles. It seemed that there was no form of creative artwork she would not attempt.

Mom passed away on a Saturday morning, June 9, 2012. She expired with her family near, her schedule clear and her work on earth completed. No family member had any sense of what life could possibly behold without her. Her happiness made us happy. Her talents filled our void. Her faith sustained her and those who were fortunate enough to coddle the moments with her.

The funeral came. The church accompanied a respectful assemblage of her friends and friends of her children. Words spoken—an endearment and a reflection meandered through meaningful sentences meant to attribute the promises of forever. The *Ave Maria* was never more lilted. A grave site gathering deepened the loss. The overcast clouds she would have painted intimated rains to come. The distant threat reserved an ellipse of time for the moisture-laden freshening breezes.

The aspect of finality is a summit that is difficult to reach. Our feelings are obscured by the last conversation or the last clutch of her hand. We internalize them. Nobody really knows just how devastated you become. My mother had been very sick, and the quality of her life had been taken. A realization is left to be measured from the experience. It is that death is not about me but about Mom. It was good that she no longer suffered. I must think of her plight, not my own.

An artist, Charlotte McQueeney raised nine children while nurturing the warmth of a loving home. *Courtesy of Olan Mills Studio.*

We grieve better when we grieve with hope. We remain tethered to an ideal, to a memory and to some unchartered timing of transitional reconnection. It is difficult to navigate the finality. Memorial services, wakes and viewings are supposed to help but seem to forestall the private sorrow in deference to the façade expected of the public theater. People are earnest to take their time to come and "pay respects," to tell you that they cared about your loved one—and that they care about you. It is a most humbling experience to accept the time and sincerity of so many kind-hearted people. And then it's over.

Coping with a profound loss is a challenge. Though I try to find solace in her virtue and a life well lived, I truly miss her every day. Though I'm not good at it, Mom seemed to always cope well. She would simply invest more into God's plan. She did so with devotion, trust and patience. The strength she found was much like the constancy of her abilities. Her artful hands were steady still at eighty-one.

And she found the artist that dwelled in the soul of others. The little stories are now the bookends of lore and legend. They happened. She lived them.

She was once asked by an aggressive hippie-era female who had noticed her with a baby—her ninth—why she kept bringing babies into a dying world. There was a pause. Others would have been insulted. Some may have even taken note of the shambled state of the young lady and returned a sharp barb. Mom was not like that. She loved all people, as her God was loving and tolerant—and she felt quite confident that the moment was not for confrontation but for explanation. She softly replied with her most kind thoughts (paraphrased): "We are fortunate to be in a place in the world where babies matter and where there are so many social, educational and career blessings. A child born in America is more likely to change the world in a positive way than a child born anywhere else. This baby or one of my other children may do something that benefits society in ways that will make your life better as well as my own. Perhaps one will cure cancer or invent something important. Perhaps they will all have a gift of compassion for others and solve problems, not make them. Perhaps they can, one day, contribute ideas, or time or a large part of their own incomes to worthwhile causes that benefit other countries or the poor right here. It may be that one of my children may grow up to adulthood and be there when you need help. Here, they have that opportunity because here in America they have that privilege. Children are our best resources for a better world. I hope that you'll remember that when you have a child."

With that, the young hippie-like lady was disarmed and befriended. Mom had changed a perspective, if not a life. Her selflessness had a long rail load of boxcars. Mom had always been like that.

To be sure, amongst her offspring there are no cancer-curers. There were no presidents, no inventor-geniuses and, to my mother's chagrin, no priests or nuns. But in profound ways, my mother was justified and certainly unapologetic about her love of children. There are grandchildren—thirty-one currently. And there are great-grandchildren—another thirteen. The law of large numbers may dictate some degree of future success that my mother would humbly cite as reference to her well-based theory. She'll have more chances to be edified in her reasoning than most.

Mom had no apology for her happiness, no dirge for her faith. Yet a lamentation of our close relationship resides within me. I wish I could have just one more conversation. It would be to thank her.

It was after her passing that my family agreed to have me, as her executor, organize the household. She had given a few meaningful things to my siblings by a simple note we had found. In the aftermath; my daughter

Katie had organized much to assist me. My mother had, by my conservative estimate, made 400 personalized pieces of pottery. She had given much away already to friends and family. She had painted and sold nearly 1,100 watercolors, another 800 oils and acrylics and perhaps another 200 pastels and drawings. All of these crafts and artwork were "originals," leaving maybe another 5,000 copies of her art to the buying public by way of note cards, prints or giclées (copied art made from a digital inkjet process). She had done all of this over sixty-seven years of her professional art career. She began selling paintings at the age of fifteen. In essence, she averaged producing four original paintings and one piece of pottery each month for a career. She did this while sometimes pregnant and many times distracted. She was prodigious in every facet of her life.

It was during this organizational period that my daughter happened upon a small portable bin of paints and brushes attached to a matching portable easel. It was a plein air set assembly—something an artist would use for an outdoor session of painting. The box and easel were materially insignificant and found up in the crowded chaos of her art room. On top of the box in her handwriting, by Magic Marker, was a note that read: "This is for Tommy."

On the surface, and otherwise, the directive plans for this item from my mother made sense. Several years ago, I took art lessons and began painting in a style of my own. Like many others, I found the hobby therapeutic and relaxing. Mom encouraged me. I even had a public "exhibition," which she attended. My "wine and cheese" speech championed her lifelong mentorship. So the gift of the plein air bin and easel would make perfect sense. It should not have puzzled me as it did.

What didn't initially make sense made tears. Mom painted well into the weeks before her passing. She never mentioned gifting anything to anyone, our family falsely believing she was making progress in the conflict of her latest obstacle. She had won many significant cancer battles before. This anguish was a brain tumor that was treated with a new age technology, *cyberknife*, or non-invasive laser surgery. As incredible as she was, we all thought she would pull through yet again. She didn't. After that surgery, she seemed better for a few days. There was a rapid regression afterward. She had trouble walking and swallowing, and she even had to relinquish driving—a major assault on her vehement self-dependence. In this rush-decline of her health, Mom went upstairs to her art room, found the masking tape and a Magic Marker and designated that small wooden bin of her specially chosen paints and brushes for me. It could have been that she was again in a state of obsessive thoughtfulness. That was a *given*. There is another theory that I ascribe to this act. After sixty-seven years of her incredible contributions to the world of art, some 2,500 original works, Mom made an intended gesture of finality. She was passing the tools. She bracketed an end. She found a place to stop. She then went back down those stairs to sit and wait to die.

Memories bind.

Within her last two months, Mom had finished a painting of a typically old European street scene in Antibes, in the south of France. It was from a digital photograph I had given to her. A few days before the photograph was taken, my brother, Danny, and I had taken her to Lourdes at the foot of the Pyrenees Mountains. Mom's desire to go to Lourdes, after nearly five years of fighting cancer, was to pray at the grotto of Our Lady of Lourdes—for my father! Dad was in difficult late-life health, after the ravages of several strokes. It was another truly selfless act, one of many my mother had authored. Danny and I lit the two largest candles available in observance of our faith in God and our prayer for His grace upon our parents. It was a solemn pilgrimage—yet a warm memory of an adventure. The three of us sat on an upper portico overlooking the small French town in the diminishing evening after dinner. We shared a bottle of the restaurant's local wine. It was a time for insights, smiles and reflections. The cool breeze of that late June evening is with me still.

That painting of an old winding alleyway in Antibes was Mom's last completed oil production. The shadows kept creeping forward as I visited and watched her progress. I remarked to her that her "shadows were getting longer and that if she didn't finish it soon, that painting would represent nightfall."

Somberly, she replied, "It's later than you think."

Mom looked at all things as what they were in an artist's view. There was never a mid-horizon or a centered subject for her brush. All views were artful turns of the eye for the placement of an obscure focal point that could be emphasized on a flat canvas. The use of positioning the eye to an indistinct object out of the center gave the dimension of depth. She saw the world for all the art that was within. Those obscure focuses enthralled her. It was truly an enchanting way to traipse through life.

Her journey had been enhanced with a companion—my father. Their devotion to each other was nearly mythical. They were complementary angles that adjoined. As such, in Mom's passing, there existed one corner of happiness in the McQueeney family. My mother's longest separation from my father was over. Who is to say that he did not again find the delight of anticipation in her joy, her warmth and her certain return to him? Would he be there perhaps hoisting an empty coffee mug or murmuring a grin-filled quip of nurturing endearment? Would she hug him tightly and call him by the name she had given him: *Bully*? Could I suppose that the God that loves me despite my innumerable flaws and shortcomings will let me see them again?

And the living sunsets that I cherish each evening will scarcely capture the colors my mother had in mind for her journey. Surely she has put away her magical paintbrush to rise to the unbridled joy and warmth of God's welcome.

For He is the artist within each of us.

Epilogue

The Cultural Upside of Our Deep Past

W e're here. Our routes may have differed over the millennia, but we made it. Life is well here in Charleston. We've arrived.

But where did we really come from, and what innovations did we pick up along the way? Everything of modern humanity is around us. Whom can we thank?

The well of life, archaeologists say, sprung forth out of Africa. It's where hunter-gatherers are, as yet, hunting and gathering. In a sense, it makes us all African Americans…and African Europeans and African Asians. The sub-Saharan culture brought much more to civilization's front porch, like farming and governing leadership, not to mention the domestication of animals. Pity the tribesman who penned in the first hyena or lion. The early tribes also had the benefit of metallurgy for tools and the wheel for transport. As advanced as the later civilizations of the American Incas, Aztecs and Mayans became, especially in the science of astronomy, they did not have these essential inventions. There was no wheel for transport, no metal tools or metal weapons and very few domesticated animals.

The Africans dispersed in directions farther south and east and presumably north into Egypt, Persia, Greece and India. China, Iberia and Rome emerged. Tribal communities extended to Mongolia, Korea, Japan and Scandinavia. Most of these civilizations evolved with little outside contact.

The Chinese made gunpowder, paper and spaghetti. They also gave us the compass. We had no idea where we were going until that directional moment.

The Persians were popular as tradesmen who interacted with the Chinese, Indians and East Africans. They invented bricks, wine, tar and the windmill. They also invented cookies, ice cream and, ahem, taxes. Republicans insist they must have been Democrats.

The people of India were inventive as well. They must have noticed seasonal clothing needs. They brought civilization cashmere wool (Kashmir), cotton clothing and the buttons to keep dungarees up (from the port town of Dhunga). They refined sugar, developed cataract surgery and unfortunately advanced a frustrating game called Pachisi (Parcheesi). Long ago, my fiancée hit me over the head with a game board when I rolled the perfect numbers to block her entrance—not a good indicator for marriage. Formal marriage came from the Chinese, we're told. They abhor Pachisi.

In the event that all of this is Greek to anyone, then let's proceed to that Hellenistic culture to find democracy, important architectural advancements and the idea of "trial by jury." The philosophers came along, like Socrates, Plato and Aristotle. The Greeks built outdoor theaters for their comedies and tragedies—never to be confused as the quietness that follows a misunderstood punch line. There were myths everywhere before the Greeks claimed them as their own.

The Babylonians, the Chinese and the Romans lay claim to the invention of the umbrella. It's simple to resolve. We just have to calculate where rain was first discovered. But give the Romans credit. They depended on gravity and water to keep their aqueducts from looking like pointless archways. Archways are never pointed. Romans made paved roads to Roman coliseums and Roman baths. And Romans were the first to wear socks. They were rarely color-coordinated with their togas.

The Scandinavians were fierce fighters, energetic travelers and tradesmen. They brought both the common safety match and dynamite to the world. The fuse came from elsewhere. They made zippers and paper clips, too. One wonders what prompted the invention of the thermometer. Just how cold was it? Ask Anders Celsius.

The Egyptians fascinate us. Those large toothy grins came from their use of toothbrushes and toothpaste. They also came up with high heels, ladies. So blame the society of the pyramids. It was brilliant that they invented locks and keys at the same time. Otherwise, we would be left with millions of keys that go to nothing. There's already a drawer full of them at my house. They also came up with wigs. Come to think of it, I have never met a bald Egyptian.

The French invented Braille, the bicycle, the pencil and the electric iron. The Spanish invented the mop. Well, they also founded the beret, the cigarette and the Molotov cocktail. That paints an interesting mental picture. The Spanish did not name this homemade bomb; the Finns did that.

The Mongols, the Jews and the Germanic tribes all had a hand in bringing civilization forward with invention. Try barbecue, bagels and beer. The Druids earned little cultural credit, except perhaps for the first rock concert. It's called Stonehenge. And the Irish, you ask? Consider whiskey and seismology, in that order. They felt the room moving and then measured it.

We should toast the Mesopotamians. They invented the chariot. They built the first plow and knew when to plant because they were the first astronomers and planned everything they did around the seasons. They were the first to write stuff down, to irrigate fields and to utilize sanitation. They invented glassware. They were the first to attach a sail to a boat. They came up with support columns and the dome. Yet we cannot thank them. The Hittites conquered the last of the Mesopotamians.[158] Hittites...that's such an appropriate name for those in hand-to-hand combat. But the Hittites had metal weapons. The Mesopotamians, in their zeal to make the world a better place, had no knives, swords, spears or arrows. It was a fatal oversight.

Cultures that emerged across the millennia brought pieces of what we are today. And now there is an American culture—of only a few centuries yet—that future archaeologists will cite for radiocarbon dating, iPads and basketball.

The favorite American and worldwide cultural invention of our generation may well be the way in which we understand other cultures faster than one can read the tales of Marco Polo. It is the favorite tool of the previously uninformed—aspiring to be the ultra-informed. We call it the Internet. It's better than tar, toothpaste and whiskey combined. And so far, it's free. And with it, this information deserves a giant electronic footnote, the last one in a book completely notated from Internet sources.[159]

So there is another sunset. It's the brilliant orb of our imagination. It could be that it is cyclical to scientists but scintillating to those of us inspired by all that life has to offer. There are other advancements beckoning, more invention and other joys to be recorded. They will likely be from the consortium of all cultures, ever aware of the presence of warmth in humanity and understanding—and always in appreciation of the radiance and luminosity of the setting sun.

Notes

1. William Shakespeare, "Sonnet 55."
2. WCSC TV, http://promotables.wordpress.com/about.
3. Mayor J. Palmer Gaillard, http://www.halseymap.com/flash/mayors-detail.asp?polID=38.
4. Alte Oper, http://www.esther-ofarim.de/fr04.htm.
5. Hong Kong Cultural Centre, http://topics.scmp.com/news/hk-news-watch/article/Expert-action-at-last-to-tackle-concert-hall-sound-barriers.
6. *Business Week*, http://www.rtbot.net/Martha_Rivers_Ingram.
7. Nashville's Parthenon, http://heritage-key.com/blogs/prad/architectural-copies-what-nashville-has-common-athens.
8. Ibid.
9. Ingram Book, http://www.ingramlibrary.com/about/distribution.aspx.
10. Reverend Daniel Jenkins, http://www.sc.edu/orphanfilm/orphanage/symposia/scholarship/hubbert/jenkins-orphanage.html.
11. County Council Election 1970, http://avery.cofc.edu/archives/Hamilton_Lonnie.html.
12. Ibid.
13. *H.L. Hunley*, http://www.history.navy.mil/branches/org12-3.htm.
14. Charlotte tragedy, http://www.postandcourier.com/article/20090911/PC1602/309119956.
15. 67,000 population, 1974. http://www.postandcourier.com/article/20090911/PC1602/309119956.
16. College of Charleston, http://www.postandcourier.com/article/20090911/PC1602/309119956.

17. Ben Tillman, http://www.northcharleston.org/visitors/attractions/museumsandart/navalbasehistory.aspx.
18. Ibid.
19. Ibid.
20. Ibid.
21. Cold War, http://www.history.com/topics/cold-war.
22. Black sea incident of 1988, http://www.informationdissemination.net/2008/11/on-february-day-on-black-sea-in-1988.html.
23. Ushanka hats, Soviet, blog.ushanka.us/2012/04/new-blog-concept.html.
24. Deputy DOD Ocean Policy Affairs, http://www.martindale.com/William-L-Schachte/352829-lawyer.htm.
25. Clemson Corps of Cadets, http://www.thetigernews.com/news.php?aid=1461&sid=1.
26. SWIFT boat, http://www.slate.com/articles/news_and_politics/explainer/2004/08/what_exactly_is_a_swift_boat.html.
27. FAC Forward Air Control. Acronym, http://www.nationalmuseum.af.mil/factsheets/factsheet.asp?id=5575.
28. Mother Teresa of Sea Islands, http://www.themiscellany.org/index.php/news-archives/78-2009/189-sister-mary-joseph-ritter.
29. Ibid.
30. Divine Savior Nursing Home, http://sistersofcharityolm.org/Sisters-of-Charity-Our-History.htm.
31. Ibid.
32. St. Elizabeth Ann Seton, http://www.catholic.org/saints/saint.php?saint_id=180.
33. Ibid.
34. Malcolm D. Haven Award, http://www.tcfgives.org/awards_haven.htm.
35. Seton Legacy Medal, http://www.gettysburg.travel/media/news_detail.asp?news_id=200.
36. Malcolm D. Haven, http://www.tcfgives.org/awards_haven.htm.
37. Grace Bridge accident, February 1946, http://www.gribblenation.com/scroads/cooper.
38. Hootie & the Blowfish Foundation, http://www.cbsnews.com/2100-500187_162-3080027.html.
39. Sisters in Charleston, http://www.cbsnews.com/2100-500187_162-3080027.html.
40. Carolyn Rucker, http://countrymusic.about.com/od/maleartistsmz/a/DariusRuckerBiography2.htm.

41. Learn to Live, http://www.umc.org/site/c.lwL4KnN1LtH/
b.4785843/k.1E88/Music_Review_Darius_Rucker_emLearn_to_
Liveem.htm.

42. CMA Award speech, http://www.lehighvalleylive.com/music/index.
ssf/2009/11/taylor_swift_darius_rucker_win.html.

43. Loutrell Winslow Briggs, http://www.preservationsociety.org/progress/
PPJUNE06CS.pdf.

44. Ibid.

45. Ibid.

46. 1887 Fire Tower No. 1, http://legeros.com/history/charleston/
stations.

47. Ed Smith Stadium, http://www.baseballpilgrimages.com/spring/
sarasota.html.

48. 2011 Oriole statistics, http://baltimore.orioles.mlb.com/stats/sortable.

49. Matt Wieters Georgia Tech, http://www.ramblinwreck.com/sports/m-
basebl/mtt/wieters_matt00.html.

50. Rebecca Wieters Moake, http://honors.cofc.edu/honorsalumni/
classof2006.php.

51. Joe Mauer with power, http://www.fangraphs.com/fantasy/index.
php/matt-wieters-joe-mauer-with-power.

52. Thomas Wolfe, *Look Homeward, Angel*, http://www.goodreads.com/
author/quotes/7921.Thomas_Wolfe.

53. Passing of Donald Conroy, the "Great Santini," http://www.nytimes.
com/1998/05/14/us/donald-conroy-77-model-for-the-great-santini-
dies.html.

54. Wellington College, England, http://www.sciway.net/movies/sc-
movie-lords-discipline.html.

55. 2001 Citadel Graduation Speech, http://externalaffairs.citadel.edu/
conroy.

56. Citadel Basketball May 1997, fundraising compiled by the author.

57. Chicco Apartments, http://www.ccpl.org/content.asp?id=15693&acti
on=detail&catID=6029&parentID=5747.

58. Prospect Hill, http://www.charlestonmag.com/home/feature/
prospect_hill.

59. James Hoban, http://www.nndb.com/people/633/000204021.

60. Order of the Palmetto, http://www.themiscellany.org/index.php/
news-archives/75-1999/1014-bishop-thompson-receives-order-of-the-
palmetto.

61. Ibid.

62. Electronic endnote, Life of Bishop Fulton J. Sheen (detailed citation given).

63. Ibid.

64. Ibid.

65. Ibid.

66. President and CEO appointment, http://www.lppc.org/committee/LPPC-Lonnie-Carter-February-2012-photo.pdf.

67· Green energy research, https://www.santeecooper.com/portal/page/portal/SanteeCooper/AboutUs.

68. Santee Cooper Board, http://www.postandcourier.com/article/20111022/PC05/310229928.

69. Ibid.

70. *Esquire*, Scott Rabb, http://www.esquire.com/features/man-at-his-best/q-and-a/bill-murray-interview-0612#ixzz1yQv5ocoo.

71. Ibid.

72. SAL Hall of Fame, http://www.kltv.com/story/18835975/bill-murray-honored-by-minor-league-baseball.

73. IMDb biography, Bill Murray, http://www.imdb.com/name/nm0000195.

74. *Esquire*, Scott Rabb.

75. Ibid.

76. John McKissick, http://www.postandcourier.com/news/2011/aug/23/23_mckissick_numbers.

77. Summerville players in all-star games, http://www.postandcourier.com/news/2011/aug/23/23_mckissick_numbers.

78. Quote from Joe Call, http://www.usatoday.com/sports/preps/football/2011-08-22-John-McKissick-enters-60th-season_n.htm.

79. Number of high school football teams in the USA, http://answers.yahoo.com/question/index?qid=20080406133141AAZYjcK.

80. Ibid.

81. Quote by John McKissick, Philip Bowman, Postandcourier.com, http://www.postandcourier.com/news/2012/feb/04/mckissick-wins-national-award.

82. Wins & Losses, Shula v. McKissick, http://www.google.com/search?client=safari&rls=en&q=John+McKissick+win-loss+record&ie=UTF-8&oe=UTF-8.

83. No Fear of Failure, Burnison, Gary, http://my.safaribooksonline.com/book/leadership/9781118000786/chapter-6-coach-john-mckissick-building-teams/lessons_from_the_coach.

84. Flowertown Festival, www.charlestonlowcountry.com/specialpages/ Flowertown.html.
85. Summerville founding, http://www.midlandterracecondos.com/ summerville-azalea-article.php.
86. Dee Norton Lowcountry Children's Center, http://www.yellowpages. com/charleston-sc/mip/lowcountry.
87. 205 million gallons, http://www.washingtonpost.com.
88. 540 million gallons estimate, www.propublica.org/topic/gulf-oil-spill.
89. Settlement BP, http://www.motleyrice.com/news/view/bp-settlement.
90. Ibid.
91. Pelvic mesh, http://www.motleyrice.com/transvaginal-mesh-lawsuit.
92. USC, http://www.postandcourier.com/article/20080412/ PC1209/304129926.
93. Charles Pinckney, http://south-carolina-plantations.com/charleston/ snee-farm.html.
94. Monsignor Egbert Figaro, http://www.belmead.com/dedication/ dedication.htm.
95. Charleston Catholic School, http://www.charlestoncatholic.com/ content.asp?name=Site&catID=15237&parentID=15207.
96. Ibid.
97. Knights of Peter Claver, http://www.newadvent.org/cathen/11763a. htm.
98. FitsNews cited objective, http://www.fitsnews.com.
99. The mace group, http://macegroupllc.com/services.
100. Dr. Barbara Zaremba, http://www.jamesamcalister.com/sitemaker/ sites/JamesA1/obit.cgi?user=barbara-zaremba.
101. Sermon, Rev. Danny Massie, March 21, 2012, part of Charleston Community Lenten Series, given at the First Baptist Church in Charleston.
102. From sermon, First Scots Presbyterian Church.
103. *Presbyterian Survey Magazine.*
104. Ibid.
105. Ibid.
106. Ibid.
107. Dr. Daniel W. Massie on Sunday, May 10, 2009, at St. Philip's Episcopal Church in conjunction with the annual meeting of the General Society of Colonial Wars.
108. September 11 Pentagon crash, http://archives.cnn.com/2002/ US/03/07/gen.pentagon.pictures/index.html.

109. 165 recommendations, http://usmilitary.about.com/cs/
airforcetrng/a/academyrules.htm.

110. St. Bernard Abbey, Cullman, Alabama, www.stbernardabbey.com.

111. Ibid.

112. Abbot Bede Luibel, http://search.yahoo.com/search?ei=utf-8&fr=aa
plw&p=Rt.+Rev.+Bede+Luibel.

113. Right Reverend Bede Luibel, www.osb.org/amcass/necrology/nec-
03.html.

114. Archbishop Oscar Hugh Lipscomb, www.catholichierarchy.org/
bishop/blipscomb.html.

115. Ibid.

116. Silas Pearman Bridge, http://www.weidlinger.com/project.
aspx?type=200&cat=&id=2121.

117. Snee Farm, http://sneefarmcountryclub.com/history.htm.

118. Ibid.

119. Ibid.

120. Edward Rutledge, 117 Broad Street house, www.hmdb.org/marker.
asp?marker=27467.

121. Cardinal Joseph Bernadin, http://archives.archchicago.org/jcbbio.
htm.

122. Carmen C. Reinhart and Kenneth Rogoff, *This Time It's Different: Eight
Centuries of Financial Folly*, http://press.princeton.edu/titles/8973.html.

123. Western Illinois University, http://www.wiu.edu.

124. PGA Section President, http://www.golfconversations.
com/2010/04/22/roger-warren-president-kiawah-island-golf-resort.

125. GPTP, http://www.pgamediacenter.com/bios/warren.pdf.

126. McIlroy quote from PGA Championship, http://www.golfchannel.
com/news/rex-hoggard/hoggard-mcilroy-wins-pga-championship.

127. Los Angeles Chargers, moved in 1961 to San Diego, http://www.
google.com/search?source=ig&hl=en&rlz=&q=Paul+Maguire&oq=Pau
l+Maguire&aq=f&aqi=g6g-s1g3&aql=&gs_l=igoogle.3..0l6j0i10j0l3.34
59.7340.0.7890.14.12.1.1.1.0.65.743.12.12.0...0.0.1dHIuNHRmME.

128. Ibid.

129. Ibid.

130. Ibid.

131. Olympic Order, http://www.falconheadcapital.com/page/
investment/59.

132. Early Evidence of European Golf, http://www.finleyongolf.com/
articles/TheEarlyHistoryofGolf.htm.

133. South Carolina Golf Club, http://www.golfstyles.net/EnewsFolder_Nov09/TravelN09.html.

134. St. Andrew's Golf Club, http://www.travelandleisure.com/articles/americas-first-golf-course.

135. Ibid.

136. Early Golf in America, http://www.finleyongolf.com/articles/TheEarlyHistoryofGolf.htm.

137. Master Golf Tournament, *Sports Illustrated*, http://sportsillustrated.cnn.com/vault/article/magazine/MAG1006444/index.htm.

138. 1939 Golf Money Winner, http://golf.about.com/od/golfersmen/p/henry_picard.htm.

139. Picard-Revolta, http://golf.about.com/od/teamcompetitions/p/rydercup1937.htm.

140. Sam Snead, http://www.thepeoplehistory.com/golfhistory.html.

141. Bobby Jones, http://espn.go.com/sportscentury/features/00014123.html.

142. Ford family championships, *Sports Illustrated*, John Garrity, http://sportsillustrated.cnn.com/vault/article/magazine/MAG1110854/index.htm.

143. Walter Hagen, http://news.google.com/newspapers?nid=1499&dat=19380405&id=tqVQAAAAIBAJ&sjid=NCIEAAAAIBAJ&pg=2221,2009402.

144. Ibid.

145. Ben Hogan, http://articles.chicagotribune.com/1989-10-29/sports/8901270181_1_henry-picard-pga-championship-pga-tour.

146. Ibid.

147. Billy Picard, http://www.calaverasenterprise.com/news/article_b6b8dd32-2cc6-11e1-a0e9-001871e3ce6c.html?mode=image.

148. Beth Daniel Induction Speech of Henry presenting Henry Picard, World Golf Hall of Fame.

149. P&C article Tommy Ford by Tommy Braswell, http://www.postandcourier.com/article/20120329/PC20/120329677&source=RSS.

150. Ibid.

151. C. Vann Woodward, http://www.amazon.com/C.-Vann-Woodward/e/B001I9S4VE/ref=ntt_athr_dp_pel_1.

152. Friendliest City in America awarded by the late cultural writer Marjabelle Young Stewart.

153. General George S. Patton, http://www.generalpatton.com.

154. NCAA College Football Winning percentages, http://en.wikipedia.org/wiki/List_of_winningest_college_football_teams.

155. Ibid.

156. Frank Beamer, http://www.hokiesports.com/staff/beamer.html.

157. *Baltimore Sun* Father of the Year, http://articles.baltimoresun.
com/2007-05-24/sports/0705240181_1_father-day-friedgen-day-
council.

158. Hittites defeat Mesopotamians, http://history-world.org/hittites.htm.

159. All cultural invention citations were derived from cruising the
Internet. If the information therein is factual, then the essay is relevant
and thusly inured with truth. The book itself relies on the same
documentation.

About the Author

Author W. Thomas McQueeney has offered another compelling insight into the characters and consequences that have vaulted Charleston to the world stage. A self-described "child of the pluff mud," McQueeney is a 1974 graduate of The Citadel, where he majored in English. The fourth of nine children, he is one of a record six McQueeney brothers to graduate from the esteemed Charleston military college. McQueeney is the author of *The Rise of Charleston: Conversations with Visionaries, Luminaries and Emissaries of the Holy City.* A recipient of the Order of the Palmetto, South Carolina's highest civilian accolade, McQueeney is a local businessman who has distinguished himself as a journalist, volunteer, donor and community ambassador. McQueeney resides in Mount Pleasant, is married and has four children and two grandchildren.

Visit us at
www.historypress.net